Helion & Company Limited
Unit 8 Amherst Business Centre
Budbrooke Road
Warwick
CV34 5WE
England
Tel. 01926 499 619
Email: info@helion.co.uk
Website: www.helion.co.uk
Twitter: @helionbooks
Visit our blog http://blog.helion.co.uk/

Text and maps © Combat Films and
    Research 2013, 2022
Photographs © as individually credited
Colour artworks © as individually credited

Designed and typeset by Farr out
    Publications, Wokingham, Berkshire
Cover design Paul Hewitt, Battlefield Design
    (www.battlefield-design.co.uk)

ISBN 978-1-804512-52-4

British Library Cataloguing-in-Publication
    Data
A catalogue record for this book is available
    from the British Library

We always welcome receiving book
proposals from prospective authors.

CONTENTS

Note: In order to simplify the use of this book, all names, locations and geographic designations are as provided in *The Times World Atlas*, or other traditionally accepted major sources of reference, as of the time of described events.

FOREWORD

There are a lot of books published on guerrilla warfare, but few record the guerrilla's perspective. Of these, some are written by participants for a political and/or autobiographical purpose (Che Guevarra, *Guerrilla Warfare*; Mao Tse-tung, *On Guerrilla Warfare*; T. E. Lawrence, *Seven Pillars of Wisdom*). There are others that are written to record guerrilla history (Edward Leslie, *The Devil Knows How to Ride*; Robert Asprey, *War in the Shadows*; Alistair Horne, *A Savage War of Peace*). There are even works of fiction about guerrillas (John Steinbeck, *The Moon is Down*; Ken Follet, *Lie Down with Lions*; Ernest Hemingway, *For Whom the Bell Tolls*). What is lacking in the literature about the guerrilla perspective are collections of the combat experiences of the rank and file guerrillas and their tactical leaders. These people seldom leave written records, yet theirs are often the most interesting accounts.

In 1994, Ali Jalali and I traveled to Pakistan to meet with Mujahideen combatants of the Soviet-Afghan War. Ali is a former Afghan Army officer, Mujahideen combatant and Voice of America journalist. We traveled, talked to numerous Mujahideen, drank gallons of tea and produced a series of vignettes that showed the tactics used by the Mujahideen. The resulting publication was a US Government book entitled *The Other Side of the Mountain: Mujahideen Tactics in the Soviet-Afghan War*. Eventually 100,000 copies were printed for allied forces in Afghanistan, with another 8,000 copies published in Dari, one of the principal languages of Afghanistan. I do not know how many unauthorized copies were published, but they are out there with remarkably shoddy black and white maps.

Dodge Billingsley and I have known each other for almost two decades. Dodge is a fellow historian and a video journalist who heads *Combat Films and Research* in Salt Lake City. When I was writing articles about the Russo-Chechen War, Dodge was wrapping up graduate school having already spent considerable time in the Caucasus. Dodge returned to the Caucasus upon completion of his studies and entered Chechnya during the chaotic interwar period where he connected with Shamil Basaev and combatants under his command. Dodge accompanied these men, and teenagers in some cases, through out Chechnya and eventually produced his first of two documentary films on Chechnya. He has since produced a number of other films based on his work in Afghanistan, Iraq and the Korean Peninsula.

In 2005, Dodge and I were in Afghanistan gathering material for our book and documentary film entitled *Operation Anaconda: America's First Major Battle in Afghanistan*. Dodge had been embedded with US forces during that battle. One evening Dodge and I were discussing the soldiers' demand for copies of *The Other Side of the Mountain* and wishing that other guerrilla conflicts were also covered from the perspective of the guerrilla as well as the opposing government force. *Fangs of the Lone Wolf* began in Kabul. Dodge maintained contacts with the Chechen community and had the reputation as an impartial journalist who did not shirk from danger and discomfort. Dodge liked the format of *The Other Side of the Mountain* and the accurate color maps and wanted to continue this approach in his book on the Russo-Chechen Wars.

Dodge set to work tapping into contacts he made while in Chechnya years previously. Finding the right Chechens was a major problem. Russian successes in Chechnya drove many of the combatants underground in foreign lands where at least a few were being hunted, probably by the Russian secret service. Many of the combatants were crippled and maimed or suffering psychic trauma. Patiently Dodge conducted his interviews, cross-walked accounts with other Chechen and even Russian accounts when available, performed countless map checks and produced the remarkable vignettes that tell the guerrilla side of the Russo-Chechen Wars.

Fangs of the Lone Wolf is a unique book. It is not so much a history as an exploration into numerous fights, large and small. There are no epic heroes of impeccable virtue, unsurpassed intellect and athletic invincibility. These are ordinary men who are fighting outnumbered and outgunned against a modern army. They are fighting for their land, family, neighbors, or just out of plain cussedness. This book is their story. It is not about right or wrong and has no political points to make. The war was what it was and this is the story of combatants in that war.

Les Grau

PREFACE

Chechen combatants continue to show up on many battlefields since the conclusion of the Russian-Chechen Wars including Syria and Iraq in the wake of the US withdrawal in 2011. They are said to have been in Afghanistan, although the evidence is lacking. However, they are deeply involved in the Russia-Ukraine war on both sides of the conflict. While Chechen strongman Ramzan Kadyrov and the "Kadyrovsky" stand firm with the Kremlin, anti-Russian Chechens fight alongside Ukraine units. In fact, the presence of Chechens on other battlefields in the post-Soviet era goes back to at least 1992. My first trip to the Caucasus occurred on the heels of the Georgia-Abkhaz War of 1992–1993. I was surprised at how much I heard about "Chechens" by both Georgian and Abkhaz combatants. I was intrigued by descriptions of the battle for Gagra (late summer/early fall 1992) and the role Shamil Basaev and his Chechen volunteers played. I have been on their trail ever since. Two years later I was sitting in graduate school studying former Soviet successor states when the conflict in Chechnya erupted. A couple of years later I entered Chechnya to see the place for myself and to make a documentary film, *Immortal Fortress*, about the Chechen warrior culture and the combatants who had won de facto independence from Moscow.

Getting there was harrowing. My cameraman and I were detained in Derbent and then Makhachkala trying to reach Grozny via Dagestan. Eventually we entered Chechnya through Vladikavkaz. The capital city was still a pile of rubble but the community was coming back. Groups of fighting-age men gathered together on street corners, perhaps waiting for the next round of conflict to begin but more likely holding on to the power that the gun provided them. I met dozens and dozens of former first war combatants, including Shamil Basaev and Salman Raduev. Each village showed its own unique scars of war. While Vedeno was more or less intact, Batumi was largely destroyed. I was also aware of the jihadists who had entered the fight. The Arab al Khattab would not talk to me because in his own words; I was "an American, an infidel, and should be beheaded."

After a couple false starts and the events of 9/11, I sat out the Second Russian-Chechen War, being pulled more and more to cover the wars in Afghanistan and Iraq. However, and maybe because of these conflicts, I remained committed to studying the conflict in Chechnya and staying in touch with combatants I knew. A book regarding the battlefield exploits seemed appropriate, and I began reaching out to various former Chechen combatants abroad. Most of the combatants I met in the 1990s are dead or in exile. Those in exile are battered and bruised. Many of these men are maimed or suffer from the effects of years of combat and post-traumatic stress. I decided that they had a story that should be told and I traveled to find them and to record their experiences.

After I finished my interviews and wrote the 30 vignettes contained in this book, I enlisted the help of an old friend, Les Grau, who has written extensively about the Soviet-Afghan War.[1] Les and I kicked around Afghanistan together and separately. Les is a Vietnam vet who knows guerrilla tactics and has also written extensively about the Russian-Chechen Wars. He and I tweaked my vignettes and provided commentary and context for our reader. Les also helped me find a publisher. He is someone I trust.

The content of this book was reconstructed through first person interviews with the participants indicated in each individual scenario. In every case the names of the Chechen combatant veterans have been changed for their own security concerns. There is still considerable fear of Russian reprisal among the veterans interviewed. In many instances we were never told the interviewee's real name. In most cases I was allowed to record the interviews and even show their hands on a map, but was not allowed to photograph or videotape the participants' faces or distinguishing scars or features.

Interviews typically lasted many hours and even days. In every case, the interviewee was asked to draw on a map the action he was explaining for clarification. This was of critical benefit, as I was able to then corroborate the hand-drawn maps with Soviet military maps of the area in question and also satellite imagery where available. One funny exchange occurred when I pulled out some Soviet topographical maps from 1984. Upon seeing the maps the Chechens exclaimed; "We never had such good maps. If we had these maps we would have won the war!" When two combatant stories intersected, every effort was made, when possible, to cross-examine the interviewees and cross-reference the transcripts for clarity and verification. I also used Russian works and sources to corroborate and add additional perspective to the scenarios whenever possible.

On a more personal note, it was apparent from the first interviews that sharing their combat experiences with me was traumatic for many of these combatants. A few simply could not reconstruct particular events, times and places. Some suffered headaches and exhaustion from verbalizing their war experiences. In many cases we were forced to take breaks in the interview process to give the interviewees a chance to regroup and in some instances the participants were not able to, or chose not to, continue the interview. In the best cases, the interview process seemed to be therapeutic.

This book does not look to take sides in the conflict. Nor does it pretend to cover the Russian soldiers' story. Rather it seeks to tell the Chechen tactical story of the war – to tell the story of the war through the eyes and experiences of the Chechen combatants themselves. Recognizing that simply telling an individual's story can be legitimizing and words carry with them political weight, the term "combatant" is used rather than "fighter," "soldier," "insurgent," or "terrorist" – all terms previously used to describe the Chechen resistance movement. Each has significant political implications. Chechens chafe being called "fighters", while Russia balks at the Chechens being given soldier status. These then are the accounts of men who have fought, often under brutal conditions, the battles that make up the Russian-Chechen Wars 1994–2009.

Dodge Billingsley

ACKNOWLEDGEMENTS

This book would not have been possible without the initial trust of a few Chechen veterans still alive, who, in turn, introduced me to many more former combatants. I thank them for their consideration; they took time to sit down with me and think about and examine parts of their history that many would like to forget but, nevertheless, were willing to share. Unfortunately I can't list them by name.

Les Grau, who believed in this project from day one and added his invaluable insight and context to each vignette, honed by decades of studying the wars and armies of the Soviet-Russian empire. Now, if we could just get our email exchanges to work more efficiently!

Art Speyer and Tamie Huston of the United States Marine Corps at Quantico who made this project possible through their encouragement and support.

Glen Doxey, a brilliant linguist and student of languages out of Brigham Young University, who was critical to conducting the interviews and, even during the writing phase, clarifying many small details that in some cases changed the direction of the scenario in question. I thank him for his willingness to learn a whole new vocabulary of military terms.

Ben Unguren, my mapmaker, who was able to grasp each and every scenario based on a stack of hand drawn sketches, published maps and satellite imagery, and produce each scenario map. He demonstrated that good technology can produce pretty images.

Aaron Perez of the Foreign Military Studies Office who improved these maps for publication.

Scott Thornton here at Combat Films and Research, who processed so much of the data into workable files from which I worked. He now knows more about the wars in Chechnya than anyone else he knows, and probably more than he ever thought he wanted to!

Also at Combat Films, Todd Sansom for shooting so many of the interviews and Mason Garcia for putting many hours into time-coding and archiving all the material for easy referencing.

Editors Harry Orenstein (whose self described "war on commas" made this work a much easier piece to read) and D. M. Giangreco.

To Jeff Ringer and Cory Leonard at the David M. Kennedy Center for International Studies at Brigham Young University, who let me bore them to tears and lecture their students on Chechen tactics, and who supported this project on many levels.

Finally, this book wouldn't be possible without the loving support of my wife Adessa, who let me traipse around the world interviewing "shady characters" in remote and far-flung places around the world.

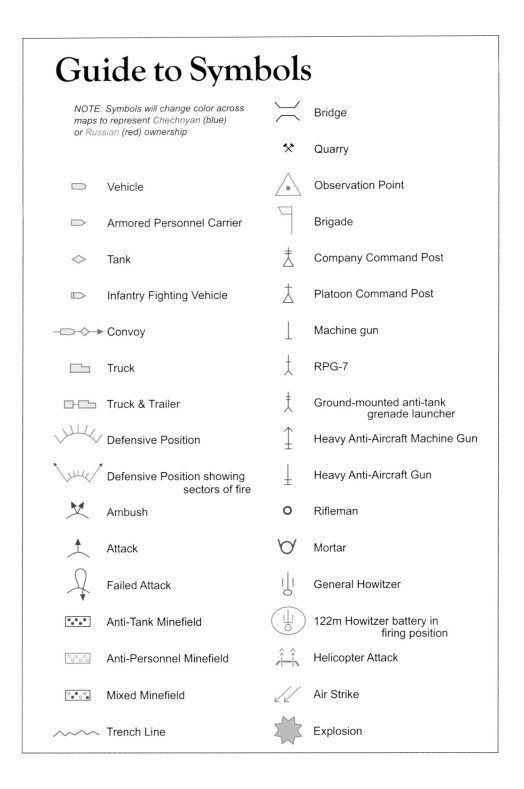

Guide to Symbols

NOTE: Symbols will change color across maps to represent Chechnyan (blue) or Russian (red) ownership

Vehicle

Armored Personnel Carrier

Tank

Infantry Fighting Vehicle

Convoy

Truck

Truck & Trailer

Defensive Position

Defensive Position showing sectors of fire

Ambush

Attack

Failed Attack

Anti-Tank Minefield

Anti-Personnel Minefield

Mixed Minefield

Trench Line

Bridge

Quarry

Observation Point

Brigade

Company Command Post

Platoon Command Post

Machine gun

RPG-7

Ground-mounted anti-tank grenade launcher

Heavy Anti-Aircraft Machine Gun

Heavy Anti-Aircraft Gun

Rifleman

Mortar

General Howitzer

122m Howitzer battery in firing position

Helicopter Attack

Air Strike

Explosion

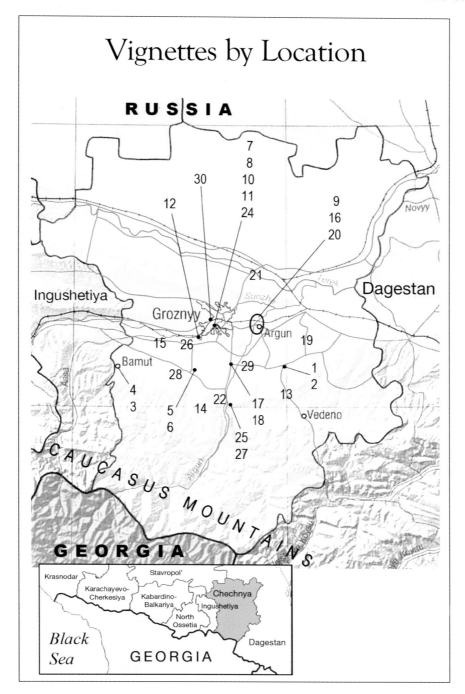

1
A BRIEF HISTORY OF THE CHECHEN CONFLICT

This work is not meant to be a retelling of the history of the Russian-Chechen War, as there have been many publications that have addressed that topic in sufficient detail. Still, when examining Chechen combatant tactics it helps to have a basic understanding of the events, conditions and patterns that make up the conflict in order to anchor the events examined into their historical context. The post-Soviet history of Chechnya, while dominated by conflict, can be characterized by and divided into the following parts; a prewar period and path to confrontation (1991–1994), the first war (1994–1996), the interwar period (1996–1999), and the second war (1999–2009).[1]

As the Soviet Union dissolved, Russian President Boris Yeltsin encouraged peoples to "grab as much freedom as they can." This was directed at the major ethnic groups in such distinct former Soviet Republics such as the Ukraine, Kazakhstan, Uzbekistan and the Baltic Republics. Chechnya "grabbed" its freedom and declared independence from Russia; however, Yeltsin, had not included the Chechens among the people that should grab their freedom for many reasons, including the following: Chechnya sits on the southern mountain wall of Russia, blocking the Caucasus region from southern peoples and empires; Chechnya's oilfields produce low-sulfur oil that requires little refining to produce high-grade aviation fuel; a major oil pipeline crosses Chechnya and Grozny was a major oil-refining center.

Chechnya is a small republic. Northern Chechnya consists of plains and lowlands and is cut off from the rest of the country by the Terek River. A long hill mass stretches east to west south of the Terek River. The hill mass is bordered to its south by the Sunzha River. The bulk of the population lives in the rolling plains that lie between the Sunzha River and the northern face of the Caucasus mountains.

Russia and Chechnya have a long history of confrontation and conflict. The path to the first Russian-Chechen war turned violent when Moscow-supported Chechen opposition forces tried to topple Chechen President Djokhar Dudaev's regime and seize power on two occasions, first in summer 1994 and then again in late fall 1994. Both attempts to destroy Dudaev's regime failed miserably. The second attempt rallied separatist Chechens when it became apparent that the coup attempt had been supported by Russian tanks and crews.

Russian mechanized forces rolled into the republic shortly afterwards, intent on seizing the capital city of Grozny and destroying Dudaev's "bandit" regime once and for all. On New Year's Eve 1994 Russian armored units struck the capital of Grozny. The three-pronged advance turned into a significant loss for the Russians as Chechen combatants were able to destroy, pin down and capture most of the enemy combatants in the capital, forcing the Russians to pull back, regroup and strike the city with aircraft and artillery. Russian military might was finally able to force the Chechens to retreat from Grozny in February 1995. The Chechen combatants fanned out from Grozny towards the second-largest city, Argun, and into the villages on the plains. Clinging to fixed positions, the Chechens suffered devastating losses against the Russians, who could bring their tanks, artillery, and air assets to bear against the Chechen positions before Chechens combatants could get within maximum effective range of their primary weapon system, the RPG.

By June 1995 the Chechen insurgency had lost all the major cities and towns. On General Aslan Maskhadov's orders the Chechen insurgency abandoned the conventional struggle and shifted to guerrilla warfare, utilizing the mountains that had always been important to Chechen national survival. It was a raid in late June 1995, however, that had the most impact of any Chechen combat during the first war. When studying Chechen tactics, most readers are likely to be familiar with what has become known as the four "spectaculars," the four large-scale hostage-taking operations on Russian territory outside of Chechnya between 1995 and 2004. The fortunes of the first war were dramatically changed by Shamil Basaev's June 1995 raid into Russia, which ended with the hospital siege at Buddennovsk. The raid led to a ceasefire in Chechnya and the safe return of Basaev and his fellow combatants to Chechen territory. His action has been widely credited within Chechnya as the turning point in the conflict in favor of the separatist insurgency.

The raid's success likely inspired others in Chechnya to do the same. In January 1996 another Chechen commander, Salman Raduev, attacked a Russian air base in nearby Kizlar, ending with a similar hostage-taking operation. However, Russia was not going to let another Buddennovsk transpire cutting off the Chechen's retreat back into Chechnya, concluding in a battle in Pervomayskoye in neighboring Dagestan. Raduev's copycat operation yielded nothing positive for the Chechen side of the war and led to increased hostilities in the spring of 1996 between Russian federal forces and Chechen combatant units.

In early March 1996 the Chechens conducted a remarkable raid into Grozny, laying siege to most of the Russian positions in the city before withdrawing three days later. Although they were forced to leave the capital, Chechen veterans of the operation claim the attack was meant to demonstrate that they could still operate against Russian forces across a broad front, while also serving as a dress rehearsal for the yet to be planned final assault on Russian forces occupying Grozny.

In August 1996 the Chechens attacked Grozny again, killing, capturing or encircling all the Russian units in the city. This third and final battle for Grozny was the last battle of the first war. Weeks later Russian President Boris Yeltsin accepted de facto Chechen independence and signed the Khasavyurt Accord.[2]

With the war behind them and the withdrawal of Russian forces from Chechnya, the Chechens set out to rebuild their fragile nation state. The interwar years in Chechnya were chaotic. Establishing a functioning state proved difficult for the Chechen leadership. Former warlords or commanders dominated politics. No single instrument of state power was strong enough to demobilize the various combatant forces. Divisions over religion were also surfacing. Rule of law broke down and kidnapping became rampant throughout the republic. Many Chechen veteran combatants state that these actions go contrary to Chechen culture and blame Russians and pro-Russian Chechens for these crimes. However, there is ample evidence that many Chechens from both camps were involved in the kidnapping trade.[3]

During the interwar period Chechen attacks against Russian positions surrounding the republic were not common, but did take place. On 22

A Chechen T-72A of the Shali Tank Regiment pictured in Grozny, 1995. (Photo via Efim Sandler)

The failed November 1994 attempt of the Russian-backed opposition to overthrow Dzhokhar Dudaev and take over Grozny. The picture shows a Chechen militant standing on an MT-LB armored vehicle in the center of Grozny, looking to repel the advance of Russian forces on 25 November 1994. (Photo by Ivan Shlamov/AFP)

On 14 December 1994 an Mi-8 helicopter of the 325th Separate Helicopter Regiment made a forced landing in Noviy Sharoy, some 30km from Grozny, after being hit by anti-aircraft fire. Two crewmembers were killed by Chechen militants on the ground, the third one died in captivity. This was the first Russian Air Force loss in Chechnya. (Photo by Mikhail Evstafiev)

was forced to retreat back into Chechen territory. Then between 4–13 September a series of apartment bombings in Russia were blamed on the Chechens, although many commentators in and out of Russia see Moscow's hand in the explosions. The short-lived Chechen incursion into Dagestan and the apartment bombings in Russia served as the casus belli for the Second Chechen War.[5]

Whatever the reasons, the Second Russian-Chechen War began in late August 1999 with the aerial bombardment of Grozny. On 1 October 1999 Russian troops entered the Chechen Republic, surrounding the capital and seizing the strategic heights in southern Chechnya. Unlike the initial battle for Grozny in the first war, the Russian forces were able to successfully seal off the southern escape routes from Grozny and methodically begin taking the city block-by-block. The Chechens holed up in the capital began withdrawing from Grozny on the night of 31 January 2000. It was not the easy walk out of the city that it had been five years earlier. Most of the force, as many as two or three thousand combatants led by Shamil Basaev and many other notable commanders, was caught in a Russian minefield and artillery barrage while exiting Grozny. As many as 600 Chechens and nine major commanders, including Lecha Dudaev and Khunkar-Pasha Israpilov, were killed. Shamil Basaev lost his foot in the retreat.

December 1997 a multi-ethnic combatant group comprised of Arab jihadists and ethnic Chechens attacked the 136th Armored Brigade of the 58th Army in Buinaksk, Dagestan. Chechen sources reported the destruction of all 300 vehicles at the base, including 50 brand-new T-72 tanks, while Russian sources reported only 10 armored vehicles destroyed and 15 damaged vehicles. The mixed force successfully retreated across the Terek River and back into Chechen territory.[4]

A year and a half later the second war began on the heels of two controversial events. On 7 August 1999, the Islamic International Brigade (IIB), under the command of Basaev and al Khattab (a Wahhabi Arab who commanded foreign fundamentalist forces in Chechnya), invaded Dagestan in support of the Shura of Dagestan. Russian units responded with force and the brigade

Chechnya has a population of about one million. Combat attrition played a significant role in changing the nature of the conflict. Senior leaders were killed and replaced by junior leaders. Personnel losses were harder and harder to replace. Two months later, in March, another major Chechen commander, Ruslan (Khamzat) Galaev, and his men were trapped by Russian forces in his home village of Komsomolskoye. Additional Chechen units and individuals who came to the village to help were trapped as well. As many as 800 Chechen combatants were killed or captured during the battle.

These two costly confrontations devastated the original Chechen separatist movement, as many of the leaders and rank and file combatants were now gone. There were still many separatists in Chechnya after these events, including Chechen president-elect

Dzhokhar Dudaev visiting the Shali Tank Regiment with Ruslanbek Iderzaev, commander of an antitank unit. The Shali Tank Regiment was the only armored unit of the Republic of Ichkeria, combining leftovers from the Russian 392nd Tank Regiment and 42nd Motor Rifle Division, withdrawn from Chechnya in 1992. (Photo via Efim Sandler)

to many Chechen combatants, Khattab's most significant contribution to the war effort was not ideology, but small group tactics. The Chechens referred to him as the "Russian tank killer" for his ability to destroy Russian armored vehicles during the first war. Khattab set up a training camp near Serzhen-Yurt between the two wars, and hundreds of Chechen combatants attended. They learned basic Arabic and studied the Quran, and, more importantly, they learned basic military tactics.

By Chechen accounts Khattab and the other international Islamic fighters in Chechnya never amounted to more than 100 personnel at any given time. The majority of these foreign volunteers were from Syria, Jordan and Turkey. Some were returning to their ancestral homes: their ancestors had been kicked out of the North Caucasus region

Aslan Maskhadov. However, many of the new combatants and leaders, such as Doku Umarov, who was a junior commander under Galaev, were more radical. Major leaders like Basaev were shifting the cause from Chechen separatism to a trans-regional Islamic jihad.

While the very rationale of the Chechen resistance seemed to be changing, the second war ground on. By late spring/early summer 2000 the Chechens had given up all fixed positions and reverted to guerrilla war. Periodic strikes against targets in Grozny and other Russian-occupied population centers occurred, but there were no significant operations against Grozny or other locations of Russian power as there had been during the first war. The Chechen forces lacked the manpower, materiel, and, more frequently, local support.

Attrition, desperation and radicalization led to an increased number of small-scale terrorist attacks in Russian territory and two additional "spectaculars," beginning with Mosvar Baraev's siege of the Nord-Ost Theater in Moscow in October 2002. This was followed by the Beslan School siege in neighboring North Ossetia in September 2004, which led to the death of hundreds of Russian school children. Neither of the hostage-taking operations of the second war led to any significant gains for the Chechen insurgency; on the contrary, they appear to have been gross miscalculations on its part. The international community was repulsed by the hostage taking at Beslan and the Chechen cause lost considerable outside sympathy and support. Within the splintered insurgency some Chechen leaders condemned these attacks, while others supported them.

The presence of foreign Islamic fighters in Chechnya had a decided impact. They clearly contributed to an ideological shift within the insurgency. By far the most significant foreigner was the Arab, al Khattab. Khattab, arrived in Chechnya shortly after the first war began in the spring of 1995. He brought with him a small contingent of foreign combatants who, like Khattab, were Wahhabi. According

by the Russians during the forced deportations of the 19th century. Their influence was not without impact. During the first war and initial stages of the second war, most Chechen combatants remained Sufi adherents and failed to embrace Wahhabism or any other form of Islam. Some Chechens did convert to these outside Islamic ideologies. Basaev is the clearest example of the debate surrounding this issue. In 1997, at the time when he was supposed to be shifting towards a more radical Islam than the Sufism practiced by the Chechen community at large, I asked him what significance Islam has in the daily life of the Chechen people. He replied, "That's not the right way to put it. Islam can't play some kind of a role in life when life is Islam in itself." While this statement is not enough by itself to pin radical Islam on Basaev, it did signify a departure from the socioreligious order by which most Chechens lived, where their distinct culture, *adat*, was the dominant force in the society for which religion was a singular part.

Initially Khattab was not immediately welcomed in Chechnya and was viewed with suspicion by many. He had to earn his place through combat, and did so. Eventually Khattab and his Islamic battalion were co-located in Basaev's area of influence on the southeastern front, specifically in the Vedeno district. The relationship between the two combatant leaders was reportedly close and Khattab no doubt influenced Basaev's thinking. This is especially evident in Basaev's idea of an Islamic caliphate that would span the North Caucasus, postulated during the interwar period (1997–1999).[6] While speaking to me near his headquarters in Grozny, Basaev stated, "It is possible to unite everyone, as a matter of fact there is a great possibility because all of the nations of the Caucuses, and I stress all without exception, want freedom and independence from Russia. They are sick of Russia."[7]

Khattab and the foreign Mujahideen continued to play a minor role during the second war until Khattab was killed by a poisoned letter delivered by an agent of the Russian security services on 20 March 2002. Another foreign Mujahideen replaced Khattab until he too was killed and replaced as well. This pattern continues.

After Khattab's death, the war continued under the often conflicting rhetoric of Chechen president-elect Aslan Maskhadov and Basaev, the insurgency's most well-known commander. Many analysts see Maskhadov's death at the hands of Russian federal forces

on 8 March 2005 as the end of the hope for a moderate Chechen leader. Russian President Vladimir Putin demonstrated no interest in seeking out or supporting negotiations with Maskhadov. After Maskhadov's death Basaev remained the dominating force behind the insurgency until his death on 10 July 2006. Doku Umarov led the insurgency until he too was eventually killed by Russian forces and replaced.

2
DEFENSE OF AN URBAN AREA

Most readers are familiar with the Chechen urban defense of Grozny. After Grozny, the fighting shifted to other urban Chechen cities and villages. This chapter deals with the fighting for Serzhen-Yurt, Bamut, and Goyskoe.

The Russian Army had learned many hard lessons in the early battles for Grozny and brought them to the subsequent fighting. When possible, the Russian Army avoided the frontal assault, where the enemy was strongest, and tried to locate and attack his flanks. The Russian Army was also careful not to expose its flanks during the penetration of an urban area. The Russian approach was methodical and attempted to spare the lives of its own soldiers. Despite harsh criticism to the contrary, in many cases the Russians also attempted to spare the lives of the noncombatants by leaving an escape route and not launching an attack immediately upon arrival, but rather giving a few days for the noncombatants to leave the area.

The Russian Army conducted reconnaissance of some type prior to the attack. The Russian attack usually began with airstrikes and then phased artillery fire, which fired in lines along the defensive sector, shifting into the depths of the defense while pummeling the area over which it would advance. Tanks would lead the attack, followed by infantry fighting vehicles or armored personnel carriers and dismounted infantry. The attacks were shallow enough that artillery did not usually have to displace during the advance. Since the fighting was through the rubble of a city or village, the pace was slow and methodical. This gave the Chechens time to react, but also permitted the Russians to keep the bulk of their firepower forward, where it was most threatening.

Vignette 1: First Phase of the Battle for Serzhen-Yurt, Early May–23 May 1995

Kair, Musa, Ilyas

Background: By May 1995 the Chechen insurgency was reeling. Grozny had been abandoned and Argun, the second-largest city, was under Russian control, as were all the villages in the plains, including Staryye Atagi, Novyye Atagi and Shali. The Chechen combatant leadership had been pushed into the mountains, while Chechen units tried to hold a line of towns and villages on the edges of the mountains stretching from Bamut in the west, Chiri-Yurt in the middle, and Serzhen-Yurt in the east. Each of these towns was strategically important for the Chechens to hold and the Russians to seize. If the Russians could control these towns, the gateways to the mountains, the Chechens would be isolated from their support bases among the population of the urban centers.

If the Russian forces could break through at Chiri-Yurt they could then fight for Duba-Yurt and the Wolf's Gate, opening a path through the mountains to Maskhadov's headquarters in Vedeno and Dudaev's base at Shatoi.

Serzhen-Yurt was equally significant, as it is at the entrance to the strategically important Vendo rayon[1] and controls the only road to Vedeno, the location of Maskahdov's headquarters and the ancestral home of Shamil Basaev, Chechnya's most significant field commander. In the third week of March, during the Russian encirclement of Argun, the Chechen general staff moved its headquarters to Serzhen-Yurt. However, a couple of weeks later, in the first half of April, Maskhadov and the general staff moved further south to Vedeno.[2] Although Basaev's family lived in Vedeno, Basaev located his individual command in Benoi-Yurt, half way between Serzhen-Yurt and his hometown. From Benoi-Yurt, Basaev was responsible for the defense of the strategic rayon. By the end of April that defense was concentrated on Serzhen-Yurt.

The Chechens gained a momentary reprieve when on 6 April 1995, in anticipation of dignitary visits honoring the fifty-year anniversary of the Second World War, President Yeltsin signed decree No. 417 suspending Russian operations in Chechnya from 28 April to 12 May. Yeltsin's decree meant little to the Chechens and hundreds of small-scale attacks against Russian troops occurred during the ceasefire. Russian forces also continued to engage Chechen positions, albeit on a much smaller scale. On 5 May a Russian SU-25 attack aircraft from the Russian 4th Air Army was shot down while on a sortie near Serzhen-Yurt. The pilot was killed and the Chechens recovered documents, including charts and maps, from the wreckage. Additional fighting near Serzhen-Yurt occurred on 8 May. Finally, on 10 May five Mi-24 combat helicopters attacked Chechen positions in Serzhen-Yurt. There were reports of seven villagers killed and eight wounded, but like so many casualty reports they are impossible to verify.

Although both Russian and Chechen forces continued to fight during the two-week moratorium, the Russians did not conduct an all-out push to take Serzhen-Yurt and Chiri-Yurt. The moratorium could not have come at a better time for the reeling Chechens. The Chechens defending Serzhen-Yurt were a collection of battered groups and individual combatants, short on ammunition, food and medical supplies. More importantly, morale was faltering among the combatants, the result of one recent defeat after another.

Shamil had two battalions defending Serzhen-Yurt, both under the command of Mohmad Hatuev, who had responsibility for the Serzhen-Yurt portion of the larger sector under Basaev's command. Realizing Serzhen-Yurt could not be held with the limited number of combatants defending the town, Basaev requested additional

Russian forces in the Serzhen-Yurt area. Serzhen-Yurt was the key to the so-called Wolf's Gate Gorge in the Shali District. Russian forces blockaded the area in February 1995 but did not move forward, having probably lost momentum. (Efim Sandler collection)

A battery of Akatsya 2S3 152mm self-propelled howitzers, along with a PRP-4 Nard artillery reconnaissance vehicle. These examples were operated by the 2nd Artillery Battalion, 166th Separate Motor Rifle Brigade, in the Chiri-Yurt area in April 1995. Chiri-Yurt was the settlement located about 17km from Serzhen-Yurt, being famous for its cement plant that saw some fierce fighting in 1995. (Photo via 166 Brigade veterans)

A Russian BMP-1 in a dug-in position. The BMP-1 and -2 IFVs were the main workhorses of the Russian Motor Rifle units. (Photo via Efim Sandler)

men and units. In response, Maskhadov ordered additional units to Serzhen-Yurt, including the Islamic battalion under the command of Islam Halimov and the presidential guard of 30 combatants, usually given responsibility to guard Maskhadov's headquarters. There were also two groups from the Nozi-Yurt district, but it is unknown if these two groups were part of the reinforcements sent by Maskhadov or if they were already defending the town in conjunction with Basaev's battalion. Problems of coordination surfaced from the beginning, as the Islamic battalion would not take orders from Hatuev, telling Baseav that Hatuev, "was not our Emir."[3]

On 11 May, hours before the official end of the cease fire, Russian armored units began pulling out of their assembly areas in preparation for an attack on Chechen positions across a broad front, including Serzhen-Yurt. The renewed assault began with a massive artillery and air bombardment of the Chechen defenses at Serzhen-Yurt, Duba-Yurt and Chiri-Yurt. The bombardment lasted days. On 17 May the Russian Army began its ground assault on these targeted cities. Sometime during the advance or the artillery bombardment Russian units seized Hill 541.6 near Serzhen-Yurt, putting them one kilometer closer to the town.[4]

The Chechen defense of Serzhen-Yurt was focused on the northern approaches to the town. "Our line, we called it the 'Serzhen-Yurt Line,' stretched across the gap west to east from the hills to the river," recalls Musa. Although battered, the Chechens had developed more "field smarts" when constructing defensive positions and had dug a series of zigzag trenches with which to protect themselves against the artillery and air strikes. According to Kair, Basaev's battalion had responsibility

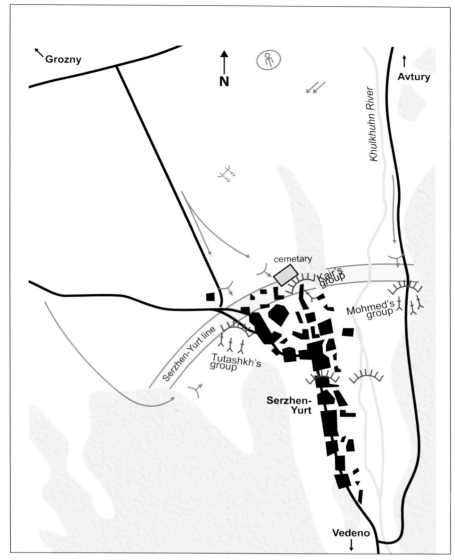

First Phase of the Battle for Serzhen-Yurt, early May–23 May 1995.

for the Serzhen-Yurt Line, but there were other units involved, such as a group from Serzhen-Yurt itself. There were at least three separate units defending the broad defensive line. Kair's unit of 17 combatants was located in the middle of an apple orchard facing an open field that bordered a cemetery. "We had three RPG men, two machine gunners, and the rest were riflemen." To his east, Mohmad[5] commanded a group of 22 combatants next to the Khulkhulan River. His unit had numerous antitank weapons, as the Chechens believed that any armored breakthrough would come on the flanks, not up the middle towards Kair's position. A third group of 14 Chechen combatants, commanded by Tutashkh, was to Kair's left, up against the hills near the main road to Serzhen-Yurt. Tutashkh's unit was also armed with numerous antitank weapons.

From Kair's vantage point, most of the Russians seemed to be positioned directly in front of him, in the cemetery. Kair and Tutashkh could both see Russian armor drive back and forth on a small road on the far side of the cemetery even before the main Russian assault skirmishes broke out. On the western edge of the Chechen line Tutashkh's unit had a clear line of sight on the road and was able to destroy two tanks on the road before the main assault began. Unbeknownst to the Chechen defenders, Russian units were also advancing through the forests to the Chechens' left flank.

On 17 May, Kair was observing the Russian positions from the safety of a concrete building to the east of his unit's position in the apple orchard. He suddenly saw Russian infantry advancing towards the center of the line.[6] "There was a big concrete fence that we could hide behind. We had an observation periscope from a BTR. The periscope was fitted to binoculars." Kair alerted his men in the orchards to take their positions. "I could see the Russian soldiers walking toward us – no armor or other vehicles – only foot soldiers." He told his group to get ready. From their trench position they waited until the Russians were in range and opened fire. The Russian infantry dove for the ground or fell among the grave stones. "I have no idea how many were killed and wounded."

A bit to Kair's left, an antitank weapon arced from the Chechen line into the field ahead of him. "There must be tanks left of us" Kair thought. While most of the antitank weapons had gone to Mohmad's group near the river, Kair's group had a homemade antitank weapon known as a Shaitan (devil). Short on heavy weapons, the Chechens had been able to devise some ingenious antitank weapons during the short duration of the war.[7]

Although a veteran of numerous battles, Kair didn't know what was happening up and down the Chechen line. The sound of the fight around him was deafening. He had not noticed that Russian armor had been able to maneuver towards Mohmad's group at the river

The fight for Serzhen-Yurt was conducted by the 506th Motor Rifle Regiment from March 1995. The settlement was blockaded but no move was made to take it over until May. The fighting was mostly an exchange of fire between Russians and Chechens that continued until the ceasefire was agreed in summer 1995. The photo shows a BRDM-2 of 506th Motor Rifle Regiment near Serzhent-Yurt in May 1995. (Efim Sandler collection)

and that the Russians had marched through the forest and begun to encircle Tutashkh's group. Fierce battles were now going on all up and down the line. Prior to the Russian assault the Chechens had placed the majority of their antitank assets with Mohmad's group at the river, concluding that the armor might try to break through at that position along a dirt road on the east side of the river.

The fighting near the river was intense but Mohmad's force was well dug in and Russian tanks, forced to attack straight ahead through a relatively narrow corridor between the river and the steep cliffs leading off the surrounding heights, could not break through Mohmad's position. Antitank fire from Mohmad's position forced the Russians to retreat. Kair assumes that the Russians were trying to flank the city along the river and get to an overlook east of the city

from which to control artillery fire. Four or five burned-out tanks littered the battle zone, a testament to the ferocity of the battle on the right flank

To Kair's left, Tutashkh's unit was in trouble. Cut off from behind, outmanned and outgunned, Tutashkh could not hold out or break through the Russian encirclement, nor could the Chechens rush significant forces to Tutashkh's aid. Kair recalls Tutashkh's last message. "I am surrounded. Farewell." This was a devastating blow to the Chechen line.[8]

"We defended against two attacks here in the apple orchard." After two days of fierce fighting, the Russians pulled back and "started to bomb us, using long-range weapons and helicopters." Kair recalls that it was the third day that they were given the order to retreat southward to secondary positions deeper inside the town. "When the first and second Russian attacks retreated we were given the command to withdraw because their forces were greater than ours." Rather than push their advantage immediately, the Russians consolidated their gains.

Commentary: The initial attack on Serzhen-Yurt lasted roughly two-and-a-half days. At the time Russians reported six soldiers killed in action, while Chechens claim three Chechens killed and two wounded. Both are likely wrong. Kair and Musa, both participants in the battle, recall that at least one Chechen unit was overrun (Tutashkh's), while also claiming to have destroyed no fewer than seven pieces of armor – two before the battle, one during the battle from Kair's position and at least four near the river in Mohmad's part of the line. Kair recalls only one of his unit being wounded while retreating to the secondary positions deeper inside Serzhen-Yurt.

The Chechens' 'Serzhen-Yurt Line' proved stubborn and difficult to break. Although the Russians had forced the Chechens from their forward positions, they were unable to seize the town after two-and-a-half days of fighting. Unable to seize Serzhen-Yurt, the Russian ground assault withdrew[9] or consolidated their limited gains. As the Russian ground forces pulled back, air and artillery strikes pounded the Chechen line. Hatuev received the order

BTRs proved to be extremely vulnerable to anything heavier than small arms fire. In Serzhen-Yurt the Chechens destroyed several Russian BTRs, mostly with RPGs. The picture shows a destroyed BTR-70 which had probably been carrying ammunition that exploded. Samashki Village, 31 January 1995. (Photo by Karsten Thielker)

to pull his Chechen units back to secondary position during the barrage. The Serzhen-Yurt Line was moving further south, ceding the northern half of the town to the advancing Russians.

Fatigue, command and control issues, and lack of sufficient arms and ammunition were but a few of the mitigating factors working against the Chechen defense of the village. Although the Chechens had the advantage of defending the narrow gorge, they had no answer for the airpower and artillery the Russians were able to apply against their positions and, as they did in every battle to this point, they retreated to the next position.

Although the Chechens describe their fight in terms of battalions, these "battalions" were not even full-platoon strength. The "battalions" had a high-percentage of antitank weapons and at this point were still fighting a conventional fight. The guerrilla phase would start once the Chechens were forced into the mountains.

The Russian instincts were good – dominate the high ground and go for the flanks instead of a head-on urban fight. The flank attacks, however, were tactical and shallow. The narrowness of the valley actually forced the Russians to attack head on along some sections of the front. For instance, while the assault on Mohmad's position east of the river would have allowed the Russians to flank the Chechens holding the center of the village, the tanks were still forced to face Mohmad's antitank weapons head on. Later the Russians would use deeper, larger-scale flanking attacks with greater success. In fact, at the very same time the battle for Serzhen-Yurt was raging, the Russians were making progress in Chiri-Yurt, from which they would pass through the Wolf's Gate and then cut back east to end up in Vedeno's rear, forcing Maskhadov's command post to abandon Vedeno.

Vignette 2: Second Phase of the Battle for Serzhen-Yurt, 24 May–end of May 1995

Kair, Musa, Ilyas

Background: After the Russian pulled back from the first assault on the town, in the midst of artillery and air strikes, the Chechens manning the Serzhen-Yurt Line fell back to secondary positions in the vicinity of Zhelimkhan's monument. Mohmad Hatuev brought a reserve unit into the line to replace Tutashkh's unit, which had been encircled and overrun a few days earlier. The Chechen formations now held a second line running from the Khulkhulan River in the east to the forested hills west of the town, past Zhelimkhan's monument on the road leading to Vedeno west of the town and up to the hills west of the town. "There were places that had been prepared beforehand. We knew in advance that we would relocate to this position. A Chechen soldier, once he takes up a new position, he begins to dig. There's gravel all over the place, rocks – it's hard to dig – and he needs a crowbar and other tools. To haul all that equipment around, in addition to your weapon and other supplies, was an extra burden. It was very difficult and an additional risk. We prepared these areas beforehand in order to prevent this additional risk."

Kair's unit had retreated straight back on the road and now maintained new positions to the right of the main road near Zhelimkhan's monument. Another unit on Kair's left flank was guarding the western flank of the town. Mohmad had moved his force further south along the river to a Soviet-era children's camp with the same mission, to deny the Russians use of the river bed or the road east of the river to flank the line and move further south towards the Chechen command HQ in Vedeno.

Recalling the repositioning, Kair stated "As soon as we were set up, they [the Russians] found out that we had taken up new positions. And they began, like I said before, to look around, like they were doing recon. They mostly went through the village center heading in our direction, along the roads, which weren't far from our positions. We watched as they prepared the area for the arrival of the bulk of their forces. This was on the second day. We had cleared out of our forward positions at night, and moved into these fallback positions. On the second day, towards the evening, the Russians had already started to make probes around here. In their reconnaissance they carefully look, learning which places are mined and which aren't. Let's say there's a freshly dug-up place in the road – they then know that there might be mines there. They take pictures of this road from an observation helicopter. They only advance once they've analyzed the pictures and reports."

On 24 May Russian artillery paused and the ground assault on Serzhen-Yurt began again. Ironically, being forced to fall back from their first line, the Chechens now occupied an even better position, as the narrowing valley concentrated their efforts. The Russians had no choice but to assault the Chechen force head-on if they were going to reach Vedeno through Serzhen-Yurt.

The first battles broke out east of the river as the Russians tried to break through the Chechen defenses along the well-worn dirt road. "I suspect they were trying to break through and get to a strategic height that would have given them command of the entire Serzhen-Yurt area and views southward towards Vedeno" recalls Kair. "The Russians were concentrated along the river. There were trees beside the river. The Russians hid behind the cover of the trees." The strip of woods was about 50 meters across. The road ran parallel to a steep cliff that had been carved out by water over the years. In this way the Russians were pinned in place. They couldn't maneuver left. If they went right they ran into the river and right into my unit. Their only real option was to advance directly into Mohmad's fire or turn and retreat."

The Chechens had positioned their line to be able to help each other in case one point of the line began to fail. "That's why the blocking positions were positioned where they were. We were sitting right below the monument and there was a reserve group on the other side of the road. From our positions we were able to direct our fire across this river and through the strip of woods" Kair recalls. "Because of the forest, we couldn't actually see their movement but we could determine where they were because they were firing at Mohmad's defenses. We just kept pounding the area with our antitank weapons." One of Hatuev's reserve groups was also on standby if it needed to relocate across the river and intercept the Russian advance pushing towards Mohmad's group. "In case they went towards this group and engaged them in battle, we could help and move to their aid."

The Russian assault on Mohmad's position ground to a halt. There was a number of destroyed armored vehicles strewn out on the road. "We burned those tanks beyond the river to hell," recalls Kair. The next day, a Russian gunship flew over the river at the scene of the heavy fighting the day before. There were Chechens throughout the town, occupying houses, garages and whatever other structures were available. All the units tracked the helicopter before a heavy machine gun opened fire from one of the reserve units near the monument. The helicopter turned away from the line of fire, but it was too late. The bullets raked the tail section and the helicopter began to smoke and spiral towards the ground. A moment later it crashed into the river. Nearby Chechen combatants ran to the wreckage to secure its

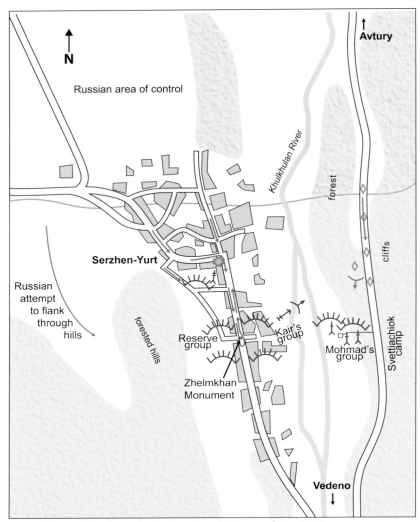

Second Phase of the Battle for Serzhen-Yurt, 24 May–end May 1995.

weapons and ammunition. The rocket pod was very important for both the tubes and the rockets.

To the west, the Russians decided against a move up the middle but sent a unit on the other side of the ridge in another attempt to flank the Chechen line from the heights on the west of the narrow valley. "The Russians, not being able to advance through the town, turned around behind the ridge and advanced upwards."

There was a pause after downing the helicopter. Then the artillery rained down. Kair and the other combatants scrambled from their positions in the houses of the village for their fortified, dug-in positions. There was nothing they could do but wait it out. The firing began to slow down and the Chechens once again returned to their lookout points. Kair could not believe his ears. It sounded like armor, this time the tracks clanking against the asphalt road. They were coming straight for his position, in the thick of the Chechen defenses. "I think their reconnaissance failed and they thought that we might have left. They could not break right through the center" Kair recalls.

From dark doorways and windows, dozens of Chechens watched as a small column of three tanks and a BTR clanked past them. "There are houses and fences there, barriers, or other things in the courtyard, parked cars, people... it was not a problem to hide there. This tank went right between our two groups. Had he noticed us, he could've opened fire on all of us with his machine gun. But he went through, not noticing us."

The column actually went right between Kair's group and a reserve unit. The arrival of the tanks surprised the Chechens taking positions in the houses next to the road. They had not expected them to drive this far south into the village. "They were most likely scouts. Maybe they thought we were all at the river defending. I don't know."

"When these four vehicles passed us, the reserve unit that Hatuev had just put in the line went after them and immediately stopped them." Two of the tanks and the BTR were engaged and brought to a halt. The Chechen combatants swarmed the vehicles. It was close quarters fighting with the Russian crews. The third tank managed to get turned around, avoided a disabling RPG strike and drove north out of the kill zone.

"The tank appeared to be home free. It slowed down to make the turn at a three way intersection. A streak of fire arced forward and hit it with a boom! The tank suffered a direct hit with a Shmel flame round.[10] "Our forces took the tank out on the corner as soon as it passed our position. And that's where it burned.

We had a flamethrower, but it's hard for me now to say exactly who had it. But we had a flamethrower; as often was the case with many groups and I don't know who actually fired it. We had guys dispersed all around the area. Our group wasn't more than 200 meters from this intersection. So, our men could destroy the tank. Men from the reserve group were also able to hit it. They were able to engage it from behind cover. It's hard for me to say exactly who from which group destroyed it. What I know is that we torched it. It burned to scrap in front of us."

Back in the kill pocket the Chechens finished off the Russian crews. There were just some bursts of fire and then it was over. All three vehicles were captured intact and the Chechens drove them into their lines and used them to fire on the Russian armor trying to get up the riverbed. The crews were either killed in the fight or as they surrendered, according to Kair. He does not recall any prisoners being taken. Kair only feels certain about the outcome of the tank crew that was hit by flame projector. "When a tank burns, it's hard to get out of it. When an antitank projectile hits the tank, it explodes, whether it is from an RPG or

Each Russian motor rifle regiment had a tank battalion of about 40 tanks, unlike the regular tank battalion of 30 tanks in tank regiments. The picture shows T-72B/B1 tank of the 506th Regiment in the Shali region, 16 June 1996. (Photo Efim Sandler collection)

a Shaitan launcher. Everyone in the tank goes deaf from the force of the explosion. They can no longer think or get their thoughts together, they don't know how to get out or where to go – that's the condition they are in. There is a loud noise and tremendous pressure from the air. The air pressure works upward. So, for the tank crews, it's one big grave."

The tank assault was a complete surprise to Kair and the others manning positions in the center of town. "Our guys were sitting right here, and there was a reserve group, and a group that was in charge of evacuating the wounded. They were the ones who attacked the tanks and BTR, forced them to a stop and then captured three of the vehicles. I don't think the Russians had any idea we were in the vicinity, maybe they thought we bugged out."

The front seemed to go quiet. A car from Vedeno arrived to deliver food and supplies. However, the captured BTR had both food and ammunition. The supplies were divided among the combatants. Soon after, the artillery bombardment began again, and Kair and the rest took cover. Sometime after the day's fighting, some of the extra groups that Maskhadov had sent in to reinforce Basaev's battalions unexpectedly withdrew.

Commentary: The Russians were never able to take Serzhen-Yurt by force. Eventually the Russian ground assault on Serzhen-Yurt abandoned the frontal attack and struck the Chechens from the rear. The defenders of Serzhen-Yurt did not know that the Russians were already making their way to Vedeno by bypassing Serzhen-Yurt and attacking through Chiri-Yurt and the Wolf's' Gate, turning east and striking Vedeno from the west. In conjunction with the armored flanking maneuver, Russian helicopters began landing airborne troops in the hills above Vedeno. On 2 June Maskadov's command was forced to withdraw from Vedeno to a new predesignated command location in Dargo, even though Basaev's battalions continued to hold Serzhen-Yurt.[11]

The remaining fighters in Serzhen-Yurt were effectively cut off, with the Russians now behind them. A few days later Basaev's two battalions split into many smaller groups and snuck out of the Russian encirclement at Serzhen-Yurt through the town of Kranoye Vedeno, again demonstrating the Chechens' ability to continually break through Russian lines. They made their way on foot to Dargo to join the rest of the Chechen fighters at the new headquarters

location. Chechens talk about this being their darkest time. Their leadership was split up with very limited means of communication, the groups were in disarray, everyone was hungry and ammunition was in very short supply.

As always casualty figures vary. According to Russian sources, on 28 May alone, 11 Naval Infantry (Marines) from the Pacific Fleet's Naval Infantry Detachment were killed in the fighting. Chechens claim that 30 Russian soldiers were killed and 10 Russian armored vehicles destroyed, while losing 11 Chechen combatants.

Some Chechen combatants continued to operate in the Serzhen-Yurt-Vedeno corridor, conducting ambushes of Russian columns, but they held no fixed positions.[12] The Chechen side had now gone entirely to guerrilla warfare. Weeks later, Basaev would lead his now infamous operation into Russia that would save the Chechen resistance movement for the time being and change the course of the first war.[13]

The Russian forces had recovered from their original embarrassing performance in Grozny and were reluctant to take on a strong urban defense head-on. Once their probes into Serzhen-Yurt failed, they bypassed the village for a 14-mile end run through the Wolf's Gate to capture Vedeno. They left enough forces at Serzhen-Yurt to hold the Chechen defenders in place and not allow them to join forces with additional Chechen units in Vedeno. The Russians were also becoming more skillful at holding a defense forward while they felt for the flanks and then unhinged the defense from the flanks and rear. Still, their scouting efforts needed work, as their unsupported entry of four armored vehicles into the middle of a village demonstrated. Ironically, Vedeno suffered very little physical damage during the war because Maskhadov opted to give up the town and relocate rather than fight it out with the Russians in this location.

Vignette 3: Defending Bamut, Mid-June 1995[14]

Musa

Background: By the spring of 1995 Russian forces had taken Grozny and the rest of the major cities in Chechnya. In May, Vedeno fell without much of a fight and the Chechen command retreated deeper into the mountains. Shatoi and Nozhai-Yurt fell to Russian

In parallel with the developments in Serzhen-Yurt, there was a fight for the cement plant in Chiri-Yurt (some 17km distant). Russian forces launched several attacks, initially with the 245th and 324th Motor Rifle Regiments and finally using the 108th Guards Airborne Regiment of the 7th Guards Airborne Division, commanded by Colonel Shamanov. The picture shows paratroopers firing a Konkurs 9M113 ATGM to destroy Chechen positions in the plant on 21 May 1995. (Photo by Alexander Nemenov)

Another picture of Russian paratroopers of 9th Company, 108th Guards Airborne Regiment, with a BMD-2 armored vehicle, after taking over the cement plant in Chiri-Yurt, on 21 May 1995. (Photo via Efim Sandler)

Responding to the call for help, many small groups began making their way towards besieged Bamut. Unfortunately for the Chechens, many of the groups traveled through or close to the villages near the forest line and were ambushed by Russian reconnaissance units operating between the mountains and the towns of Gekhi-Chu, Orekhovo and Staryi-Achhoi. Other units, recognizing the danger of traveling so close to the Russian lines, went deeper into the mountains before swinging westward to arrive at Bamut. This was difficult and time consuming. Some units arrived only a couple of days before the Russian assault and barely had time to prepare themselves or their positions.

"It was mandatory to inform the sector commander that you had arrived, the strength of your unit, as well as providing any additional information, so that you could be placed in the defense according to your capability and as the need required," noted one of the group leaders. In this way Boris was able to get a clear picture of the forces at his disposal, assess their strengths, and build a defense based on available resources. As the arriving units and individual combatants checked in with Boris, he assessed the needs and placed the various combat elements where he thought they could be used most effectively.

The Chechen units spread across the defensive perimeter west of Bamut frantically dug a series of zigzagged trenches to withstand the pending Russian assault. The Chechens also dug trenches into the wooded hillside east of Bamut, where it hugged the contours of the gorge leading south into the mountains. A casualty collection point was also established in the wooded hills east of the village. The Chechens used boards to construct pedestrian bridges across the Fortanga River on their way to the village and their fighting positions west of the village. Normally, building materials might have been in short supply, but Bamut was a village of destroyed houses, providing ample materials to construct makeshift defenses and fortify approach routes.

The trenches west of Bamut were in several rows, with their forward positions a mere 50 to 100 meters from the charred ruins of what used to be houses. The Chechens spread their positions over a

forces on 13 June. Bamut was the only sizable village still under Chechen control. Previous Russian attacks on Bamut had failed and the village lay in ruins. Burnt-out Russian tanks and BMPs littered the main road through the village, testifying to the fierce fighting that occurred there.[15]

With Shatoi in their control, the Russians refocused their effort to take Bamut. While much of the eastern front, including Bamut, fell under Ruslan (Khamzat) Galaev's command, the individual commander for the on-the-ground defense of the village was a Chechen called Boris. Observing Russian forces mobilizing on the plains facing Bamut for a final strike, Boris sent out an SOS – a request for help from any Chechen combatants or groups that could help. At the time, Bamut's defenders were male volunteers from the village and other local area volunteer groups.

series of trench lines, a tactic that had been perfected over months of painful experience based on the Chechen principle of "attack and retreat, attack and retreat." The general idea was to constantly displace during battle, maintaining mobility and not relying on any fixed position that could be targeted and destroyed by Russian air strikes, artillery and mortars.

The attack for Bamut began as the Chechens expected: air strikes followed by artillery. The Chechens were familiar with the pattern and considered it "the old way of fighting – the Soviet way." They could easily see the Russian positions in the flat lands north of them. The positions were more than a kilometer away, beyond the effective range of their only antitank weapon – the RPG.[16] The Chechens could only hunker down in the relative safety of their dugouts in the tree line and wait for the barrage to end. Finally the shelling stopped and the Chechens ran to their forward trench positions to meet the armor and infantry that had begun moving southward along the main road towards the village.

The Russians also feigned an attack from the direction of Achkoi-Martan. It is unclear how the Chechen's knew, but they expected this, recognized it as a diversionary action and did not take the bait. They maintained their positions against the Russian column that was advancing toward them from the northwest. As the Russian column approached Bamut, individual units broke off and spread out along a broad front facing the defending Chechens.

While Boris had overall command for the entire defense of Bamut, each specific unit commander was in charge of his own place in the line and his men. He was also free to employ his own specific tactics, including how he and his unit fought on the line. Because of this, the battle for Bamut on the first day became a series of individual skirmishes between a continuous Russian line, breaking up under the fog and friction of combat, and Chechen strong points, each attempting to maintain secure flanks. Individual Chechen units fought separate actions, each in its own way and according to its own plan.

Once in range, the Chechens poured RPG and automatic fire into the oncoming Russians, being careful not to stay in any one position long enough for the Russians to call in and adjust effective supporting fire. Two significant battles along the line broke the Russian assault and forced the Russians to retreat. The Chechens on the left flank were able to trap and encircle a portion of the Russian force (see map detail 2). A Chechen unit on the right flank had come to Bamut with antitank mines, and devised its own tactics to strike a blow at the advancing Russian force (see map detail 1).

Knowing that they would have to displace, and hoping to suck the Russians into their abandoned positions, the unit mined their own trenches with the antitank mines, linked together for remote detonation. Under intense fire, but as planned, the Chechens then withdrew to secondary trenches. Russian infantry pursuing the retreating Chechen group jumped into the abandoned trench line and began to consolidate the newly captured position. The Chechen unit detonated the mines from their secondary trenches and the whole position was destroyed, killing all the Russians occupying the trench. With its infantry gone, the Russian armor withdrew under fire. "These trenches were completely blown up. But we weren't able to get the armor. The armor went back without the infantry. They retreated back 300–400 meters because without infantry they would quickly be covered with fire" recalls Musa.

The Russian advance stalled and then retreated back to its pre-assault positions beyond Chechen RPG range. Artillery again pounded the Chechen line, but the Chechens again displaced to their positions in the hills, carrying their wounded and dead off the

A Russian Mi-24 launching an attack with unguided rockets on a target in the Shali District in early 1995. Russian strike aviation was not very active at this period, being mostly prohibited by the orders of Moscow. (Efim Sandler collection)

T-80B/BV tanks of the 166th Separate Motor Rifle Brigade seen in the Shali District. 166th Brigade was very active during the mountain war in Chechnya and was one of several Russian units that employed T-80 tanks in 1995–96. (Photo via Efim Sandler)

front line. The next day the Russians attacked again, but the battle was short. It was possibly a probing attack to see if the Chechens had stayed to defend or had melted away into the mountains as they had done so many times before. After meeting determined resistance, the Russian assault pulled back. According to Musa, the entire fighting during the second day lasted less than a half hour.

The same night, the Russian force sent a reconnaissance team to breach the Chechen line and operate in the Chechen rear with the intent to call in air and artillery strikes on Chechen coordinates (see map detail 3). They tried to sneak right up the middle of the line, but a Chechen position of four soldiers noticed and engaged the team. A brief but deadly firefight ensued and 10 of the 11 Russian soldiers in the reconnaissance party were killed. One was taken prisoner. Under interrogation, the prisoner told the Chechens that his unit's objective was to "get through the line, take a position in the village, discover the Chechen positions, and then call in fire on those

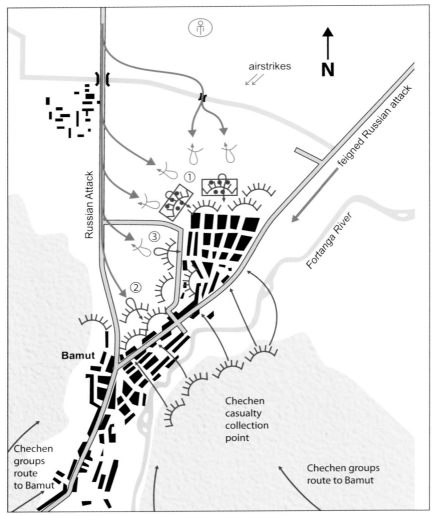

Defending Bamut, mid-June 1995

coordinates." The POW was also asked about the strength of his forces because, having beaten back the Russian advance twice, the Chechens had begun to entertain the idea of going on the offensive and attacking the Russian position. The Russian soldier's account of his forces compelled the Chechens to drop any offensive plan, as it was considered too dangerous. The Russians were just too numerous and a counterattack would not be worth the risk with the chance of success minimal.

The Chechens continued to dig in, treat their wounded and wait for the next Russian attack, which many believed would be much more fierce. However, no Russian assault came. The Chechens defending Bamut received word over the radio of Shamil Basaev's raid into Russia and the resultant negotiations and truce. Both the Russian and Chechen lines at Bamut ceased hostilities as the war paused for the next few months.

Bamut was the last Chechen stronghold and was sure to fall to Russian forces in time. However, due to the truce following Basaev's raid into Budennovsk, Bamut was spared Russian occupation in 1995. Russian attacks on Bamut resumed in 1996 but the Chechens were able to successfully defend the village and it was actually never under Russian control during the first war (1994–1996).

Commentary: The first day's battle lasted no more than two hours. Although the Chechens constantly displaced and the Russians were severely bloodied on the left and right flanks, Chechen unit commanders on the line say they had many killed and wounded.

There are no accurate numbers for the casualties, nor is the actual number of Chechen defenders known. Chechen veterans of the battle suggest as few as 100 and as many as 300 Chechens defended Bamut during this time. One Chechen commanding a line unit suggested that only Boris knew the exact number of defenders, a precaution taken to minimize the chance that the Russians might acquire the same information by taking a Chechen prisoner.

Russian unit size and casualties are not known, but Chechen participants suggest many Russian casualties and some destroyed armor. However, as in other battles, both sides tended to minimize their own losses while exaggerating their enemy's.

The Russian unit deployed in the main attack was at least a mechanized infantry battalion reinforced with a tank company and supported by self-propelled howitzers. The artillery likely fired the standard four-phase artillery preparation for an attack on a prepared, defending enemy, but apparently stopped after phase two, since this was not a defense in depth and there would be no breakthrough and pursuit of a mechanized enemy. The maneuver unit deployed using the basic battalion battle drill for moving from battalion column to platoon line. A lot of effort was directed toward maintaining a contiguous line with maximum firepower forward. The Chechen opposition, however, was not linear, although their prepared positions were. The opposition was not even in their positions during the artillery preparation. The artillery fire support and maneuver were not fully coordinated, since the Chechens had enough time to move forward into their defensive positions after the artillery quit and before the tanks and infantry arrived.

The Russian diversionary attack was probably company-strength. It was not pressed, although it had the potential to unhinge the entire Chechen defense, threatening their defenses from the rear and limiting their escape routes to constricted areas that could be easily interdicted with artillery fire boxes. The Chechens probably knew the size of the diversionary attack, since it moved on a separate axis where local Chechens could perform a quick vehicle count.

The Chechens effectively practiced centralized command with decentralized control – a technique that the Germans introduced in the battlefields of World War II. The Chechens were not reading old German manuals or doing this deliberately, but rather Chechen culture made this type of command arrangement inevitable. It was effective but cost the Chechens heavily in fratricide and the inability to coordinate effective covering fire from outside their own unit.

Vignette 4: Encircling Russian Forces on the Left Flank of the Defense of Bamut, June 1995[17]

Musa

Musa received the call for help from the defenders of Bamut and sat down with his unit to discuss their options. His men had some reservations regarding the pending journey, but all were in favor of

The Fortanga River. Bamut is on the left side and consisted of about 1,200 households (5,000–6,000 population) in the west of the Chechen Republic, close to the Ingushetia border. Some 6km from Bamut were four silos for R-12 Dvina (SS-3 SANDAL) ICBMs of 178th Strategic Missile Regiment that was disbanded in 1980. (Photo via Efim Sandler)

going to the defense of the last village not under Russian control. Musa recognized the danger of traveling too close to the Russian lines and decided to go deeper into the mountains to the south before swinging westward to get to Bamut. It took Musa and his band of 13 men nearly 34 hours to traverse the mountain passes on their way

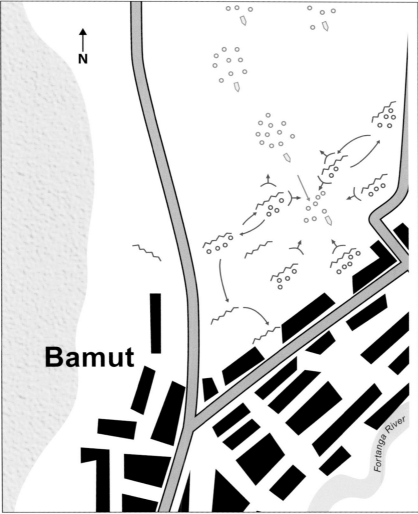

Encircling Russian forces on the left flank of the defense of Bamut, June 1995.

Although the Russians believed there were no more than 300 fighters, members of the Bamut Battalion operated in highly mobile and well-armed groups. Initially Bamut was defended by the Gananchozh Regiment that included the Bamut Company, later evolving into a battalion. After the First Chechen War the battalion was transformed into the Dzhokhar Dudaev Bamut Regiment. (Efim Sandler collection)

8th Special Detachment of the Ministry of the Interior, "Rus", in spring 1995. The first assault on Bamut was mostly undertaken by the 2nd Operational Division of the Ministry of the Interior (MVD). Several Special Detachments took part including "Rus", "Vityaz" (6th OSN) and "Rosich" (7th OSN). The heaviest daily losses were suffered by 7th Detachment on 18 April 1995 when it was ambushed and lost 10 killed and 17 wounded. (Photo via 8th OSN Veterans Association)

(northeast) flank. Musa's group was one of the larger units and he was given a larger section of the defense.

Musa led his small group to their part of the line and began to dig in. Their forward trenches were not in the village but out in front and alongside it. They dug their defensive positions 30, 50, or 100 meters from the village edge, depending on terrain and favorable digging conditions. They had learned to dig zigzag trenches to contain and deflect explosions that landed in trench sections from the artillery and air strikes that would surely precede the Russian ground assault. Since the beginning of the war many Chechens had been killed by the shock waves of the large ordnance hitting linear trench lines. It was a lesson learned the hard way. Musa recalls, "If a fighter was hit with the shock wave, he was thrown out of the trench and blood came from his ears. Blood came from his mouth. So in order to preserve our men we did a lot of things, including digging zigzagged trenches." Musa also dug positions within the village, using the walls of the destroyed houses as concealment. He was careful not to place his trenches too close to remaining structures. One hit could topple a wall down on top of him and his men.

The Chechens well knew to move from position to position, trench to trench, every 15 to 20 minutes as required. Staying in one place for too long would invite mortar and artillery fire on that position. Musa also conferred with the group commander to the right of his position about working together against the impending

to Bamut. They ate but they did not sleep. They also did not run into a single Russian unit. Other Chechen units that skirted the plains were spotted and attacked by Russian forces enroute to Bamut.

Upon arriving in Bamut Musa went directly to Boris, the sector commander, offering his services. After a brief discussion assessing the strength of Musa's group, Boris gave Musa and his men part of the left flank. Other units were already stretched out across the breadth of the village from the left (southwest) flank to the right

Russian assault. Together they devised a plan.

Musa and his group had been working on their positions for three days when the bombing began. The Chechen combatants knew what to expect. The air strikes would be followed by an artillery barrage before the Russian armor and infantry would begin to move forward. Musa and the others moved across the river into the relative safety of their positions in the wooded hillside. Finally the air strikes and artillery barrage were over. Musa and the rest of the Chechen line

Russian forces near Bamut in April 1995. The major effort was undertaken by the 8th Separate Operational Brigade of the Ministry of the Interior and elements of the Russian Army. During the failed attempts on 18–19 April, the brigade lost at least 24 men killed. (Photo Efim Sandler collection).

Chechen fighters on a T-72B tank destroyed during the assault of 18 April 1995. The tank probably belonged to 324th Motor Rifle Regiment. During this day Russian forces lost three tanks, two BMPs, and about 30 men killed. (Efim Sandler collection)

A Russian T-72B named 'Lidiya' pictured near Bamut in May 1996, moving with forward elements of the task force of General Vladimir Shamanov. The task force included 2,610 men, 45 tanks, 144 APCs, 50 artillery pieces, attack jets and helicopters. (Photo Efim Sandler collection)

ran to their trenches to await the Russian assault. Every combatant had a partner – no individual fighter was left alone.

Musa's plan was simple on paper but hazardous to execute. As the Russian tanks and infantry moved forward, Musa hoped to suck some of them inside their trench lines and then reoccupy the forward trenches behind the advancing Russian spearhead to cut them off and encircle them. They anticipated that the Russian armor, seeing an opening, would take it. The trick was not to let in a big group that they could not handle. For this reason, they had to entice a small

Russian aviation hammering Bamut in May 1996. Despite being a widespread belief, Chechen fighters did not use the old Soviet ICBM complex, but a wide network of trenches and underground shelters dug under the basements of the houses. (Photo AFP)

part of the Russian force to move forward of the general advance and isolate them before they could turn and encircle the Chechen front line. Musa noticed that the Russian groups deployed in groups of one or two armored personnel carriers and 15–20 dismounted infantry. Musa considered these as manageable numbers. If he could get one of these groups behind his forward defensive position, he was sure he could finish them off.

The left flank had only 33 to 35 men in four groups. Musa's group of 13 was the largest and better armed than most of the others. Musa's group was in the center of the left flank at its most vulnerable spot. There were at least two or three combatants in every position, located every five to 10 meters apart, depending on the terrain. Most of the group was armed with RPG-7s and RPG-18s (Mukhas).[18] The smaller groups were positioned further left, closer to the tree line and rougher terrain, as the village snaked its way into the gorge. The Chechens considered the terrain on the far left inaccessible for armored vehicles. Musa noted that there were many more men and groups in the center and right flank of Bamut, where they were more exposed to the Russian advance against the village.

At the height of the battle, Musa's men on the right of his sector withdrew from their position. As planned, the group adjacent to Musa's did the same, opening a noticeable gap. "We fought running from one position to another. This was our plan. Dig a lot of trenches and fight on the run." Musa and the other group hoped the Russians would notice the corridor and seek to break the Chechen line at this location. Musa's orders to his men were to let the Russian armored vehicles and infantry pass through their line. Musa was sure the Russians did not know that most of his men were sitting in three other defense positions nearer to the village, ready to engage the Russian vehicles and infantry.

As planned, the Russian BMPs and infantry passed through the gap and were met by RPG and Mukha fire from 12–15 men in a semicircle of three groups opposing them. They hit the Russian unit hard while Musa and the adjacent unit fought hard to retake their abandoned positions and encircle the small group of Russians. Encircled, the Russian unit tried to retreat, but Musa instructed one of his two RPG men to turn to his rear and attack the Russians who had just slipped through the gap in the line, once they tried to retreat towards them. "They thought they could break through, take our positions, occupy them and go on the defensive. But they didn't know that there was a group waiting here for them." He instructed his remaining RPG gunner to continue to fight northward against the main Russian attack, to beat back the rest of the advancing

Another T-72B tank destroyed at Bamut. In Bamut Russian losses throughout the war amounted to hundreds of men and dozens of armored vehicles. The majority of assaults failed due to incompetent planning and poor, despite the large number of troops and firepower involved. (Photo by Alxander Utrobin)

Members of the Bamut Battalion. Chechens operated in a small groups of about five men including commander, sniper, machine gunner and antitank gunner. This was the standard composition throughout the war. (Efim Sandler collection)

A Russian MT-12 100mm anti-tank gun near Bamut in May 1996. In many cases direct fire was ineffective against dug-in defenses, while heavy mortars were much appreciated. (Photo AFP)

Russians, forcing them to retreat and further isolate the Russian group, now fully encircled. The adjacent group did the same.

Commentary: The encircled Russian unit fought hard, inflicting Chechen casualties, but Musa and the adjacent Chechen unit were able to successfully trap and wipe out this portion of the Russian line. "Our strategy was to close it off while fighting." This small victory, combined with the actions of another Chechen group on the right side of the line that destroyed a portion of the Russian line

Bamut was finally taken on 24 May 1996 by a joint force of 166th Separate Motor Rifle Brigade and the 876th Separate Company of Special Forces. Despite the large number of units that took part in the fighting for Bamut, there was always a mixture of elements from different units usually having no connection to each other. (Photo via 166 Separate Motor Rifle Brigade veterans)

by mining its own defensive position, seemed to turn the tide and force the Russians to retreat.

In the aftermath, as the Chechen groups surveyed the situation and took care of their dead and wounded, word of Musa's tactic has spread up and down the line. The other Chechen groups made preparations to carry out similar ploys during the next assault. However, the Russian attack the next day was only a probe, with no serious attempt to break the Chechen line.

Musa recalls many more BMPs than tanks in the Russian advance. Previous Russian assaults on Bamut included many more tanks and, in fact, by the time of this particular battle, the few streets of Bamut were strewn with burned-out tank hulls and turrets, blown off by Chechen RPGs. Musa's unit had taken casualties, killed and wounded. While the greater Russian army and Chechen leadership negotiated in the wake of Shamil's raid on Budennovsk, Musa conferred with Boris and decided to leave with his wounded. His unit had one horse and they loaded the wounded man on it and set off back to their positions near Shalazhi. Again they took the longer mountainous route to avoid Russian patrols in the foothills. Looking back on the village, Musa thought to himself, "Bamut wasn't ever given up, but it was completely destroyed."

It takes leadership to get a dug-in soldier to leave his defensive position under fire. These Chechens may have had some military experience; still, the leadership, discipline and unit cohesion of these Chechen units is exemplary. Inexperienced troops do not realize that most bullets do not find their mark and that they will likely emerge unscathed from what seems like a hail of bullets and that movement increases the chances of survivability. Of course, continued exposure increases the odds of meeting that one on-target projectile.

Vignette 5: Holding the Eastern Flank of Goyskoe Against a Russian Armored Attack, sometime between 21 March– 5 April 1996

Hasmohmad

Background: 14 March 1996. Hasmohmad and his small group of seven combatants from the village of Goity had just arrived in Goyskoe. He was not the leader of his tiny group, just one of the seven volunteers from his village under the command of S. E. Dangaev.[19] They had just taken part in the three-day operation to attack Russian positions in Grozny and now, like hundreds of other combatants, they were in Goyskoe because there was a base located in the village where they could rest between operations. Akhmed Zakaev, the commander of the 1st Sector of the Southwest Direction of Chechen forces, was also in the village. Hussein Isabaev, his subordinate, was also there. Isabaev was from Goyskoe and was key in establishing and coordinating the defenses.

Hasmohmad and his group from Goity received their instructions directly from Isabaev. There were at least 17 other groups in the village according to additional Chechen accounts of the battle. Hasmohmad recalls hearing that there were around 160 Chechen combatants in the village.[20] The Chechen command set up a base along with their headquarters in the town center, while various groups spread themselves out along the village perimeter. Half of the force was kept at the base and in the town center as a reserve.

On the night that they arrived in Goyskoe Hasmohmad heard that Chechen intelligence knew that the Russians had tracked the Chechen forces there and were going to surround and attack it the next morning. Around 11:00 PM, Hasmohmad and the rest of his group were assigned to a position on the perimeter and began to dig in. They were located near the canal on the eastern edge of the village near some garages. Beyond the garages lay vast open fields. If the Russians were going to attack, they would most likely establish their staging positions in these fields beyond the range of Chechen weapons.

The next morning before dawn, as intelligence had indicated, the Chechen observed the headlights of hundreds of Russian vehicles beginning to encircle the village. From Hasmohmad's vantage point it looked as if the whole Russian Army was in front of him and that the village was being surrounded, although, in reality, the Russians established their positions to the north and east of Goyskoe only. The west side of the village was protected by the city of Urus-Martan, while the south was protected by the city of Komsomolskoye.

The sight of Russian units massing for attack sent the villagers into a panic and for at least three days there was a steady stream of civilians leaving the town. There were also refugees coming up the road from the direction of Komsolmolskoye. Hasmohmad was not sure where they were coming from, but they were traveling through Goyskoe to get to Urus-Martan and elsewhere.

At one point in the day a tractor with a large white flag and a trailer full of refugees came up the road towards their position. The Russians began shelling the vehicle and the driver panicked and jumped out of the cab. It looked as though the tractor were going to end up in the canal. Dangaev jumped out of his position and leapt onto the tractor, grabbing the wheel before it careened off the embankment. He brought the tractor under control and stopped it to let the civilians off before sending them on their way, all under sporadic Russian fire.

Although the Russians had arrived in force and fired into Goyskoe occasionally, they seemed intent on preparing their own positions, giving the civilians in the village time to flee and the

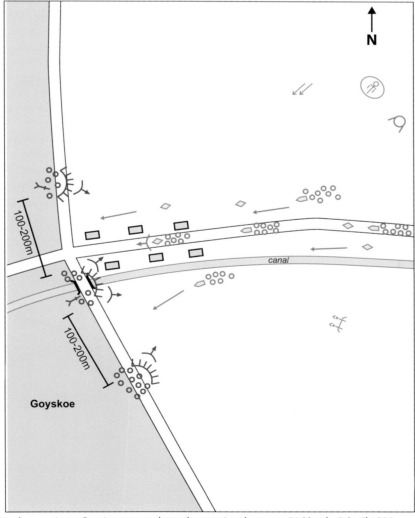

Holding the eastern flank of Goyskoe against a Russian armored attack sometime between 21 March–5 April 1996.

combatants more time to fortify their positions. The sides agreed to a parlay and the Chechen and Russian commanders went out to talk. The popular story among the Chechens is that "the Russians said that we needed to surrender, and our commander said they should surrender to us. He said, 'If you surrender, we'll let you go.' We gave them certain conditions. If they would surrender we would feed them and provide everything they needed, and then we would send them home. But they said just the opposite, 'No, if you don't surrender, we will destroy you.' In conclusion, our commander wrapped it up and said, 'Then let's fight.'"

Military activity began to escalate about a week after Hasmohmad's group arrived. There was no direct attack, but fixed- and rotary-wing aircraft began pounding the Chechen positions. The attacks then died down again. "The Russians were only 500–600 meters from us. We could see them. We could also hear them. At night, when it was quiet, we could hear their conversations."

On 31 March the Russians conducted a reconnaissance-in-force, probing the Chechen defenses along the northern and eastern perimeters of Goyskoe. The Russians facing the Goity group were still out of range of the few weapons the group possessed. "In my specific group we had only one RPG and six rockets. For my rifle,

Two of the commanders of Chechen forces in Goyskoe – Akhmed Zakaev and Dalkhan Khozhaev pictured together in Urus-Martan in December 1995. Brigade General Khozhaev was also a writer, historian, and head of the archives department of Chechen Republic government. He was killed by a sniper in 2000. (Efim Sandler collection)

I had eight magazines and something like five packages of bullets. One package of ammunition is enough to fill one magazine. We had to make do with that. So we were forced to fire single shots as accurately as possible. We couldn't miss. Our trophies were basically whatever we had taken and could take from the Russians. That's the only ammo we had."

Hasmohmad felt fortunate to be where he was. They had dug a large fighting position that he called a "wolf pit" right up against a very strong asphalt road supported by gravel shoulders. "We dug in deep in order to survive. We were under attack from airplanes, artillery, tanks. We had to protect ourselves to keep casualties to a minimum. We were lucky because this road was asphalt, and it was laid on gravel. We were able to dig in deep, and when we came under fire we would go into the pits."

The Chechens made similar dugouts and defensive positions along the perimeter. The distance between the Goity unit and their neighbors was roughly 100 to 200 meters. This was deliberate. "We kept our spacing so that we could catch the Russians in intersecting fires when they attacked."

The next three days were quiet all along the front, since the Russians did not conduct any attacks against Goyskoe. Rumors spread during the lull that other units in the city had knocked out some Russian armor and even downed a helicopter, but it was impossible to know for sure. "Somewhere in the village we even fired on the Russians from a BMP, but I don't know who had it or where it was."

Suddenly, on April 3rd, the Russians attacked the middle of the eastern side of the village, perhaps trying to split the village into two sections, using the canal and parallel road to divide the Chechens defending the village. "Their tanks and artillery fired, and then their airplanes flew over, and then their helicopters attacked. The Russian armor seemed to be attacking right down the road in front of us. Then their infantry got out and attacked. We started firing at the dismounted infantry when they got about 300 meters from us. We could see them clearly."

Using intersecting fires, the Goity group and the group north of their position fought without a break to stop the Russians from penetrating their perimeter. They were woefully short of ammunition. It was the reserve forces who rushed to the line that

Russian forces near Goyskoe. The task of taking over Goyskoe had been assigned to the 324th and 245th Motor Rifle Regiments. In April 1996, several attempts were undertaken: all were unsuccessful with numerous losses. (Photo by Antoine Gyori)

saved the day. Eventually the Russian advance stalled and retreated due to intense RPG fire from the Chechen side.

The day's events were only the beginning. The next day, the Russian forces tried to squeeze the Chechen defenders in a pincer movement, attacking in force on the northern and southern flanks. Reserve units rushed to those parts of the line and a massive battle for the village raged into the early hours of 5 April.

The Chechens held their ground and the Russian units again withdrew to their positions east of the village. The battles continued on and off for another month until the Chechens withdrew from Goyskoe. "It was impossible to continue. There were no more medical supplies, no food. We were starving. What's more, we didn't even have the weapons to continue the resistance." Akhmed Zakaev gave the order and everyone left. "They went to their various villages. As I recall, there wasn't really one main base. So they went to Goity, Urus-Martan, and other places. Gekhi, Alkhazurovo, Komsomolskoye. My unit went to Tengi-Chu."

Commentary: The battle for Goyskoe destroyed the village and the Chechens consider it one of the three worst battles of the first war. It was also costly for Has-mohmad and the Goity unit. Hasmohmad was wounded and had to be evacuated in late April. Dangaev, the commander of the group, was killed.

From Hasmohmad's vantage point the Russians clearly had suffered losses, but he had no idea what they were. He did know that his unit knocked out at least one Russian tank on the road next to the canal back on 3 April.

By spring 1996, the Chechen forces had all but given up defending fixed positions, with a notable exception (Bamut). Why the Chechen leadership decided to dig in at Goyskoe is unclear. It could have had as much to do with the sector leader, Akhmed Zakaev, as any other factor. Or, since the Goyskoe fixed position had multiple escape routes to the south and west, perhaps the Chechens decided that it was a good place to make a stand and bloody the Russians.

In the battle for Goyskoe, while the Russians did destroy the village via air strikes and artillery, all the civilians had already left by the early stages of the operation. The defense of Goyskoe also proved the value of well constructed fighting positions with overhead cover and interlocking fields of fire. The Russian forces concentrated on penetration along roads leading to bridges into the village and at the Chechens' narrowest defensive perimeters in the flanks. They wanted to seize bridgeheads and to degrade the Chechen force through air and artillery strikes.

Vignette 6: The Battle for Goyskoe, 21 March–7 May 1996 (Focus on 3 April–5 April 1996)

Hasmohmad[21] and Khuseyn LIskhanov[22]

Background: Goyskoe is a small farming community southwest of Grozny with a pre-war population of only 2,500 people. It is rectangular in layout, stretching north-south on the west side of the main road running between Komsomolskoye and Urus-Martan. The village is split in the middle, east to west, by a canal. There are no mountains in the immediate vicinity. Chechen units withdrew to Goyskoe on the heels of their three-day March assault on Grozny.

The primary Russian unit battling the defenders of Goyskoe was the 324th Motor Rifle Regiment, based near Chiri-Yurt to the east. In order to surround and assault the village from the west the 324th

A Russian BMP-1P near Goyskoe, April 1996. (Photo via Efim Sandler)

One of the numerous Russian Special Forces Detachments, 1995–1996. (Photo via Efim Sandler)

A knocked-out BMP alongside Russian soldiers killed during the failed attempt to capture Goyskoe in April 1996. (Photo by Antoine Gyori)

and attached units would have needed to pass near Urus-Martan to Martan-Chu. These villages were not under Russian control and would have exposed the Russian supply line to attacks in their rear. Nor could the Russians move to the west side of Goyskoe from the south, as they would have had to travel past Komsomolskoye, another city not under Russian control.

The defense of Goyskoe was conducted by the Chechen 1st Sector of the South-West Direction, under the overall command of Ruslan (Khamzat) Galaev. However, operational command for the village rested with Akhmed Zakaev. Chechen accounts suggest that as many as 18 different groups participated in the Chechen defense, often numerically designated as a particular company of a particular battalion from a particular regiment. However, according Khuseyn Iskhanov those designations should not be taken too seriously. "The defense was made up of portions of various units. It wasn't a specific 'army' or 'regiment' that took specific positions. For example,

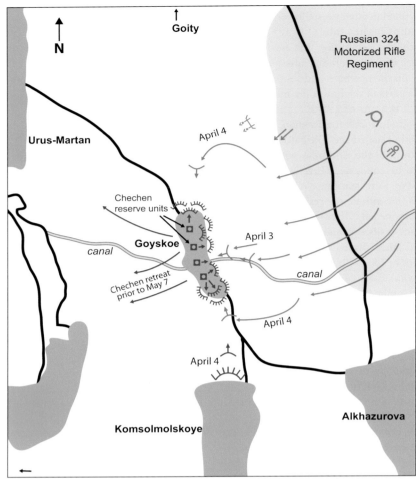

The Battle for Goyskoe, 21 March–7 May 1996 (Focus on 3 April through 5 April 1996).

there were 20 men in this or that unit, there were 50 men from the presidential guard and 50 men from Zakaev's unit, and another 50 men who didn't take orders from anyone. They were militiamen who came simply to help out."

Zakaev assigned sectors to the various units according to a master defensive plan drawn up by the leadership. "I was right in that village literally a half hour before the battle started" Khuseyn recalls. "I spoke with Akhmed Zakaev and other military leaders, after which they went to their positions, where the defense had already been well laid out. Trenches and foxholes were dug, and even crawlspaces were built out into the fields so that we could conduct a good defense invulnerable to enemy fire."

"I remember most of all that there was such a ringing silence before the battle that it left an impression on me. No chickens, or birds, or animals, made a sound, no one made the slightest sound. It was strange. But this silence, this premonition of a huge tragedy, cut me to the core. A half hour after we left [the forward positions], the Russians began their attack on Goyskoe." It was 20 March 1996, at 0900, when Russian artillery fire began to pound Goyskoe.

The artillery barrage was followed by helicopter gun runs over the village defenses. The Chechens were well dug in and could wait it out. Still, some Chechens took offensive actions. One helicopter was damaged by Chechen machine-gun fire and began to trail smoke as it left the area of operations. Chechens claim that a Russian tank and a soldier's tent were also destroyed by a Fagot antitank missile.

The shelling and probing of the village by Russian forces eventually petered out, and there was a lull in the battle until 31 March. Then the Russians struck in force around 1100, probing the Chechen lines with a massive reconnaissance-in-force across the

entire front. Again the attack started with artillery fire, followed by fixed- and rotary-wing aircraft. Then armor began moving toward the village perimeter. They stopped short at a distance of 400–500 meters from the Chechen line of defense and, safely out of the range of most of the Chechen arsenal, began to bombard the Chechen positions.

But it was not all stand-off attack. Some Russian armor and dismounted infantry attempted to break through the fields and into the village perimeter. They were pushed back. By day's end, the Chechens claimed two more Russian tanks destroyed by Fagot antitank missiles, while another tank was destroyed by RPG fire. "We had colossal experience and no one was afraid, knowing where to hit which type of armor, which point to aim at to destroy them, and which direction was more advantageous." Khuysen recalls, "We didn't have any problems fighting against the armor. Absolutely none." Hasmohmad, who was deployed near the canal in the middle of the village perimeter, recalls, "Our positions were laid out with ample room between units, 100 to 200 meters. In this way we could catch the advancing Russian armor in intersecting fires."

A BMP-1 "Borz" cannon, under the command of Said-Khusein Tazbaev, destroyed a Russian tent. According to Chechen sources only two combatants were injured during the day's fighting, both from Dadaev's detachment. Chechen combatant accounts also claim that two Russian tanks were fired upon and destroyed by their own helicopters. Chechens believe this was to compel the armor to move forward, to attack.[23]

Although artillery and helicopters continued to strike the village defenses, another lull in the ground battle occurred from 1–3 April. The Russian military, perhaps startled by the loss of their tent and

Mortars proved to be very effective against entrenched defenses. A Russian soldier operates an 82mm battalion mortar against Chechen positions in Goyskoe in April 1996. (Photo via Efim Sandler)

A Su-25 of the 368th Separate Attack Aviation Regiment shot down by ZU-23-2 fire over Goyskoe on 4 April 1996. The pilot ejected and was instantly picked by a passing Mi-8 helicopter and transported to the base at Khankala. (Efim Sandler collection)

the realization that the Chechens had at least a couple of weapons that could reach out and hurt them, used the time to fortify their positions.[24]

On 3 April the Russians attacked again. This time the attack came at the middle of the defenses along the canal where Hasmohmad's group was defending. The attack was an apparent attempt to break through the Chechen defenses in the center of the line and split the village into two parts. "Some of us were forced to engage in close combat with the advancing Russian units, but mostly it was a circular

A Chechen defender of Goyskoe. (Photo via Efim Sandler)

Russian troops near Goyskoe in April 1996. (Photo via Efim Sandler)

battle hitting us all along the front. It lasted a few hours, something like from morning until noon." The Russian armored thrust was repelled by heavy RPG fire and retreated. Again the Russian attacks had faltered. Russian losses from 20 March through 3 April were four tanks, three helicopters and two tents. According to the Chechens, their losses during the two-week defense of Goyskoe were 17 men.

The fighting continued the next day. At midnight on 4 April heavy artillery, multiple rocket launchers, mortars and armor began pounding Goyskoe. At 0200 the Russians began a massive air bombardment. The ground and air fire assault continued until 1230. At 1230, under cover of the fiercest artillery fire yet, the Russians launched another armored assault on the village. Again the armor moved to primary positions along the entire front, just out of RPG range. Simultaneously the left and right armored flanks attempted a flank penetration.

The night before, the right flank or southern portion of the Chechen perimeter near Komsomolskoye was weakened when

A Russian D-30 122mm howitzer. Russian artillery took part in major battles of the Chechen wars. (Photo via Efim Sandler)

Goyskoe was taken by General Shamanov's troops on 7 May 1996. On the right is the commander of the Reconnaissance Company of 166th Separate Motor Rifle Brigade, Aleksey Efentyev 'Viper'. (Photo via 166 Separate Motor Rifle Brigade veterans)

a company under Khachukaev, at Gelaev's command, was moved out of the line. Reportedly, Zakaev had not been informed of the decision and was unaware that the Chechen line was so thin at that location. As a result, the Russian armored thrust was able to enter the village from the south, under heavy covering fire. At least three Chechen units were forced to retreat and take secondary positions within the village perimeter as a result of the Russian penetration.[25] All the Chechen combatants but one in the Minchuria group were wounded and incapable of continuing the fight.

Not only did the three retreating units create a breach in the line, but they also enabled the Russian armored assault to encircle another Chechen unit of six combatants. Fierce close combat ensued. In the end three Russian BMPs were destroyed, but at a high cost. Only one of the six combatants lived through the battle. The lone survivor, Sultan Mutiev, was severely wounded.

The Chechen command responded by rushing a reserve unit under the command of Bazhiev into the broken line to stop the Russian penetration. At the same time, reserve groups under the command of Ali Itaev and Dokka Umarov struck the Russians in their flank from the village of Komsomolskoye. The battle lasted most of the day, but by 2000, the remaining Russian soldiers, retreated to their primary positions, leaving destroyed armor, dead and wounded on the battlefield. The Chechens suffered eight dead, including two unit commanders, Salaudi Mutiev and Visita Dikaev, and 14 wounded.

At the same time, the battle for the northern perimeter (left flank) was equally brutal.

Under massive artillery support the Russians were able get their armor right up to the trenches. However, they were halted and driven back by massive RPG and small-arms fire from Nikaev's, Bakaev's, Magomadov's and Apti's detachments. Advancing Russian armor was halted when a Fagot antitank missile from Ismailov's group destroyed a BMP. "There were even attempts to penetrate the village, driving armor at high speed, and one was destroyed right on the spot because at the time we had a great deal of experience fighting armor." A significant number of Russian armor and personnel were destroyed, while the Chechens on the left flank lost four dead and five wounded. The total Chechen losses that day were 12 dead and 21 wounded.

The Russians finally retreated around 2100 on the 4th. Chechens counted five tanks, and 12 BTRs and BMPs destroyed. Khuseyn states "It was simply a frontal attack by the Russians, which we successfully fought back. BMPs and BTRs were destroyed, and there were large losses among their soldiers."

The Chechens also had some success against Russian aviation. Two MI-24 helicopters were shot down and an SU-25 ground attack aircraft was shot down by machine-gun fire and crashed north of Goyskoe, close to the village of Goity. Chechen combatants from Khachukaev's group, observing the pilot's parachute, made an attempt to take him prisoner, but were thwarted in their plan by Russian Spetsnaz, who laid down suppressive fire while he was evacuated by helicopter.[26]

But the fighting continued. Mopping up operations were conducted into the early morning hours of 5 April on the southeast edge of the village in order to root out Russian soldiers who did not or were not able to retreat with the rest of their force.

Commentary: The battles for Goyskoe continued for another month, when Russian forces finally took the village on 7 May. However, as in many battles before and since, most of the Chechens were able to retreat to the west before the final Russian assault. "There wasn't any reason to hold the village any longer. It wasn't strategic for us. The decision was made to leave and our units retreated in the direction of Urus-Martan, Gekhi and surrounding villages." Hasmohmad recalls.

Geographic necessity forced the Russians to attack Goyskoe head on from the east. This was a significant benefit to the Chechens, because it meant that at no time were they surrounded, and they could focus their military efforts on the Russians in front of them. The Chechens also had an open back door. When the time was right they simply withdrew through the village in a westerly direction. Commenting on the successful withdrawal of Chechen units, Khuseyn recalls. "Our rear was protected. We held the rear so that the units in Goyskoe could leave the battlefield at will or whenever needed."

The Chechen force held out for a significant period of time against significant combat power. The Russian army was confronted by a series of thin, elongated towns built along the north-south roads. Bypassing these towns to take them from a flank would expose their own flank to an attack launched from the next population center. The Russians pounded their way through each belt of towns, slowly and methodically.

Chapter Two Summary

The Chechens countered the Russian attack with a truly mobile defense. They built multiple defenses and trench rows, but occupied portions of them for short periods of time to avoid being targeted by the feared Russian artillery. Chechen use of bunkers and zigzag trenches helped them survive when trapped by Russian artillery. Each unit moved when it wanted to unless ordered to stay in one position. Consequently, there was little flank security and each unit tried to provide its own. There was coordination among defending units, but the physical tie-in was often lacking, or tended to come apart under pressure.

Chechens preferred to stop Russian advances on the approaches to urban areas. Once the Russians gained entry into the urban area the Chechens tried to canalize them along narrow streets, where they could be trapped and slowly reduced.

The RPG-7 was the optimum weapon of the Chechen resistance and the Russian Army learned to stay out of its maximum effective range until the final minutes of the assault. Then, hopefully, artillery fire, machine-gun suppressive fire and supporting infantry would keep the RPGs from engaging the armored vehicles.

The Chechen decision to defend the urban centers initially provided them an opportunity to bleed the Russian Army. However, once the Russian Army recovered, such a defense provided the Russians with concentrations of Chechen resistance that could be reduced methodically and effectively. The Chechen resistance lost many of its best commanders and many combatants during this time. Overwhelming Russian military strength focused on these separate centers of resistance, which were often not mutually supporting, and took them down one after another. The fight for the urban centers eventually sapped the Chechen resistance fighting strength, cost them popular support among the populace and forced them into guerrilla warfare and the loss of control of the population centers, economic centers and access to adequate medical care, food and supplies.

3
BREAKING OUT OF AN ENCIRCLEMENT

Breaking out of an encirclement can be conducted by massing a large force at one point or exfiltrating smaller forces at several points. Much depends on the surrounding force's disposition and strength, as well as the escaping force's immediate follow-on mission. The Chechen resistance conducted small and large breakouts, but the smaller breakouts were usually more successful. Large breakouts could be more easily spotted and be decimated by air strikes and artillery. The Chechens seldom rehearsed large or small breakouts and seldom planned supporting fires from Chechen mortar crews and heavy weapons.

Most encirclements during the Russian-Chechen Wars involved cities or villages. Russian and Soviet encirclements historically involved inner and outer lines of encirclement. The inner encirclement prevented the surrounded force from breaking out and the outer encirclement prevented external forces from breaking in to the surrounded force and relieving them. Since the Chechens lacked sufficient forces and mobility, there was no threat of an external relief force, and so the Russians only established inner lines of encirclement. The original purpose of Russian encirclements was to prevent the breakout of mobile, organized units and their equipment. Therefore, the Russians focused their attention on strongly securing roads, bridges, tunnels and rail lines. These encirclements were fairly porous for small groups trying to escape as long as they

focused on difficult terrain with adequate cover. The Chechens tried to break out with intact units, but they were seldom able to evacuate their vehicles and artillery pieces. Chechens managed to carry out their wounded and man-portable weapons, but left their heavy systems, severely wounded and remaining supplies behind. Often the Chechens fought until their supplies were exhausted and then attempted a breakthrough. This gave the Russians additional time to improve their encirclement.

During the early stages of the first war, the Russians left a "golden bridge" in their encirclement of Grozny – an open corridor through which noncombatants could escape the encirclement. The Chechen combatants were quick to take advantage of this corridor for reinforcement, troop rest and supply. Later, the Russians closed

Chechen fighters in Grozny in January 1995. (Photo by Peter Turnley)

Tumen OMON outpost near Grozny in 1995. The T-72B1 tank belonged to a Russian Army motor rifle unit – it was a common practice to have a mixed force of troops from the Ministry of the Interior and Army. (Photo by Alexander Efremov)

The fight in Minutka Square between Volgo-Vytsk SOBR (Special Rapid Response Unit of the Ministry of the Interior) and Chechen fighters on 7 March 1996. Chechens attacked Russian forces in Grozny on 6–8 March. Although this attack was repelled, at least 70 Russians were killed. (Efim Sandler collection)

close the corridors, however, the Russians were in a constant frontal attack, smashing their way steadily forward but not limiting the Chechens' ability to maneuver, reinforce, supply and evacuate their wounded. The Russians stated that they left the southeast corridor open so that Grozny's civilians could escape the fighting (the bulk of Grozny's population was ethnic Russian and many of them used the corridor to escape). Finally, in February, the Russian Army closed the encirclement and the Chechens' ability to withstand the Russian assault was severely restricted.

Many of the Chechen volunteers fighting in Grozny in January and February 1995 came and went as they saw fit. By this time Aslambek had been in and out Grozny for almost two months. Nine other volunteers from his village were still with him. Two days earlier a Russian air strike wounded him, but he could still walk and carry a rifle. Squeezed by the Russians and chronically low on food and ammunition, most Chechen units were beginning to retreat from the besieged capital. Everyone in his unit was armed with assault rifles and one carried an RPG, but there were very few rounds left, so this weapon was employed sparingly. As Aslambek and the other volunteers from his village prepared to exit

the corridor and established "filtration" points through which noncombatants could slowly exit the area after close inspection and interrogation.

Vignette 7: Small Unit Retreat from Grozny, 20 February 1995

Aslambek

Background: After their initial failure to take Grozny in a coup de main, the Russians pulled back, reconstituted their force and prepared to conquer the city systematically. They encircled the city but, curiously, did not complete the encirclement. They left a large section to the southeast of the city open, and the Chechens were able to move forces and supplies in and out of the city through this corridor, as well as through other exfiltration routes to the south and southwest. The Russians brought in massive quantities of artillery and retook the city block-by-obliterated-block. Since they did not

the capital, their group merged with other small groups and now numbered 50 fighters.

Navigating around and through the Russian positions inside Grozny was difficult. Finally Aslambek's unit entered the 56th District and the suburb of Gekalovsky. Their exit route of choice was blocked by a much larger Russian force, so the hastily assembled group of 50 was forced to march around and over the Chernorechensky Reservoir Bridge in western Grozny.

After sneaking across the Chernorechensky Reservoir Bridge in the dark, the unit, using a band of dense forest for cover, continued south between the road to Alkhan-Yurt and a small river. A kilometer or so from the capital, the road veered off to the southwest, where it would connect to the M-29 Rostov-Baku Highway at the Chernorechensky intersection. It was now broad daylight.

Scouts in the lead reported that the M-29 Highway was filled with Russian columns, while the Chernorechensky intersection, home to an old GAI station, was occupied by at least a Russian armor company consisting of 20 or more armored vehicles.[1] Moving

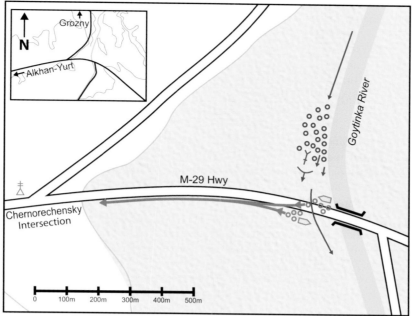

Small unit retreat from Grozny 20 February 1995

BTR-80s of 165th Naval Infantry Regiment of Pacific Fleet at Mt. Syurin Kort near Khankala, April 1995. (Efim Sandler collection)

A group of Chechen fighters probably pictured in Grozny in August 1996. (Photo via Efim Sandler)

southwesterly toward the intersection would also be further to walk. The Chechens decided to continue due south through the forested area adjacent to the river.

However, Aslambek's unit still had to cross the M-29 Highway. In addition to the numerous Russian convoys running back and forth, the scouts reported that there were two BTR-80s and 16 to 20 Russian troops positioned right in front of them on their exfiltration route, just west of the bridge over the Goytinka River, which they were paralleling.

The Chechens were tired and hungry – some had not eaten in days. A good number were also wounded, and getting them quickly into hospitals outside of the Russian encirclement of Grozny was critical. The only other option was to cross the river to the east and venture out onto the plains, where they would surely be spotted and attacked by Russian air and artillery. After a brief pause roughly 100 meters from the BTRs on the M-29 Highway, the Chechen leaders decided that they would have to attack the BTR position in order to break through the Russian encirclement and continue on to their next positions.

Getting into position, under tree cover, about 50 meters from the BTRs on the M-29, the unit waited for a break in the stream of Russian military traffic. They noticed that the BTR nearest to them had its 14.5 mm KPVT machine gun facing away from

them. However, the BTR across the road had its main gun barrel facing directly towards the hiding Chechens and posed the greatest immediate threat. A gunner armed with one of the few functioning RPGs waited for the "go" signal and then fired a single shot from 50 meters at the furthest BTR. It was a direct hit, blowing unsuspecting Russian soldiers to the ground and causing a general panic among the Russian troops at both BTRs.

The entire Chechen unit rushed from the cover of the trees yelling "Allah Akbar" and fired their assault rifles and PK machine guns at the BTR position. The surviving Russians broke and ran west down off the embankment into tree cover and toward the Russian armored position at the Chernorechensky intersection a kilometer away.

Aslambek's unit did not pursue the retreating soldiers. Rather, their objective was to get across the highway and continue south into Chechen-held territory. Lead elements took positions on the road to defend against any Russian counterstrike from the highway from either direction. Others quickly searched the undamaged BTR for food and weapons. The majority of the unit ran up to the road, between the two BTRs and down the embankment on the other side, continuing southward towards Goiti and then Staryye Atagi. They made no attempt to destroy the undamaged BTR. A very brief discussion broke out in Aslambek's unit about whether or not they should take the surviving BTR. Nobody in the unit knew how to drive it and no one was sure what they would do with it. They decided to leave it.

The whole action took less than 10 minutes. There was no immediate counterattack by Russian forces, either by helicopter or from the Chernorechensky intersection a kilometer west of the attack. There were no Chechen casualties. Several Russians from the burning BTR were killed.

Commentary: The Russian motorized infantry were reluctant to move away from their BTR-80 armored personnel carriers. They huddled close to the vehicles and did not push out patrols, picquets or outposts into the forest paralleling the highway. They also failed to deploy some trip-wire "flash-bang" flares for early warning. They had no apparent artillery fires registered around the position. The audacity of the Chechen attack carried the day. The Russians made no attempt to slew the gun of the second BTR around and get it into action. Amazingly, the Chechens made no attempt to disable the vehicle, only pausing to strip it of food, ammunition and weapons. The Russian force at the GAI post was also timid and had no apparent plan to rescue or reinforce their two BTRs holding the bridge. The small Chechen force, strung out in a column and carrying wounded, was an easy target. The Chechen force did establish flank security as it moved its force across the highway, which made it less of an easy target.

The porous, almost haphazard nature of the Russian encirclement of Grozny and the outlying areas allowed the Chechens to engage and escape with minimal contact. The Chechens, given the tactical advantage of their small numbers and implicit knowledge of the terrain and surroundings, frequently were able to break through Russian lines using concealment and quick decisive violent action. In many cases Chechens acknowledged that Russian soldiers and commanders were often aware that Chechens were moving through their positions, but apparently did not want to risk contact and

A Russian BMP-1 in an ad hoc caponier in Grozny in 1995. (Photo by Grigory Tambulov)

A Russian armor graveyard near Grozny in 1995. (Photo via 245th Motor Rifle Regiment veterans)

would let the Chechen fighters pass, often acknowledging each other with the wave of a hand.

Vignette 8: Escaping Grozny, Mid-February 2000

Isa and an Anonymous Member of His Group

Background: As the Russian noose tightened around Grozny in January 2000, the Chechen leadership faced a dilemma deciding how long the bulk of their forces should be committed to the capital. In the first war the Chechen combatants were able to come and go in Grozny at the time of their choosing because Russian forces were never able or willing to seal off the southern approaches in and out of the capital. However, the Russians finally appreciated that the Chechens were able to rest, refit and supply their forces through this corridor, and by January 2000 Russian units were encircling the city, sealing off the Chechen combatants operating in Grozny.

Isa claims that there were about 4,000 Chechen combatants defending Grozny at the time. "There were many different units there, and I had about 1,000 combatants under my command." According to Isa, "there was a meeting which was attended by the following generals of the Chechen Army: Aslambek Junior, Shamil Basaev, Khamzat Galaev, Lecha Dudaev, Doku Umarov, and myself. This was our last meeting before the withdrawal. We met in a basement and decided right then and there to withdraw from Grozny."

Isa was given separate instructions. President Aslan Maskhadov, who had already relocated from Grozny, ordered Isa and his men to remain in the city to act as a decoy and rear guard while the rest of the Chechen forces withdrew to their previously prepared mountain

T-72B1 tanks with mounted infantry in Grozny in 1995. The habit of infantry riding on top of tanks had been revived in Afghanistan and instantly spread across units. Later it was forbidden due to numerous incidents and several fatalities. (Photo via Efim Sandler)

Russian TOS-1 Heavy Flamethrower Systems seen during the Second Chechen War near Grozny. (Photo via 276 Motor Rifle Regiment veterans)

bases in the south. Isa protested. "I told Maskhadov that we had suffered many casualties and had very many wounded warriors. Maskhadov conceded and suggested that I withdraw several of my battalions and then remain in Grozny with only 300 men, or three battalions. So, I withdrew most of my battalions from Grozny as I was ordered."

Isa and his three battalions remained in the city, while the retreat from Grozny turned into a dismal chapter for the Chechen insurgency. A large group of Chechen combatants left Grozny heading in a southwesterly direction, following a narrow path near the Sunzha River past the settlement of Kirova.[2] It had been snowing for days. The snow-covered ground obscured the path and the Chechens walked right into a minefield. Chaos erupted as the first Chechens in the field began detonating the mines. Alerted by the commotion, Russian artillery and mortar fire began to zero in on the long Chechen column.

Making matters worse, there was panic and many combatants moved in different directions further into the minefield. Finally, the commanders were able to regain order and push the combatants through in more or less single file, forging one lane through the mines rather than multiple lanes. The Chechen commanders led the way and as a result nine of 16 prominent commanders were killed during the withdrawal. Shamil Basaev lost his leg below the knee, but a surgeon saved him from death on an operating table in Alkhan-Yurt the next day.[3]

As the retreating Chechens struggled through the minefield, Isa and 300 of his men were scattered around the village of Kirova. He had five or six subordinate commanders. One of his battalions defended a chemical plant near the Sunzha River, another defended the village of Kirova, and a third provided the rear guard for the withdrawing column. Many of his troops were dug in around a power plant. The retreating Chechens passed through this position on their way out of the city before entering the minefield. Isa also had a half dozen Russian prisoners with him, including one Spetznaz soldier.

"My understanding was that I was to stay there. None of us thought that any of us would leave there alive. We all thought that we would die there. I stayed in order to attract the Russian fire onto my position. I would get on the radio and say that I needed help, but I didn't. We had worked this all out ahead of time. I simply needed to deceive the Russians in order to get the other Chechen units out of Grozny alive."

Isa's forces did not seek contact with Russian forces. They struggled enough trying to defend their positions, eat, and stay healthy. "We did not have the strength to attack. Someone had to be the decoy. As fate would have it, we became the decoy." However, Isa's men were caught up in the fluidity of urban warfare. "There were times when the Russians actually entered our rear area. Sometimes we were in their rear area. There would be 50 of us fighting, and all of a sudden we would notice Russians behind us and Chechen troops ahead of us. It was confusing."

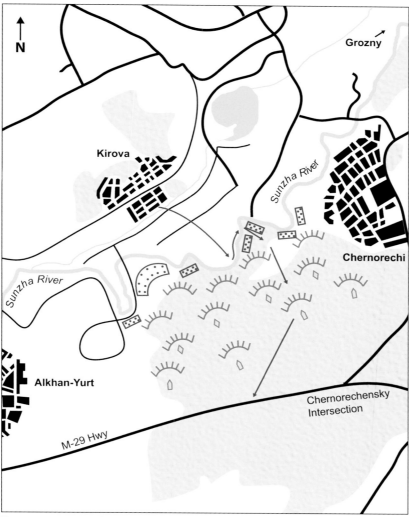

Escaping Grozny, mid-February 2000.

Isa and his three battalions remained in Grozny for almost three weeks. "On the 17th day, we had completely run out of ammunition. There was hardly any food. We hadn't eaten for nearly a week. All we could do was eat snow. There were about 50 wounded, including myself. I had a shrapnel wound that went clear through my leg. We had no other choice. Finally, I gathered all of my commanders together and told them that we couldn't stay any longer."

Information operations played a key role in Isa's unit's ability to operate in the city after most of the other defenders had pulled out. "I would get on the radio as if asking for help, that we were losing the battle, that things were bad. I would say that I was withdrawing this way or that way. After I would deceive them like this on the radio, they would move entire units to the area that I had stated over the radio. At the same time, we also had another communications network that the Russians had a difficult time decoding. They could still decode it, but it would take them one or two days. This is how we communicated among ourselves."

The disinformation campaign helped during Isa's breakout. "The Russians truly expected us at a different place, but I chose a different route. I did not tell even one officer or soldier with me which route we would take. I made that decision myself, and then led them, with the help of Allah." But Isa's position in the city was tenuous and his unit struggled to avoid contact, as this would risk their being wiped out or overrun. The morning before the planned departure, Isa spread his men out and positioned them on the roofs of the higher buildings. The Russians apparently knew they were in the area and deployed units into the sector where they were hiding. The Chechens lay low to avoid being noticed and forced into combat. "They actually walked right past us, perhaps they thought we had already left. When the Russians left the area in the evening, we escaped."

At 0030 in the dead of night, Isa gathered his soldiers and said that it was time to leave. The wounded were divided into several groups and placed at the rear of the column. Isa chose 25 soldiers who were "the healthiest, the toughest, the strongest, and armed them with heavy machine guns. We found whatever ammunition we could and gave it to the machine gunners." He then led them out of Kirova and towards the Sunzha River. "I didn't expect any of us to get out alive," Isa confided. In addition to having to cross the frigid Sunzha River, the south bank was sown with mines and defended by three rings of Russian positions. A motorized rifle regiment was closest to the river, backed by armored vehicle positions and finally the Tambov Assault Brigade.[4]

"I was in the front with a rifle, because I did not have the strength to carry a machine gun. We put our wounded inside our column and moved forward." Once at the river, Isa and his men waded downstream, in the dark, for what felt like an eternity. Isa estimates that they were in the water for nearly a kilometer before exiting on the south bank near a steep incline. As they climbed up on the river bank "a Russian special forces soldier that we were holding prisoner fell back into the river. The current was carrying him away, but a couple of Chechens were able to snag him and drag him out of the river. We eventually sent him to his parents via Ingushetia. He is still alive today."

Facing the steep incline, Isa and his men prepared to scale the cliff. "There were some athletes and special forces soldiers with me, and they stood on each other to create a human ladder. They climbed up, dropped a rope, and we began to climb up this rope, directly into the Russian rear area. The Russians were not expecting us at this spot." Isa had crossed the Sunzha in an area the Russians were not expecting the Chechens to cross and so they were not defending this stretch of the riverbank.

The terrain was forested and Isa's scouts led the long column of men to the right of the Russians' first line of defense. They methodically picked out a path for the column of starving combatants and their Russian prisoners. A few minutes later they were beyond the first line of defense. Cautiously they approached dug-in tanks that were part of the second line of Russian positions. Estimating that the tanks were at least 100 meters apart, they quietly snuck between two dug-in positions. So far the escape had been successful. Isa's men began to be hopeful. "We penetrated the Russian infantry, crossing their trenches and tanks."

The Chechens continued on. Isa's scouts could see no way around or through the third Russian line. "We ran right into their assault teams," recalls Isa. "It was the Tambov Assault Brigade, and they were well positioned with a series of trenches and dug-in BTRs." There was no option but to assault the nearest position. If it could be done quietly there was still a chance of breaking out of Grozny unseen. If they were forced into a firefight "we would likely all die there, in the middle of the Russian defenses."

They knew they had to keep going. The Chechen scouts advanced briskly in the dark to the Russian positions. Apparently, since this was the third line of defense, the soldiers were not alert or awake. "They were completely shocked when we ended up in their rear area. They were not expecting us." Isa's friend, who is strong and tough, "pulled two Russian soldiers out of the trench as if they were children, and asked 'where is your officer?' They couldn't even speak. They were just so surprised." The Chechens swarmed over the BTR and Russian trenches. They were careful not to make any noise. A gunshot was out of the question. Any killing that would take place tonight would have to be done hand-to-hand. The Russians were so surprised, no killing was necessary. "We took their weapons, we took trophies, and found some food in the BTR. We were hungry." Minutes later, with the Russian lines at their backs, Isa's column was on the move again.

Isa's force of 300 combatants continued out of Grozny in a southwesterly direction, passing east of Alkhan-Yurt for about 20 kilometers, using the patches of forests and tree lines for concealment. "Thanks to the small supply of food that we found at the Russian position we were able to survive. We were able to gather strength. We were able to feed the wounded," Isa recalls. "After we escaped I separated the wounded and sent them to where they needed to go, and then the rest of us went into the mountains. Very early in the morning, before sunrise, we escaped into the forest."

Commentary: According to Russian accounts there were limited skirmishes with small handfuls of Chechen combatants who were left in the city after the main withdrawal on 31 January, but within a few weeks the city was firmly under Russian control. There is no mention of Isa's defensive action or that the Russians might even have been aware that there was a significant-sized rear guard left in the city after the other Chechen commanders and their forces had left the city. Unlike the first war, the Chechens were never able to attack Grozny again in force. The loss of so many combatants and commanders on the main withdrawal from the city and the loss of hundreds more that would occur near Komsolmolskoye a few months later severely drained the Chechen insurgency of manpower.

Musing about the successful rear guard action, Isa reflected on their remarkable escape. "That is the path we took. It was an extremely difficult path. It was the highest point that I had reached in my entire life. We were all ready to give our lives at any minute, but

33rd OBRON (Separate Operational Brigade of the Ministry of the Interior) during the Second Chechen War, 1999–2000. (Photo via 33rd OBRON Veterans)

a raid or attacking a strong point, since many of the same tactical considerations apply. In most cases the Chechen intent was never to occupy Russian positions, but rather to break through their positions to reach a better position or designated objective elsewhere, in many cases bases or field hospitals outside the Russian zone of occupation. During the battles for Grozny and other urban centers the Chechens were constantly fighting from within a Russian encirclement and eventually had to fight their way out.

When possible, for larger breakouts the Chechens designated rear guard units. Rear guard duty is normally hazardous, particularly during a breakout. The Chechen command apparently did not spend a lot of time planning and establishing control procedures for breakouts. There is little evidence of control through assembly areas, time or event phasing, or movement control. There was no fire support. On the plus side, the Chechen higher command had logistics support and medical facilities positioned immediately outside the breakout area.

The Chechen force was as good as its platoon- and company-sized unit leadership. In the Chechen forces these sized units were normally well organized and well led. Most often they were also grandly designated as battalions. Multi-battalion and front commanders led through force of personality and reputation.

The rear guard action in the second vignette is interesting. The rear guard avoided direct contact with Russian maneuver forces. Rather, they used radio traffic to divert artillery fire onto their transmission locations. During the withdrawal there was no plan to collapse the rear guard through the breakout corridor to protect the withdrawing column. Rather, 300 men in three "battalions" were abandoned inside Grozny with no specific follow-on mission. Only one-third of the column served as the rear guard. The rest defended a chemical plant and an outlying village that flanked the withdrawal route. Once the survivors of the withdrawal had escaped, the rear guard spent weeks avoiding contact and finally broke out on their local commander's volition. The higher command was no longer immediately concerned with them. Chechen commanders enjoyed a great deal of flexibility and independence, so the commander's decision was not unusual.

not one of us lost their [sic] life through all of this. It was amazing. We didn't select the right side or the weak side. We chose the most foolish path, one that nobody would have taken. I didn't go to the right or the left. I made the toughest decision, to move right toward the Russian front, but it worked out. Later we found out that we had passed through a few minefields on the way. We had passed their tanks and their infantry, and their third and final line of troops. We had taken a very difficult route through all of this. We were all wet, and I can't remember another time when it was that cold."

Breaking out, or, more accurately, slipping through their lines, was a chronic problem for the Russians. In one instance after another, Chechen groups were able to find a way out of Russian encirclements. Aslanbek was part of a group that broke out of Grozny past Russian units in January or February 1995. The defenders of Serzhen-Yurt were able to slip past the encirclement near Krasnoye Vedeno in June 1995. Combatants on the Southwestern Front were able to slip through a defensive line of Russian special forces after attacking Shalazhi, Gekhi-Chu and Roshni-Chu in the summer of 2002. Part of the Russian problem was a lack of patrolling within stationary blocking positions. Electronic sensors were available to Russian forces, but they were not always placed to the front, flanks and inside their positions. Russian distribution of night-vision devices was also limited when compared to Western armies. Although this was an improved army during the Second Russian-Chechen War, the Russians still suffered from the lack of professional noncommissioned officers.

Chapter Three Summary

There is a certain ad hoc nature to smaller breakouts, and weapons and force positioning are often similar to those used when conducting

4

RAIDS

A raid is a surprise attack designed to seize an objective, exploit success and then withdraw. It is a temporary measure to capture equipment, kill the enemy, destroy tanks and checkpoints, bait traps

to draw enemy reactions and attack morale. The Chechens primarily conducted raids to capture weapons and ammunition and to demonstrate their ability to strike the Russians with impunity. Raids

Ruslan Labazanov, the Chechen Robin Hood, professional wrestler and criminal, once a Dzhokhar Dudaev supporter, then his enemy and the opposition leader responsible for attacking Dudaev's forces in October–November 1994. Prior to his death in 1996, Labazanov was a mediator between Russian and Chechen forces though without much success. (Photo via Efim Sandler)

require fewer supplies than an attack since there is no intention to hold the objective for any length of time following the raid.

Most Chechen raids were at night and depended on surprise and rapid execution for success. Russian artillery was responsive, so the raiders had little time to act before drawing return fire. There was no standard pattern for organizing Chechen raiding groups. An assault group, a fire support group and a security group are normally considered the minimum necessary for a successful raid. The Chechens frequently did without the fire support group and the security group.

Vignette 9: RPG Attack on Russian Armored Column near Argun, late December 1994

Elimpash

Background: Elimpash worked for Usman Imaev, the General Prosecutor under the Dudaev regime prior to the outbreak of war in late 1994. By mid-December Russian armored units were tightening the noose around Grozny. The Chechen command watched the developments as they prepared to defend the capital. Imaev was ordered to confirm reports of a Russian column advancing down the Petropalovsk Road toward the Permykanie Junction west of Argun, presumably heading to Grozny.[1] Crammed into two cars, Imaev, Elimpash and seven others set out from Grozny. To get there Imaev's group took the road out of New Sunzha to Berkat-Yurt and into the new housing development of Novyy Tsentoroy. From there it was only a few hundred meters to the bridge over the east–west railroad. Elimpash parked his car on the road just north of the bridge, while

Imaev parked below near the railroad tracks on the west side of the overpass.

They were not the only ones interested in tracking the Russians' movement. A group of some 20 combatants from Shali, as well as Shamil Basaev and his men, was also near the bridge location. Arriving after dark, the Chechens milled about, peering into the frozen landscape searching for the enemy. One of the other Chechen units that had been tracking the column knew that it had pulled off the road and onto the fields east of the road. But finding it was more difficult as there was not much night sky and the column had apparently shut down for the night. Suddenly Russian illumination flares lit up the night sky. The Chechens hustled off the bridge to avoid being seen. The glare of the light off the snow seemed to turn the landscape into midday. There it was, the Russian column, sitting way out in the field, more than half a kilometer away. Elimpash and the others made some quick estimates and determined that there were at least 40 tanks and APCs in a column. The Russians were using the flares to make sure there were not any Chechens trying to sneak up on them in the night.

Imaev was emphatic about attacking the column and the unit from Shali agreed. Basaev, who was conducting his own recon of the Russian column, tried to discourage Imaev, saying, "there is no need to attack the Russians here. There is no need to risk it." Still, Imaev seemed frustrated at his inability to do anything meaningful and, grabbing an RPG, he exclaimed "armed with these weapons, one can make an attack. Let's go along the railroad to the strip of woods, let's do something. They're advancing unopposed and we aren't doing anything. Let's attack them for once."

At approximately 2100 hours Imaev, Elimpash and the rest of their tiny band, plus the 20 combatants from Shali, checked their kit, broke into pairs and scuttled across the road, onto the tracks and into a small ditch running alongside. Each two-man team was armed with an RPG and a handful of RPG rounds. Elimpash carried his AKS in addition to the RPG.[2] Many had some sort of white winter camouflage to blend into the snowy background. Some had wrapped a white sheet over their jackets, while others had no white camouflage at all. Elimpash thought that it actually did not matter because it had not snowed for a few days and there were plenty of brown patches.

When they got to the narrow wooded strip straddling the railroad they dispersed in pairs to find concealment and a good firing position. The two-man teams positioned themselves 20–30 meters apart in the tree line and along the railroad tracks. There were no fixed distances between pairs but everyone made an effort to spread out while retaining any advantage they could get from the terrain. Elimpash himself used the railroad bank for cover, positioning himself and his loader on the embankment. Elimpash estimated that the rear end of the column was only 150–200 meters from their position, well within RPG range.

Imaev's instructions were short and easy to follow. "I'll shoot first. Then everyone try to get off three shots – at least two!" Imaev fired the first shot and the Chechens let loose a volley of RPG fire into the rear elements of the Russian column. "I fired my first shot and quickly reloaded for a second," Elimpash recalls. Russian counterfire was immediate as the tanks and armored vehicles fired up their engines, turned on their lights and manned their guns. The Chechens took heavy machine gunfire into the tree line and railroad tracks. It seemed earth-shattering to Elimpash, "it was as light as midday, and there was so much debris being kicked around as the Russian fire began to cut down the trees and bushes that I was afraid to open my eyes."

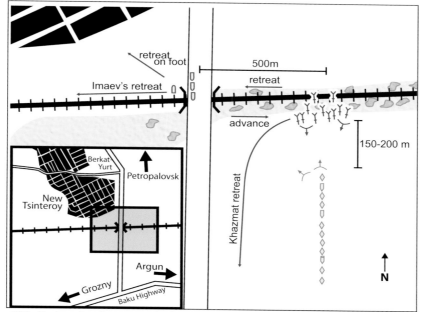

RPG attack on Russian armored column near Argun, late December 1994.

After firing the first shot Imaev was severely injured by shrapnel from an exploding tank main-gun round that struck him in the chest and exited out his back only centimeters from his heart and lungs. He also took shrapnel in his arm. His co-gunner, a relative, dragged him to the relative safety of the ditch under extreme enemy fire.

Elimpash and his assistant gunner were only 30–40 meters from the safety of a depression in the terrain that he had spotted when selecting his position, but he recalls that slithering on the ground to get there seemed to take an eternity and they "barely made it out alive." The retreat was more chaotic than the approach and not really planned at all. It was every pair for themselves but moments of heroism prevailed. While the rest of the group was retreating west under fire, Elimpash's friend Khamzat stumbled upon a wounded man from the Shali group. Instead of moving west like the others, he picked him up and moved directly south through the field, parallel and close to the column.

Still under heavy fire, Elimpash and the others finally made it back to the Petropalovsk highway. Imaev was stable but severely wounded and needed to get back to a hospital immediately. Two other combatants suffered non-life-threatening wounds. However, they now had a new problem. The Russian gunners had tracked the retreating Chechens west and had now spotted the cars near the bridge. Tank fire erupted, destroying one of Imaev's cars and damaging at least one of the vehicles belonging to the Shali group. Imaev was smart to have parked his car down below the road on the west side of the embankment. His relative helped him into the vehicle and sped out toward the military hospital in Grozny. With their other car burning on the road above them, Elimpash and the others, minus Khamzat, had no choice but to begin walking towards Novyy Tsentoroy.[3]

It is only 400 meters from the road through the fields to Novyy Tsentoroy, but only minutes later, while walking to the village, they were startled by Grad fire coming at them seemingly from somewhere northwest of Berkat-Yurt.[4] Thinking they were under attack from a second Russian position, they sprinted into Novyy Tsentoroy to close the gap between themselves and the Grad launcher, which was now sending rockets streaking overhead and landing behind them near the column. Only later did they discover that the Grads were under the command of Basaev, who, after conducting his own

recon, had ordered the systems to engage the same Russian column. Elimpash wished that Basaev would have mentioned that he was going to attack the Russian column as well.

Commentary: Usman Imaev, survived his wounds to continue guiding his small group of combatants against the Russian invasion. Elimpash and the rest of the group spent the night walking back to Grozny, arriving at their positions in the city around 0530. Khamzat and the wounded Chechen from the Shali group made it without further incident to the Permykanie Junction and to safety. Upon reuniting, Khamzat laughed, telling Elimpash and the others, "I wasn't worried, all the Russian fire was directed at you guys – they weren't looking at me. So I just went south alongside their column." Elimpash later found out that one of the Shali combatants was never accounted for and listed as missing in action. Elimpash's battle buddy was traumatized by the whole event, turned in his weapon and returned to his ancestral village to try to sit out the war (it is unknown whether or not he was successful). This is an important event in a culture that prides itself on its warrior culture, where it is every man's duty and life-long mission to oppose Russia by combat if necessary. The fact is, there were many Chechen men who did not want to fight and this is but one example.

The debate on the bridge between Imaev and Basaev illustrates an issue that plagued Chechen forces throughout both wars. Basaev had told Imaev not to bother, that the operation Imaev was contemplating was too risky. In the vast fields and plains that make up northern Chechnya, Chechen forces were limited by the range of the RPG in their ability to attack Russian armor. At the same time Russian armor had the ability to strike targets far beyond maximum effective range of the RPG-toting Chechens. Imaev's group was fortunate to have not suffered far more casualties conducting this raid against an entire Russian armored column.

Elimpash and most of the others were able to get off at least two shots before retreating under heavy fire. Still, the strike was inconclusive, as many Chechen attacks were, but the Chechens were able to bleed the Russian forces, even if they could not beat them. Elimpash recalls the group talking about seeing six or seven pieces of armor burning, but he admits he had no idea what damage was inflicted, and felt lucky to have gotten out alive. It must be remembered that for most of the Chechens involved this early in the conflict war was a new experience. Reflecting on the attack Elimpash mused, "it seemed like a success at the time. It was our first attack."

Seeking a place to stop for the night, the Russian column pulled off the road, 500–600 meters into a field, giving them a pretty good field of fire and putting them outside maximum effective RPG range from the west, south and east. However, being only 100–200 meters south of the tree- and shrub-lined railroad track made them vulnerable to attack from the north. Nor did they push out a guard force to the tree line, which may not be surprising. This Russian column is likely the same one that had fought pitched battles with Chechen groups in Petropalovsk and skirmishes in the wooded areas south of Petropalovsk only days before. They may have determined that to push out a guard force or to pursue the Chechens into the tree line was a very bad idea and that they would take their chances using illuminating flares and the openness of the fields to give them protection and extensive fields of fire. The quick reaction time to return fire suggests the Russian column was ready to respond to an attack.

Vignette 10: Attack on Russian Tank Position in Grozny, 10–19 January 1995

Musa

Background: By early January Russian forces had moved within striking distance of the Chechen command center, which was still located in the Presidential Palace. Russian tanks were actually on the square pouring shells into the Chechen command post at point blank range, while Russian infantry occupied the former KGB and MVD buildings directly north of the Palace. Although Chechen units were still moving in the city north of the Sunzha River, most of the Chechen force had withdrawn to the south bank, creating a defense against the Russian forces with the river between them.

Musa had his own group of 16 combatants at this time and occupied one of the many older five-story apartment buildings along the south bank of the Sunzha River. His group was one of many groups holding these forward positions, keeping an eye on the Russian movements across the river and looking for chances to exploit any opportunity to strike the Russian forces. The upper floors were usually occupied by Chechen snipers.

In addition to the other tanks closing in on the Palace, two tanks backed into a movie theater between the Kavkaz Hotel and the Parliament building to the east of the Palace. Using the building as both cover and concealment from Chechen forces just across the river, the tanks settled in and began to blast away at the Chechen command post, where Chechen General Maskhadov and others had taken refuge in the basement of the building. Russian sentries were placed around the tanks outside the building to prevent any Chechen attack on the position.[5]

Observing the withering fire against the Palace, Musa and his men determined to do something, but crossing the Lenin Street Bridge over the Sunzha was out of the question. The bridge itself was not occupied by either the Chechens or Russians, but both had

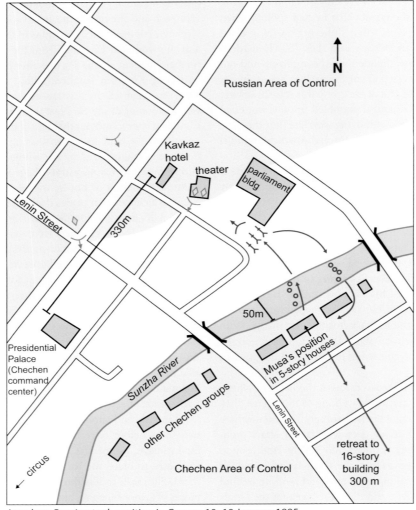

Attack on Russian tank position in Grozny, 10–19 January 1995.

a clear line of sight on the location. Both Chechen and Russian snipers were very active and neither side could put its infantry on the bridge. Still, Musa was determined to get across the river and attack the tanks firing at Maskhadov and the others still operating in the basement of the Palace. The bridge further west, past the circus, was still open but it too was dangerous, and once the attack was finished it would be a long, if not impossible, retreat.

Musa gathered some automobile tire inner-tubes and split his force into two groups of eight each. "We decided to float across the Sunzha River and strike the soldiers and destroy the tanks." Half his group would continue to occupy their position in the five-story apartment building on the south bank of the Sunzha River, while he and the other seven would inflate their inner-tubes, float across the river and destroy the two tanks, and retreat back across the Sunzha in their inner-tubes.

Musa crossed the river under the cover of the other half of his group. It was January and cold. "The Russians would never suspect us getting across the river this way." Knowing that his men were covering their slow and arduous crossing gave Musa a feeling of confidence. They reached the north bank and checked their gear. They were obviously cold and wet as they set out on foot toward the Russian tank position. The route was strewn with rubble, including debris from the Parliament building. Musa guessed they made it to within 50 meters of the Russian tanks. They opened fire but quickly came under Russian return fire. Musa did not even notice the cold. A Chechen RPG struck the closest tank, setting it on fire, but they could not get a clear shot at the second tank. Several rounds missed. Out of RPG ammunition and under increasing small arms fire from the Russian infantry guarding the position, Musa shot a flare into the air signaling his retreat.

Seeing the flare, the other half of Musa's group went into action. Until now they had silently observed the firefight from the security and vantage point of the upper story floors they occupied. Now they opened fire on the Russian position. This was according to plan, and, instead of retreating straight back to the river, he led his men eastward out of the line of fire before heading south to the river. They reached the banks of the Sunzha and once again floated across the river in their inner tubes. They were still full of adrenaline from the fight and the water did not seem as cold this time.

Safely across the river, the second half of the group ceased firing and joined Musa and the other wet attackers for a 300-meter walk back to a 16-story apartment building. By the time they entered the building Musa really noticed the cold. He and the others who had crossed the river stripped off their clothes while the others built a fire against one of the back walls. Warm again, Musa and the others settled into a nap.

Commentary: There were many skirmishes around the Presidential Palace during the final days that the Chechen command continued to occupy the building. The building itself, General Maskhadov's headquarters for a few days longer, was more symbolic than of military value. When Maskhadov gave the order to evacuate days later, he and the others headed southwest along the Sunzha, crossing the river at the next bridge. The Chechen groups held the buildings on the southern bank as the Russians claimed the Presidential Palace.

Musa's group sustained no casualties in this action but he did not consider it a complete success. "We succeeded in destroying one tank but not the second. We didn't have enough combat power." The tanks were well positioned within the crumbling building and Musa's attack group could not get an angle on the second tank without assaulting right up to the building, which they could not

do against Russian infantry fire. He recalls killing Russian infantry but estimates the number as small, perhaps only a handful. The important thing was that his unit escaped and survived to fight another day.

Although the Russians were trying to conduct an urban fight with some degree of linearity, order and control, at this point the Groxny fight was still a battle for strong points constructed around prominent buildings, street intersections and factories. Tall apartment houses were valued for their observation and sniper opportunities. The fight for the Presidential Palace was symbolic and the theater location provided a direct shot at it. Tank fire would never bring down the palace, but shelling it was symbolically important. The theater location provided flank and rear protection for the tanks. Even Musa's oblique assault could not engage both tanks.

Vignette 11: Failed Raid on Russian Position Near the Former Chernorechie Prison, sometime in mid-January to early February 1995

Elimpash

Background: By mid-January, despite fierce Chechen resistance, Russian forces were tightening their grip on Grozny, seizing most of the territory north of the Sunzha River. However, there were still considerable pockets of Chechen combatants operating in and around the city center. Former General Prosecutor Usman Imaev and his unit were now located in the Chernorechie area below the Sunzha River in southwestern Grozny. Like dozens of other semi-autonomous Chechen units, the Chechens under Imaev's command constantly monitored Russian movements in the city, looking for targets of opportunity. The Chechens were chronically low on supplies. Raids to secure weapons and ammunition were as important as attacks to bleed the Russians. Imaev was frustrated at his inability to inflict any sort of real damage on the Russian juggernaut enveloping the city, declaring, "We're constantly leaving. We're not attacking. Let's do at least one attack!"

Elimpash and the other combatants in his group began to reconnoiter Russian positions across the river, looking for positions they could attack with a strong chance of success. Many of the bridges across the Sunzha were blown up in order to slow the Russian advance. This gave the Chechens, who operated totally on foot, an advantage, as most of the disabled bridges were still crossable by foot but incapable of supporting a Russian armored thrust across the river. Khamzat noticed that the Russians were moving into a house on the other side of one of these bridges. The house was next to a water pumping station and both were protected by a short brick perimeter fence of about 75 meters. Khamzat and another combatant snuck across the Sunzha to get a closer look at the Russian position. It appeared that there were no more than five or six soldiers preparing a forward post for a larger unit, likely a company-sized element, occupying the grounds of the former Chernorechie Prison another 400–500 meters further west.

Khamzat liked what he saw and reported back to Imaev and the rest of the unit, suggesting that an operation be carried out against the position before the Russians had time to fortify it further. Imaev agreed and 10 men were selected, including Khamzat and Elimpash. Moving in pairs, the unit left in the middle of the night, crossing on an industrial pipe leading to a chemical factory that was roughly one kilometer north of the objective. Once across the river, the group

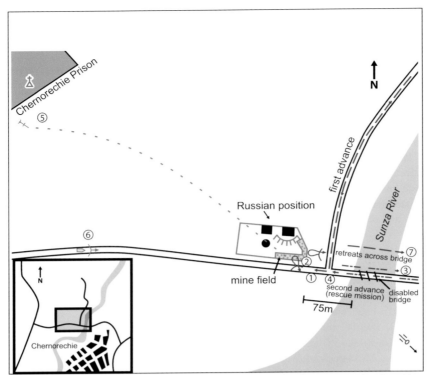

Failed raid on Russian position near the former Chernorechie Prison sometime in mid-January to early February 1995.

planned to move down a dirt road towards the water pumping station and approach the Russian position from behind. Each Chechen carried two to three magazines of ammunition and two grenades each. One had an RPG and Elimpash carried a PKM.[6] They were not as well armed as Elimpash would have liked. Ammunition was scarce. He only had 100 rounds for his machine gun. The objective was to strike the Russian position hard and fast, gather up any equipment that they could and retreat across the disabled bridge to the east before the larger Russian position at the prison could react. Imaev would be waiting at a predesignated spot on the other side of the river.

The group had not even gotten across the pipe when Russian flares illuminated the night sky. Crouching near the riverbank, Elimpash wondered, "Could the Russians have known we were coming? Or was it pure coincidence? And now what? Should we continue with the operation?" Flares continued to light up the skies over the position and Imaev decided to abandon the operation for the time being. The next night was the same, Russian flares were fired during the night. Finally on the third night it was calm. There were no flares, just the darkness the Chechens had been counting on. Imaev decided to carry out the operation. Again the group prepared itself for combat.

The 10-man Chechen force scuttled across the pipe and onto the west bank of the Sunzha without incident and began moving silently south towards the Russian position. Soon they could see the brick fence and the house and pumping station behind it. It was eerily quiet. They picked up the pace as they approached the corner. One of the Chechens threw a grenade over the fence at the house as they rounded the corner, signaling the attack. Elimpash did not have time to pull the trigger before Russian fire erupted from the windows of the house. The Chechens dove for cover. Khamzat ran towards the fence at one of the Russian blind spots to assault the house. Elimpash was surprised by the amount of Russian fire back at them: "It seemed like they were firing from every window. There

were far more than the five or six Russians we had expected. And they seemed ready for us."

Elimpash opened up with his PKM and quickly fired all the rounds in his ammunition box. Another Chechen carried an RPG, but Elimpash is not sure if he even got a shot off. There was no way to get beyond the fence to attack the building under so much Russian fire. If it were not for the fence, they would all be dead. Elimpash tried calling for help on the radio but it did not work. He was sure the Russians had jammed it.

Under fire, and quickly losing the initiative, the Chechens fell back to the river. Everything was dark, punctuated by bursts of light and noise. It was confusing. They managed to get across the disabled bridge and retreat further into the relative safety of Chernorechie. Imaev was waiting at the rendezvous point. Elimpash dropped his empty PKM. The attack had been futile. Worse, Khamzat and one other combatant were missing. Khamzat was an experienced combat veteran of many battles and everyone assumed he would make his way across the river somehow to link up with the group here at the rendezvous point. They were less sure about the second man. He was new and had little combat experience. The minutes passed and neither one showed up.

Determined to find them, the eight remaining group members reloaded and prepared to head back across the river. Elimpash had no more rounds for the PKM so he borrowed an AKM and two 30-round magazines from one of Imaev's personal guards. It was dawn as they crossed back across the disabled bridge and approached the water pumping station. Once again it was eerily silent. "Had the Russians retreated back to the prison or were they waiting?" Elimpash could not be sure. Reaching the brick fence for the second time, Elimpash and the others began quietly calling "Khamzat, where are you?" It was the second missing man who answered. Elimpash rushed toward the voice where he saw the man laying badly wounded in a small depression near the fence. He was in bad shape: "I am all shot, up and down. I'm as good as dead. Go help Khamzat." He motioned through the fence and Elimpash crept near a hole to see what was on the other side. There was Khamzat. He had jumped through the same hole in the fence only to step on a mine.

Acknowledging defeat, Khamzat handed Elimpash his assault rifle and said he would fight to the death with a Japanese sword he always carried with him. As Elimpash and the others assessed the wounded and prepared to get them back to Chernorechie, fire erupted from the house. The Russians had not retreated. Elimpash emptied both magazines as he instinctively fell back, rolling across the road. A moment later Russian automatic grenade fire began to pound their position. Elimpash was grazed by shrapnel and a combatant next to him was hit in the kidneys. They knew they had to get out of there immediately if they wanted to live. As they began to bound the 75 meters back to the river, a Russian BTR emerged a few hundred meters west of them from the direction of the prison, firing its 14.5mm KPVT and 7.62mm PKT machine guns. The small group was in a precarious situation. Elimpash recalls, "it was absolutely impossible to recover our wounded and get to the other side of the river." Leaving the wounded behind Elimpash and the others retreated across the pipe for the second time. The operation was over. They had not recovered any supplies. They had no evidence that they killed or wounded any Russians, but instead were forced to leave two of their own.

Commentary: The raid and the failed rescue mission lasted nearly four hours, beginning around 0400 and ending around 0800. The Chechen action was driven in part by a feeling of hopelessness at a deteriorating situation and the need for resupply. Raiding Russian positions to get equipment, ammunition and supplies was essentially part of the Chechen battle plan. However, this particular operation probably should not have been undertaken since the rationale behind the raid was to hit the Russians where and when they were not numerically superior, and where they were not yet dug in. Since the Chechen raid was postponed for two nights, the Russians had time to strengthen their position and increase their numbers. The Chechens seemed completely unaware of the minefield in the yard protecting the Russian blind spots.

The Chechen unit did have prearranged artillery support from a single field piece located in Chernorechie and manned by another autonomous Chechen group.[7] However, Russian radio jamming frustrated Elimpash's calls for help. The artillery unit was able to observe the raid and tried to engage the house and other buildings of the water pumping station once it was clear that the Chechens were retreating, but the gun jammed and was inoperable when it was needed most.

Khamzat and the other wounded Chechen were never recovered and left to the Russians. Khamzat had told Elimpash that he would never be taken alive. At a truce negotiated the next day, their dead were to be exchanged for two Russian prisoners who had been taken earlier. Days later Chechen and Russian military delegations met on the same dirt road that the group had used between the water pumping station and the chemical factory to reach the Russian position. The Russians arrived with only one body rather than two. In the end, the Russians gave back Khamzat's body for two Russian prisoners. The second Chechen body was never recovered.

Vignette 12: Attack on a Russian Tank Position near Shalazhi Summer 1995 (likely before Shamil Basaev's raid on Budyonnovsk 14–19 June)

Musa

Background: As Russian forces consolidated their gains on the plains of the tiny republic, Chechen combatant forces were forced to live in and operate from the mountains, which afforded them both cover and concealment from Russian military operations. The Chechen command had planned on this eventuality, but living in the mountains was hard work and much of the Chechen war effort was consumed by logistics – supplying the forces with adequate quarters, food, and equipment. This was the situation when Musa and his group of 17 men arrived in the wooded foothills next to the village of Shalazhi.

As Musa organized a position for his men, he constantly kept an eye on the Russian units below him on the plains. The Russians had dug in a number of tanks on the north side of the road approaching Shalazhi and seemed to stretch out in all directions. Russian reconnaissance units were also being continually sent into the mountains to search out and destroy Chechen groups such as Musa's. More and more the Chechen mountain sanctuaries were eroded by Russian advances and there was constant pressure to preserve their men from the elements.

Musa and his men constantly assessed the Russian positions below them, looking for weaknesses and a chance to strike a blow at their enemy. Musa scanned the horizon with his binoculars. He counted dozens of tanks dug in across the stretch of plain west from Salanzhi. All were well out of effective range of the Mukha and on the edge of effective range for the RPG-7. Since they were dug in behind berms, only the turrets would be vulnerable to a ground attack. There did not seem to be a lot of options. The tanks were also spread out, "at least 100 meters apart," Musa guessed. "Even if we could get to one of the tanks and take it out, it was only one tank. It wasn't worth the risk." Musa recalled.

About a week after Musa and his group had arrived in the area, another Chechen commander operating in the same location suggested that they work together against a specific Russian position, two tanks near the entrance to Shalazhi. Musa took a look.

The two tanks were dug in behind berms like the others he had spied. One barrel pointed towards the village, the other towards the mountains. It appeared as if the barrel were pointing right at him. Unlike the tanks spread out across the plains, these two were close together. The tanks looked to be no more than 20 meters apart. They were also dug in near some hilly terrain before it flattened out westward. Musa estimated that they were approximately 50 meters from the hills, giving the Russians minimal field of fire but also affording a Chechen strike group ample concealment from which to get close.

Musa liked the odds and the two commanders began to rehearse the plan. Musa would take his group west through the mountains to a point where the forest jutted northward and closest to the Russian tanks positioned in the plains. The other commander would take his team and, using the hilly terrain, sneak up on the two Russian tanks to strike them from close range. It would be risky but the fact that the tanks were only 20 meters apart and the terrain was favorable for most of the way convinced the Chechens it was an operation worth executing. The two groups worked on the details for a couple nights,

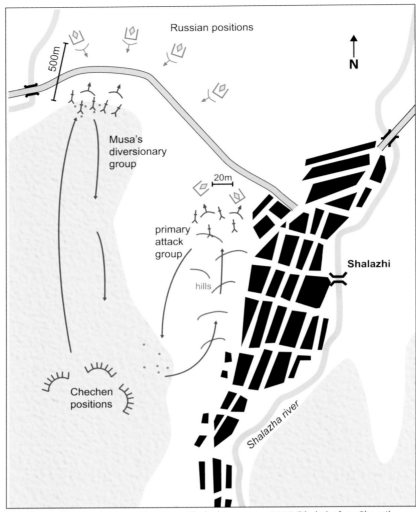

Russian positions

500m

Musa's diversionary group

20m

primary attack group

hills

Shalazhi

Chechen positions

Shalazha river

N

Attack on a Russian tank position near Shalazhi summer 1995 (likely before Shamil Basaev's raid on Budyonnovsk 14 – 19 June).

conducting what amounted to a dry run to make sure they could get the basics down – get their men to the desired locations and know their routes of exfiltration.

A few nights later the two groups moved towards their predesignated positions. Musa took only five members of his group, "I didn't send them all because the group was large, and the more people, the more noticeable it is." The primary strike group from the other unit was also comprised of only five men. The night sky was clear but it was not particularly bright. There was no moon. "The other group would have to get much closer than the protection of the hills, some 50-odd meters from the Russian position," Musa thought. To minimize the risk further they set out well after midnight. "We wanted to attack at 0300 or 0400 because, even if the Russians weren't asleep, they would be groggy, sluggish."

Both groups crept towards their positions. The primary attack group crept to the edge of the hills, so close that they could hear the Russians talking. Musa, too, moved his diversionary group out to the edge of the tree line, facing the Russian positions in the plains. He spread his team out to give the appearance of a much larger group. He also wanted to preserve his force. He did not want a single lucky mortar or tank round to take out the whole group. Spreading them out would minimize this risk.

Musa leaned his assault rifle against a tree, raised an RPG and fired. Immediately the rest of his men did the same, each firing an RPG or Mukha towards the Russians in the distance. He had no illusion he would hit anything; he was still hundreds of meters away

from the tanks spread out in front of him. His job was to make as much noise as possible to get the Russian positions to focus on his location. RPGs streaked towards the Russian tanks. Musa fired a Mukha, dropped his launcher, picked up his assault rifle and began to fire. His group even threw some hand grenades just to make noise and direct attention to their position.

Hearing the commotion, the primary attack group sprung into action. They had crept within 20–25 meters of the dug-in tanks. Although the moon was not out they could see the turret, the only part of the tank that was visible behind the earthen berm. The Russian sentries had stopped talking as they realized that another part of their line was under attack further west. Before the Russian soldiers could focus on their own sector, one of the Chechens rose to a knee and fired off a Mukha round, hitting the turret and causing the tank to go up in flames. Other Mukhas streaked into the second Russian tank, setting it on fire. The Chechens dropped their disposable launch tubes and sprayed the positions with automatic weapons fire as they withdrew. While retreating, they threw hand grenades to confuse and maybe even kill the Russian infantry around the position.

Musa could not see the primary objective being hit by the other group. He was now in a serious fight of his own. Although his weapons were ineffective, the diversion worked. Musa estimates that it was less than two minutes before Russian heavy machine-gun and tank fire returned fire on their position. "We knew we had to get out of there quickly. We couldn't run away, we had to crawl away as fast as we could." Remarkably, none of Musa's team was hit and they began to turn eastward through the forest back towards their staging base. Traversing the hillside, Musa caught his first glimpse of the two burning tanks in the distance near the entrance to Shalazhi. He knew the action had been successful.

Commentary: Both Chechen groups met up at the staging area and congratulated themselves on carrying out the action successfully while not taking any casualties. Musa has no idea how many Russian soldiers were killed by the primary attack group. After hearing the other group's recounting of the action, he estimated between six and 10 soldiers were killed. There was no confirmation that any of the infantry around the position had been killed, but Musa assumed the standard tank crew of three would have been killed outright by the direct hits to the turrets.[8] From the safety of his position, Musa watched the two tanks burn into the early morning hours.

Although small in scale, the attack was a morale booster for both groups. For months there had been a noticeable shift from the early battles, when Chechens were constantly attacking, to now, when Chechens were more often than not on the defensive. This bothered Musa, "We went where the battles were. The warrior's goal is to fight, not to lie low and wait for them to attack you. We had fixed positions. They were always attacking. We didn't have the means to attack. We could only attack at night and immediately leave."

This reality was heightened by the fact that, with the cities and flatlands under Russian control, the Chechens were forced to operate almost exclusively from the mountains. "We could only attack at night and only with small groups because it was easier for a small group to attack without being noticed and escape."

These conditions betray a more significant problem facing the Chechen combatants. The Chechens did not dare mass. As this battle illustrates, the risk to large groups was not worth it so the Chechens operated in small groups to husband their resources and reduce risk. Musa could have taken his entire group of 17 but choose to conduct the action with only five. "I didn't send them because the group was large, and the more people, the more noticeable it is." The unfortunate side effect of this is that without massing it became more difficult for the Chechens to carry out any actions of significant scope or devastating enough to have any lasting impact on the overall Russian war effort. While the loss of two tanks and the likely death or injury to a handful of soldiers may have represented a tactical victory for the Chechens, it would have barely been noticeable to the Russian high command.

Chapter Four Summary

In the earliest raid examples in this chapter there were never any rehearsals. There was a tendency to give general guidance and then let the situation sort itself out as it occurred. Over time, the surviving Chechen units started rehearsing their raids, working on coordinating events by time, better communications and rally/check points.

Once a raid has failed and the element of surprise has dissipated, it is time to depart. In the third vignette, the raiders do not realize that they have lost two members of a ten-man team until they had crossed a river and traveled over a kilometer. They then decide to recross the river and return to the raid site to find their missing men. They arrive in the area at dawn and survive only through luck and lack of aggressive Russian patrolling.

The Chechens seldom had the strength and ammunition for large attacks. In order not to surrender the initiative completely, the Chechens relied on raids and ambushes to carry the fight to the Russians and make the statement that they were still there to contest the turf. Since the Chechen resistance never enjoyed the complete backing of the population of Chechnya, such demonstrations were necessary.

5
AMBUSH AND COUNTER-AMBUSH

The ambush was a favored tactic of the Chechen resistance, as it provided the opportunity to mass forces covertly, attack the enemy, seize supplies and retreat before the enemy could react. During the first war large-scale ambushes were common, but as the Chechen forces diminished, the size and frequency of ambushes dwindled. Ambushes could also be used to slow down enemy advances in difficult terrain and tie down considerable numbers of enemy soldiers in security missions and convoy escort.

Chechen forces tried to avoid fratricide, so they seldom positioned ambush forces facing each other on both sides of the road. Rather, depending on the terrain, the ambush force could be on one side of the road or the other, but not directly across from each other. After the ambush, the ambush parties would leave the area on their side of the road. Chechen forces were careful not to cross the road, as that would put them directly and openly in the surviving enemy's sights.

Chechen forces tried to initiate the ambush from positions that were close to the road and, consequently, safe from Russian artillery fire and air support. They often would not occupy these positions until after the Russian scouts had gone through the position. The standard Russian convoy kept a group of armored vehicles at the front of the convoy with more armored vehicles spaced throughout the formation. Another group of armored vehicles, plus recovery and maintenance vehicles, brought up the tail. Helicopters or a road-clearing detachment might precede the convoy. Combat units in convoy would normally bring their own artillery on a unit move, but supply convoys relied on artillery support from fire bases along the route.

When hit, Russian soft-skinned vehicle drivers tried to drive out of the kill zones while armored vehicles responded with direct fire. The Russians also used smoke whenever possible to deny Chechens visibility of the road area as they moved vehicles out of the kill zones. Should any Russian vehicle be hit and block the exit from the kill zone, the Russians would attempt to push it out of the way immediately.

Vignette 13: Ambush of Russian Column Between Benoi and Vedeno, end of May or Early June 1995 (after Chechen defenders retreat from of Serzhen-Yurt)

Musa

Background: The Chechens had just lost Serzhen-Yurt, the last remaining strong point before the Vedeno Gorge, where General Maskhadov and the Chechen command were located. Carrying their dead and wounded, Musa, Aslan and the rest of the Chechen combatants retreated as far south as Nizhneye Vedeno. There was some discussion as to whether or not they should defend the road in the vicinity of the small town of Benoi, but Maskhadov had ordered all the Chechen combatants into Vedeno and the surrounding mountains. Still, many Chechen combatants thought that the road to Vedeno ought to be defended.

After regrouping and rearming the best they could, four group commanders (Musa, Aslan, Naib and Musadi) decided on their own initiative to move back toward Benoi and set up an ambush for the Russian column they knew would arrive. For better or worse, it was common for Chechen combatants and units to determine their own actions and their own timelines.[1] They traveled on foot at night to avoid Russian scouts or pro-Russian Chechens who might turn them in.

They were very familiar with the road, but, just to be sure, they surveyed the road again. They decided to set up an ambush at a bend in the road near a bridge adjacent to a gorge running east into the mountains. Having settled on an ambush location, the four groups hiked up the narrow gorge until they found a location that gave them a commanding view of the road from Serzhen-Yurt. From this position they would be able to see the Russian column through binoculars as it moved out from Serzhen-Yurt towards Vedeno. Musa estimates that their overwatch position was 300 or 400 meters from the road.

The Chechens knew that the Russians would take a few days to consolidate their position in Serzhen-Yurt before advancing on Vedeno. Cautiously, they worked at night to fortify small attack positions 30 to 40 meters along the sides of the road. They were careful moving back and forth from the heights to the road below. They knew the Russians would send scouts along the route before any advance. They did not want to engage the smaller force, preferring to engage the column and slow down the larger Russian advance towards Vedeno.[2] Musa wanted to arrive at the ambush site after the scouts but before the main column. It is one reason he chose an overwatch position so far from the road.

Through his binoculars, Musa could see the Russian column begin moving out from Serzhen-Yurt. He and his men had been at their positions for four days now and they were anxious to engage the Russians. They hastily made their way down the gorge and traveled the 300–400 meters to the road. Musa and the second group, with

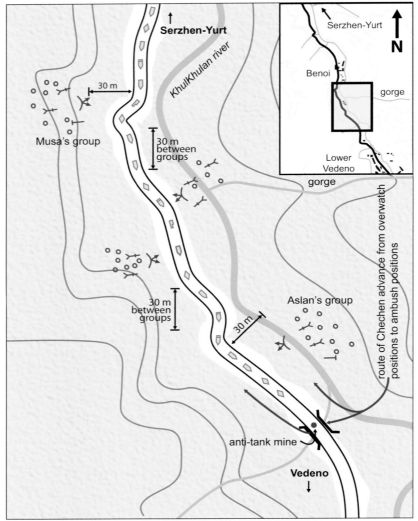

Ambush of Russian column between Benoi and Vedeno end of May or early June 1995.

A Chechen T-72A of the Shali Regiment. The Shali Tank Regiment was formed under command of Saypudi Isaev in the second half of 1992 and was based on the Russian 392nd Tank Regiment of 42nd Motor Rifle Division that had left Chechnya. Of 42 tanks only 19 were in serviceable condition but during fighting with the opposition and a failed attempt to take over Grozny, more T-72 and T-62 tanks were added to the inventory, bringing the number to about 30. After the conflict with Dzhokhar Dudaev, who blamed Saypudi Isaev for passiveness during the opposition assault on Grozny in November 1994, Issa Dalkhaev took command. Before the Russian operation in December, all Chechen tanks were marked with light colors – white, grey and blue – depending on the availability of the paint. Some had the full turret and upper hull painted, others only sides of the turret, with numbers overpainted. Chechen tanks could very often be seen with flags despite the obvious conspicuousness. (Artwork by David Bocquelet)

A Russian Federation T-72B1 of 2nd Company of the tank battalion of the 276th Motor Rifle Regiment, commanded by Sergey Bunin, deployed near Kurchaloy in the summer of 1996. As was common for the majority of tank units in Chechnya, the battalion was at only about half of the nominal strength of 40 tanks. The tanks were all T-72B1s in various conditions – from very old machines that had been used from the beginning of the war to brand new tanks from the storage depots. The tanks of 276th Regiment carried all kinds of artworks depending on the creativity of the tank commander; in this case a skull and cross bones (almost obscured by mud and dust) has been crudely applied on the rubber side skirt, and the logo from the *Ghostbusters* movie has been painted onto the searchlight cover. (Artwork by David Bocquelet)

A Russian Federation PT-76 light tank of the Mechanized Company – commanded by Sergey Golubev – of 8th Separate Operational Brigade of the North Caucasian Department of the Ministry of the Interior. PT-76 tanks took part in the fighting in Grozny in February–March 1995. During the assault of Bamut on 18 April 1995, Lieutenant Golubev used his tank to provide cover to infantry that had become trapped under heavy fire. The tank was hit by several RPGs and destroyed. After the war, the Mechanized Company was transferred to the newly formed 93rd Mechanized Regiment of the 100th Operational Division of Internal Troops. The tanks used in early 1995 were painted in two tone camouflage and carried the Internal Troops emblem, and the emblem of the North Caucasian Military District of the Ministry of the Interior (inset). No numbers were visible on these vehicles. (Artwork by David Bocquelet)

A Chechen BTR-80 captured during a raid by a team from the 45th Separate Reconnaissance Regiment of the Airborne Forces (VDV) along the Bass River Gorge on 6 April 2000. During the raid, a huge ammunition depot was found along with several vehicles. This BTR belonged to *Jundallah* ('The Soldiers of God') – an Islamic extremist faction. It is not clear whether this was connected to the Iranian-supported *Jundallah* organization, as there were several Jamaats in Chechnya from 1995 that called themselves *Jundallah* – some from Saudi Arabia, some from Jordan and Iran. In the majority of cases the mechanized assets of the Armed Forces of Ichkeria belonged to the National Guard. It was very uncommon to see a BTR in the hands of the Islamic groups after 1998 when Wahhabist units were disbanded by the decree of Aslan Maskhadov. (Artwork by David Bocquelet)

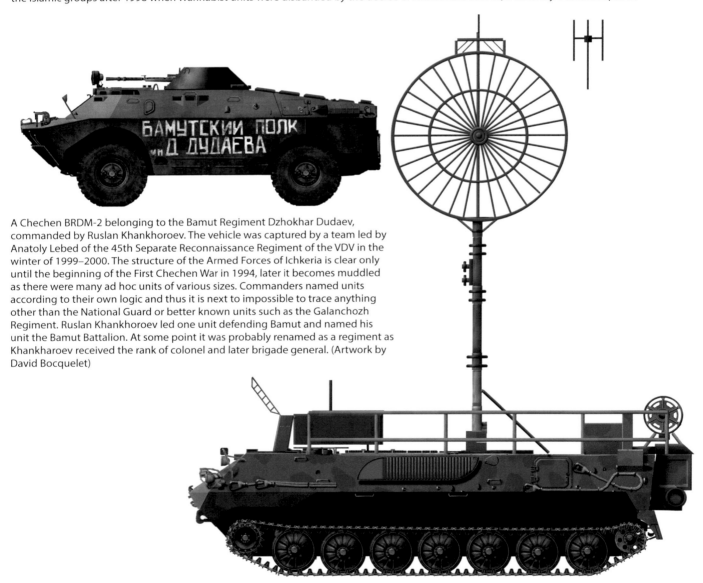

A Chechen BRDM-2 belonging to the Bamut Regiment Dzhokhar Dudaev, commanded by Ruslan Khankhoroev. The vehicle was captured by a team led by Anatoly Lebed of the 45th Separate Reconnaissance Regiment of the VDV in the winter of 1999–2000. The structure of the Armed Forces of Ichkeria is clear only until the beginning of the First Chechen War in 1994, later it becomes muddled as there were many ad hoc units of various sizes. Commanders named units according to their own logic and thus it is next to impossible to trace anything other than the National Guard or better known units such as the Galanchozh Regiment. Ruslan Khankhoroev led one unit defending Bamut and named his unit the Bamut Battalion. At some point it was probably renamed as a regiment as Khankharoev received the rank of colonel and later brigade general. (Artwork by David Bocquelet)

An R-381T1 vehicle – based on the MT-LBu – of the Taran signal reconnaissance complex used in both Chechen wars. This system was developed in the early 1970s, accepted by Soviet Army in 1980 and was used in Afghanistan from 1985. It could intercept and pinpoint enemy transmitters at a distance of up to 40km. In December 1994, the 1st Tactical Group of Radio Reconnaissance – including R-381T1 and R-381T2 vehicles of the Taran complex – were deployed in Vladikavkaz with 107th7 Battalion of Electronic Warfare, and in Mozdok with the 1919th Battalion of EW and Navigation. The complex was used to intercept Chechen transmissions, and to guide Mi-8PPA/MTPP helicopters for jamming or to direct aviation and artillery strikes. Additional Taran vehicles were deployed with the increase of the number of EW units. No specific markings were observed on the vehicles. (Artwork by David Bocquelet)

A BMP-1 of 33rd Separate Operational Brigade – commanded by Pavel Dashkov – during Second Chechen War, circa summer of 2000. The brigade took part in the painful assault on Grozny in January 2000 and was then deployed to Argun and took part in bloody fighting in the so-called Argun Triangle. After the situation stabilized the brigade held numerous outposts in central Chechnya. The camouflage pattern dates from the late period of 2000 when the majority of fighting was over; the fighting vehicles of the period were not commonly as neat and clean. The winged sphinx emblem is the 33rd Brigade's logo. (Artwork by David Bocquelet)

A BTR-ZD of 108th Guards Airborne Regiment of the 7th Guards Airborne Division. This is, essentially, a BTR-D (the turretless APC member of the BMD family) equipped with a twin-barreled 23mm ZU-23-2 anti-aircraft gun. The armor assets of the airborne units were not fully adequate for the war – they were underpowered, poorly protected and had insufficient firepower. Though nominally armed to a similar standard to the BMPs of motor rifle units, the paratrooper's BMDs were much less effective due to structural issues, not to mention that 30mm cannon-armed BMD-2s were available in lesser numbers. The BTR-ZD was used as a gap-filler. Compared to the standard BMD it had a longer and heavier chassis with an extra road wheel but gave absolutely no protection to the gun crew – similar to a gun-truck. The vehicles were used for patrolling duties, perimeter security and convoy protection. Needless to say that any encounter with antitank weapons would result in catastrophic damage. (Artwork by David Bocquelet)

The 2S4 Tulpan (Tulip) was a self-propelled version of the M240 240mm heavy mortar. These were deployed during Second Chechen war with 24th Special Mortar Battalion in Argun. Half of the 2S4s were employed in the Argun-Shatoi area while the other half shelled Grozny. Targeting was conducted by PRP-3 vehicles. The 240mm mortar fired 53-F-864 high-explosive bombs, laser guided 1K113 "Smelchak" (Daredevil) munitions, and a rocket-powered 3O8 Nerpa cluster munition. In Grozny, the Smelchak rounds were used against buildings, where they would penetrate 3–4 floors before detonating, totally devastating the interior. The last Tulpan round to be fired in Chechnya was on 30 July 2000. The 24th Battalion was later decommissioned and evolved as part of 45th Artillery Brigade. The 2S4 vehicles were in one-tone camouflage with no visible markings. (Artwork by David Bocquelet)

A 2S3 Akatsiya (Acacia) of the 50th Guards Self-Propelled Artillery Regiment, 42nd Guards Motor Rifle Division of North Caucasian Military District, circa 2002. Artillery was a major component of Russian forces in Chechnya and the 152mm 2S3 and later 2S19 Msta-S were game-changers in many fights when infantry could not move forward. The regular artillery component of the motor rifle divisions was an artillery regiment with heavy assets like the 2S3 and BM-27, and an artillery battalion in every motor rifle regiment with a mixture of D-30, 2S1 and BM-21s. The vehicles had a very neatly applied camouflage with divisional tactical marks and numbers, and several stars on the barrel marking combat deployments. (Artwork by David Bocquelet)

A 2S23 Nona-SVK of 61st Separate Naval Infantry Brigade of Northern Fleet. The 2S23 Nona-SVK was a 120mm gun-mortar system, developed from the 2S9 Nona, and adapted to the BTR-80 hull for use by the Naval Infantry. In early January 1995 the Russian Command decided to deploy the units from the Naval Infantry to make up for the lack of troops required for the assault on Grozny. Each Naval Infantry Brigade/Division sent a joint battalion that arrived by air during the second week of January; none of the Naval Infantry formations had any vehicles with them. The convoy of vehicles followed later by ground and mostly got to Chechnya in late January–early February. The Nona-SVK of the 61st Brigade probably came from 1611th Self-Propelled Artillery Battalion assigned to the Northern Fleet, commanded by General Alexander Otrakovsky. One of the vehicles was destroyed in late January during the ambush of a Russian convoy near the village of Samashki. All vehicles were painted in three-tone camouflage, with no numbers or visible markings. (Artwork by David Bocquelet)

A Russian MT-LB of the Engineering Reconnaissance Platoon, 1052nd Commandant Company of the Shelkovskoy District of Chechnya. MT-LBs were widely used by all kinds of Russian units as transports and APCs. Though extremely mobile – having been specifically designed for use over soft ground and arctic conditions – the basic version was also very light in firepower, carrying just a single 7.62mm machine gun. Engineering Reconnaissance was tasked with checking roads for possible mining and sabotage, to ensure the safety of military and civilian transportation. On 12 July 2003 this vehicle was engaged by a large radio-controlled IED near the village of Benoi-Vedeno in Nozhay-Yurtovsky district. The district was infamous as a hotspot of Chechen resistance well after the end of the active phase of the war in 2001. (Artwork by David Bocquelet)

A T-62 tank belonging to the opposition forces commanded by Ruslan Labazanov, captured in Argun during the failed attack on 9 October 1994. Labazanov's troops, sponsored by Russia, proved to be incapable of standing against Dzhokhar Dudaev's well trained and experienced National Guard, the majority of whom were veterans of the war in Abkhazia. Labazanov blamed Russia for supplying outdated equipment like BTR-60s and T-62s. The tanks had no markings, as was common with Chechen vehicles of the pre-war period, and there was no way to tell which group they belonged to. In some areas the settlements were controlled by different groups of militants with little visible difference; these groups were in a state of "cold peace" with each other until a spark initiated conflict. (Artwork by David Bocquelet)

A T-62M of 3rd Tank Company, 1st Battalion, 160th Guards Tank Regiment (commanded by Yuri Budanov), 5th Tank Division, deployed in Argun during late 1999. In December, the regiment took part in fighting over Urus-Martan, and then in Duba-Yurt to relieve the troubled forces of the 84th Battalion in the Wolf's Gate gorge. Later the regiment took part in the assault on Komsomolskoe in March 2000. The tanks of the regiment were of mixed types – T-62M and T-62 mod 1972, in various conditions – with no markings other than tactical numbers. During the war no T-62s of the regiment were lost, though several were damaged by mines and ATGMs. Shortly after the active phase of the war, in 2001, the 160th Regiment was disbanded, leaving its aging tanks for the 42nd Guards Motor Rifle Division. (Artwork by David Bocquelet)

A T-80BV of 133rd Guards Separate Tank Battalion of the 45th Motor Rifle Division of Leningrad District, commanded by Igor Turchenyuk, deployed in Kurchaloy in the summer of 1995. The tanks of the 133rd Battalion were the first to experience the bitter fighting on 26–29 December 1994 during the fight for Khankala that also appeared to be the major tank-versus-tank battle of the war. After taking part in the Battle of Grozny, 133rd Battalion was employed in the Russian offensive against Argun and Gudermes. The tanks of the battalion were of different camouflage patterns ranging from fading to sharp. They also had numbers running in the range of 5xx, painted on the side ERA blocks, or boxes on the sides and the back of the turret, while some tanks, such as this example, were observed without numbers at all. The emblem of the battalion, the "Black Wing", was painted on the searchlight cover (shown inset). (Artwork by David Bocquelet)

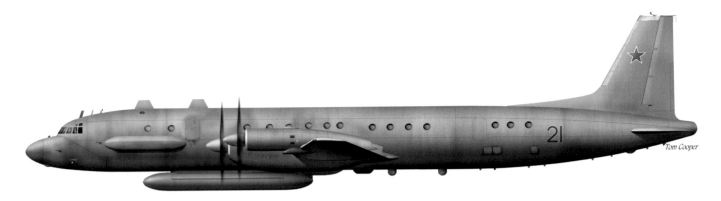

One of the most important aircraft in service with the Russian Air Force during the late phases of the Chechen War was the Ilyushin Il-20M. Based on the Soviet-era Il-18 turboprop airliner, and in operational service since the early 1970s, the Il-20Ms were deployed for a wide range of tasks. With the help of their primary sensor – a side-looking radar, installed under the forward fuselage – they could track the movement of enemy vehicles. The *Vishnya* signals intelligence (SIGINT) system (antennas under the rear fuselage); the *Kvadrat-2* electronic intelligence (ELINT) system (antennas in housings on the side of the forward fuselage); and the SRS-4 *Romb-4* ELINT system, as well as a comprehensive communications suite, enabled the aircraft to detect and track enemy communications, analyze them, and – when functioning as an airborne command post – guide friendly forces into attacks on them. All the Il-20Ms were painted the Russian equivalent to the camouflage grey (BS381C/626) overall, with national markings applied in six positions, and two-digit bort numbers in red, outlined in white, on the rear fuselage. (Artwork by Tom Cooper)

The workhorse of the Russian Air Force in Chechnya was always the Mi-8 series of helicopters, the sub-variants of which were deployed in reconnaissance, air assault, fire-support, and transport roles. The mass of helicopters belonged to the Mi-8MT variant. Many were veterans of the Afghanistan War, and saw action in Chechnya before their periodic overhauls, meaning that many still wore a badly weathered camouflage pattern with grey-green (BS381C/283 or FS34424) and green (FS24138) on upper surfaces often being bleached into different shades of light green or even sand. Undersurfaces were always painted in light admiralty grey (BS381C/697 or FS36329), and all had the Red Star on the bottom of the cabin. Bort numbers were always crudely overpainted, usually in black, and this example – former bort 55, sighted at Budyonovsk in 2001 – appears to have received the Russian national crest with a twin-headed eagle on its cabin doors. (Artwork by Tom Cooper)

A little-known task performed by Mi-8MTs was that of serving as COMINT platforms. Such examples had different aerials under the cabin and on the top of the boom, and participated in several 'man-hunts' for the leaders of the Chechen militants. This Mi-8MT – originally with bort 18, now crudely overpainted in black – seems to have undergone a periodic overhaul by the time it was sighted at Grozny-Severny Airport in summer 2000, because its camouflage pattern in grey-green (BS381C/283 or FS34424) and dark oak (BS381C/241) on upper surfaces was still relatively fresh. As usual, the undersides were painted in light admiralty grey (BS381C/697 or FS36329), but it should be kept in mind that the exact shade of this color always depended on the manufacturer and applicant, and thus often varied from aircraft to aircraft. (Artwork by Tom Cooper)

As of 2000, most Mi-24s of the Russian Air Force and the Ministry of the Interior deployed in Chechnya were grouped into the Joint Helicopter Unit, based at Grozny-Severniy Airport. The majority were veterans of the Afghanistan War in the 1980s, but were yet to undergo periodic maintenance. Thus, as in the case of the Mi-8s, most had badly weathered "sand and spinach"'camouflage patterns (usually consisting of grey-green and green on top surfaces and sides). This Mi-24P had previously worn bort 03 and a rectangular Russian flag – the latter applied on the forward part of the cabin. By late 1999, when it was sighted at Kalinovskaya, its PZU air intake filters were painted in bright orange, while the flag was covered by a cartoon of a black shark, earning it the radio callsign *Akula*. It is illustrated in standard configuration for this variant, including a B-8M pod for S-8 80mm unguided rockets under the winglet, and one or two 9K114 Shturm anti-tank guided missiles. (Artwork by Tom Cooper)

The majority of Su-25s deployed in combat during the First and Second Chechen Wars were veterans of the Afghanistan War: most had not undergone any periodic overhauls during the 1990s, and thus had a badly weathered camouflage pattern, usually consisting of green (FS24138), dark green (FS34088), sand (FS30450), brown (FS30372) or dark brown (FS30045 or FS30219) on upper surfaces and sides, and light admiralty grey on undersurfaces (BS381C/697 or FS36329). This example, Red 27, underwent an overhaul by the time it was sighted in Chechnya in 1999–2000, wearing a relatively fresh pattern consisting of camouflage grey (BS381C/626), dark green (BS381C/641) and middle stone (BS381C/362) or sand (FS30450). The aircraft is illustrated in standard configuration for the Second Chechen War, including a drop tank on the innermost hardpoint, and two B-8M pods for S-8 80mm unguided rockets. (Artwork by Tom Cooper)

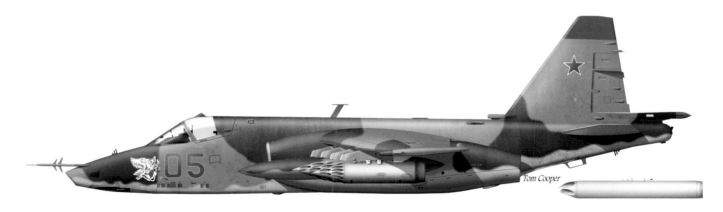

Assigned to the 461st Attack Aviation Regiment, the Su-25 Red 05 served in Uzbekistan and Tajikistan before its first deployment to Chechnya in 1994. Five years later, it was back to Chechnya and decorated with the insignia of the "Dog Squadron". It was written off on 14 June 2011, in a crash that killed its pilot, Lieutenant Colonel Yuriy Yakimenko, and his wingman, Captain Oleg Podsitkov. Red 05 was originally painted in dark green (FS34088) and grey-green (BS381C/283, or FS34424) on upper surfaces and sides, but by 2001 the former was bleached into olive drab. As on most of Soviet/Russian combat aircraft since the 1970s, undersurfaces were always painted in light admiralty grey (BS381C/697 or FS35329). Shown in the lower right corner is a B-13 pod for unguided 122mm rockets; although having entered service back in the first half of the 1980s, this weapon became available in larger numbers only during the wars in Chechnya. (Artwork by Tom Cooper)

Destroyed building, Grozny, Chechnya. (Photograph © Combat Films and Research)

Yakob, a consultant under the command of Shamil Basaev. (Photograph © Combat Films and Research)

The turret of a destroyed Russian 2S1 Gvozdika 122mm self propelled howitzer, on the road to Vedeno, Chechnya. (Photograph © Combat Films and Research)

Russian tank destroyed along the road from Serzhen-Yurt to Vedeno.
(Photograph © Combat Films and Research)

Old Chechen warriors, Vedeno, Chechnya. The man on the right carries an SVD 7.62mm marksman rifle. In the foreground is an AGS-17 Plamya 30mm automatic grenade launcher.
(Photograph © Combat Films and Research)

Rubble wall, Grozny, Chechnya. (Photograph © Combat Films and Research)

Russian tank turret, Bammut, Chechnya. (Photograph © Combat Films and Research)

Young Chechen combatants in Vedeno, Chechnya. (Photograph © Combat Films and Research)

Destroyed Russian T-72 main battle tank, Bammut. (Photograph © Combat Films and Research)

A combatant under Shamil Basaev's command with AGS-17 grenade launcher, Vedeno, Chechnya.
(Photograph © Combat Films and Research)

The turret of a destroyed 2S1 Gvozdika self-propelled howitzer in the snow near Serzhen-Yurt.
(Photograph © Combat Films and Research)

Map of the region covered in the text. (Map by George Anderson © Helion & Company)

ambush positions on the west side of the road, crossed the road under the bridge and then moved northward to their positions. Aslan and the fourth group took their positions on the east side of the road. Aslan placed their only antitank mine on the north end of the bridge. They hoped they would not need to use it. If Aslan could destroy the first vehicle as planned, it would force the column to stop and give the other groups time to engage. Their intent was to stop the Russian column before it reached the bridge.

Aslan positioned his 23 combatants closest to the bridge. His objective was to hit the lead vehicles and stop the column. Naib's (20–21 combatants) and Musadi's (23–24 combatants) ambush sites were staggered another 30–80 meters north. They were going to hit the mid section of the Russian column. Musa and his group of 19 combatants were on the west side of the road and a good 120–150 meters north of Aslan. Musa's group would be the final ambush position. In this way, the Chechens sought to hit the front, a middle section, and a section towards the rear of the column.

Aslan's group triggered the ambush from their concealed positions. Their withering fire struck the lead vehicle, a tank, and set it on fire. The column ground to a halt. Naib and Musadi then began to engage the Russian column in their sector. Finally Musa's group unleashed its own fire into another section of the Russian column. The fighters in each unit were positioned in pairs roughly three to five meters apart, depending on the terrain. There was no set position for the RPGs, but "I told the commanders to position them to engage the front and the rear of the column." Musa's RPG gunners' first target was also a tank. Just like Aslan, Musa's group blocked the road with a heavy vehicle so that the Russians trapped in the ambush could not easily push the vehicle off the road to escape.

Not every group had the same weapons or experience. In addition to two RPG gunners, Musa's group had two snipers positioned a bit further from the road with a clear field of fire on the road. Everyone else carried two Mukhas and 10 magazines for their assault rifles. "I learned in Grozny that several snipers and RPG gunners allowed me to split my group in two and still have sufficient fire power."

Musa himself was well armed, "I carried a Kalashnikov, the older 7.62mm model, not the smaller 5.45mm model. The larger round is much better than the 5.45mm because it is less likely to ricochet in urban and forest fighting. Several of our people were killed in Grozny from friendly fire – ricochets from the 5.45mm round."[3]

"Because I was a commander, I also carried a pistol and three or four magazines. I carried 12 magazines for my AK. Eight of these I carried in a four-pocket combat vest. I put two magazines in each pocket. That was my body armor. I carried an additional magazine on my back, directly covering my heart and another on my side protecting my kidney. I carried six hand grenades strapped across my stomach. So my arsenal was also my flak vest. It wasn't perfect, but good enough."

"My AK had an under-barrel grenade launcher, so I carried a bag of 10 grenades for that weapon.[4] Like all my men, except for the RPG gunners, I carried two Mukhas. I also carried some signal flares which were essential for conducting ambushes involving more than one group. My personal load was about 35 kilos."[5]

The fighting lasted all of 20–30 minutes. After the Mukhas and RPGs were gone the Chechens threw hand grenades. Finally the Chechens unleashed a torrent of automatic fire at the Russian column. According to plan, Aslan shot off a red flare, indicating that his group was down to its last magazines. This was the signal for retreat. This signal could have come from any of the commanders. Whoever was the first to run out of ammunition was to signal to break contact. Musa and his men began retreating immediately

into the forest and then swung southward to rendezvous below the bridge.

The Chechens also sustained a number of casualties and had to evacuate their dead and wounded. Musa himself lost four fighters KIA. Aslan's group lost seven, while both Naib and Musadi's groups lost three or four fighters each. Each group carried its dead and wounded with them.

Musa was not able to count the Russian dead, but he estimates 100 Russians killed. A day later he returned to the ambush site. There were 18 burnt-out Russian vehicles on the road. He had a picture of himself taken on the road with the twisted hulks behind him before melting back into the wooded mountains that had afforded him concealment the day before.

Commentary: *Ambushes are critical to the guerilla or insurgent force, especially so in Chechnya. Chechen units continued to depend on the ambush to inflict casualties, to replace weapons and radios and to obtain critical supplies, such as ammunition, fuel, medical supplies and food. In this case, however, Musa makes no mention of being able to pillage the column before retreating. They were more concerned with getting out of the ambush site before Russian helicopters and fixed-wing aircraft arrived to support the column.

At the beginning of the war the Chechen fighting units were usually small (one–two squads) and often came from the same village, organization or group of friends. However, as the war dragged on, a reshuffling of the Chechen order of battle occurred. Combatants who demonstrated a willingness and aptitude for fighting often left their volunteer units, banding together in more effective fighting groups as compared to those organized around a village, school or some other social grouping. By this time in the war Musa's men had evolved into one of these groups, built around desire and ability. As a result Musa's group was very effective, as were the other participating groups in this case, although little is known of their composition. (None of the other group commanders who took part in this ambush survived the war.)

Because of the small size of the unit it was common to combine units to undertake actions requiring a larger force. Often the command and control measures were inadequate and preparation and rehearsal time was limited. There were few standards and each unit fought to its own pattern and experience. The *ad hoc* unit would dissolve into its component parts during the retreat.

Musa's ambush is interesting because he and his group were particularly well armed. Ammunition continued to be a chronic problem for the Chechen insurgency as a whole, but some units were much better armed than others. In particular, units like Musa's, which constantly hunted Russian targets, were much better armed than volunteer units organized around a village or district holding defensive positions.

Based on experience, Musa did not believe the Russian column would get air support because helicopters were constantly being harassed and shot down over the wooded mountain roads. The ambush location was ideal for shooting down helicopters. Air strikes were possible, but Musa addressed this issue by positioning himself and the other fighters close to the kill zone (30 meters). Russian SU-25 ground attack aircraft could have provided close air support, but at great risk to the Russian column itself. Less than a week earlier, during the battle for Serzhen-Yurt, a Russian fighter plane had been shot down near the ambush location.*

Vignette 14: Ambushed in the Woods, Spring 2001

Musa

Background: By spring 2001 the surviving Chechen groups were more splintered than ever before. Command and control was a chronic problem. Musa and his group, like most others, were not able to communicate safely via radio or cell phone. As a result, the units had to travel in person to command posts to get supplies and instructions. On this occasion Musa's group was moving through the woods south of Alkhazurova in the direction of Chishki, with the intention of locating a headquarters east of Chishki.

Meanwhile, having recently secured the village of Alkhazurova, Russian units were sending patrols frequently into the wooded

mountain areas to cut off Chechen supply lines, isolate Chechen units and individual combatants and destroy them with a combination of small unit action and supporting fire.

Musa and his group had recently fought Russian units in the area and were now moving to reconstitute supplies and get further direction from command elements. Although his unit suffered casualties, there was no shortage of willing individuals to replenish the ranks. Still, Musa kept his group more or less the same size since the early days of the first war – 17 men. His primary consideration was taking care of his men. "I was responsible for arming, supplying and feeding my men. A hungry soldier isn't a soldier at all."

Musa considered his men to be well-armed and ready to fight, but past casualties meant new men in his ranks. Traversing the forest this close to the Russian-populated open plain was dangerous. Rather than walk single file, as they might do deep in the safety of

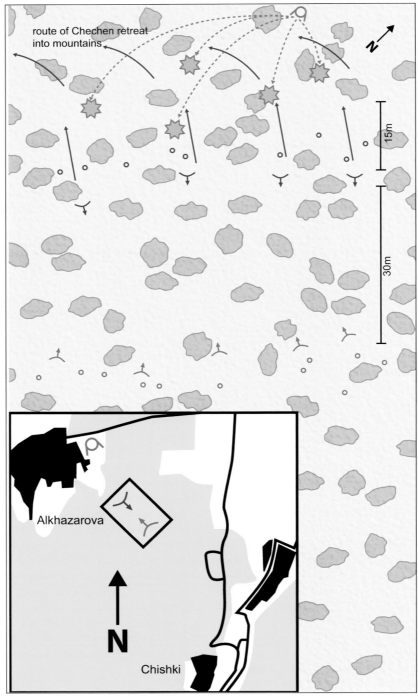

Ambushed in the woods, spring 2001.

the mountains, the Chechens fanned out across their line of march, walking three to five meters apart, depending on the terrain. It was slow going but absolutely essential. Musa knew the Russians patrolled this area just as he did, and he had to be ready to confront the enemy at any time.

Suddenly a burst of automatic fire rang out. Then another burst. Then a barrage of deafening fire. Five Chechens fell to the ground dead. Musa dove behind a large tree for cover and instinctually began to return fire. He could see the Russian muzzle blasts 30 meters in front of him. The Russians were well concealed and were using the terrain for good cover. The Russians had apparently seen the Chechens coming and took their positions and waited for the Chechens to walk into their trap. The Russian unit seemed to be about the same size as his own group, spread out more or less in an arc in front of them.

"Maybe there were a few more men, maybe 20, but no more than that."

While returning fire against the Russian positions, Musa assessed the situation. Although he had five dead, everyone else answered his call and fought. Shouting in Chechen, Musa ordered his men forward to drive the Russians out of their positions. These were his mountains. Using the terrain, Musa and the others began to inch forward. He was close enough to hear the Russians shouting orders amongst themselves. They were not leaving and instead seemed intent on destroying his group right there and then. Musa took a grenade from his vest and lobbed it at the Russians. Other Chechens threw more grenades but the Russians remained in place.

Although he could not dislodge the Russians, moving forward had its advantages. As long as they were close to the Russians, the Russians could not call in mortar or artillery fire on them. Still, they could not make any headway against the Russian fire. Musa was impressed at their resolve and his inability to force them to withdraw. Musa realized they were not making any headway. The Russians seemed well positioned. They were not dug in but were using the trees and other terrain features of the forest well. Musa had to make a decision, and make it quickly. How long could he stay engaged without further casualties, and what about ammunition? He also had dead he needed to take care of.

Seeing that the Russians were holding their ground, he gave the order to withdraw. "We yelled to each other in Chechen, 'They aren't leaving. We need to go! They are going to call in mortars!'" The Chechens grabbed the dead and began to bound back in short intervals, covering each other as they retreated. He didn't have to tell his men to move fast. Musa fired another burst from his assault rifle and then sprinted four or five meters back to a grouping of trees, turned and fired again. His men did the same, bounding tree-to-tree, dragging their dead. This was not the first time that they had been under fire and they were well versed on getting out of a kill zone. Moving straight back from the point of ambush, Musa estimated that they had another 20 meters to go before the mortars started. "Whoosh, whoosh, whoosh, mortar rounds seemed to be coming down all around us." Many rounds landed in the trees, some detonated in the branches, sending splinters and debris down on the retreating Chechens.

The Chechens continued to pull back in groups of two and three. First they went straight back, then southwest towards the safety of the mountains and away from the mortar fire. Under no circumstances were any of his men supposed to break away from the unit alone. Musa made a point of this during training. If they were hit while alone there was no one to help them. The buddy system was an unwritten commandment and the men broke from the ambush in this way. "We ran, dragging our dead."

Commentary: Eventually Musa's group cleared the ambush site and outran the mortar barrage. They were finally out of the kill zone. They also knew that the Russians they had encountered in the woods would not come after them. After all, it was the security of their positions that forced the Chechens to retreat. "No way they would give up that position, sacrifice that advantage to press the attack against us." This had been a chance meeting between two forces. The Russians detected the Chechens first and reacted effectively. But the Russian force was not strong enough to pursue a force that was withdrawing in good order. Operating in the mountains was often treacherous for Russian forces. During the two wars many Russian units that went into the mountains hunting Chechens were destroyed, some never heard from again.

Sensing safety, the group stopped retreating and began to rest. Regrouping, Musa assessed his unit's condition. Remarkably, except for the five killed in the first moments of the ambush there were no additional casualties. Musa credits the forest for saving his life during the retreat. Most of the mortars hung up in the tree tops, some not detonating; others had detonated high in the branches, which deflected the blast from the men below. Still, it was a precarious moment and Musa was glad to have escaped with most of his men.

They then dug five shallow graves for the dead and marked the location on the nearby trees. Musa and his men waited until nightfall. Two men from the group then crept into Alkhazurova under cover of night to let the villagers know about the dead and instructed them where to find the graves. They asked the townspeople to rebury the fallen in their village cemetery. The two men crept back the group's position a few hours later. Not only had they passed on the message, but they also came back with bread, given to them by the townspeople. Musa and the others took the time to enjoy the welcomed treat before putting their gear back on and moving deeper into the mountains on their way to Chishki.

On a personal level, Musa had had enough. This was his last engagement. He turned his unit over to a sector commander, took off his military equipment and made his way back to his home village. He was later taken into custody and beaten severely while interned by the Russians. His family came to his aid, buying his way out of captivity. He would make his way out of Chechnya shortly thereafter.

Vignette 15: Ambush of Russian Convoy on the M-29 Highway, August 2004[6]

Isa Xtanaev

Background: By 2004 Russian forces had control over most of the Chechen territory, but the Chechen resistance was still able to conduct operations against Russian targets throughout the republic. Months earlier Chechen combatants had killed the Russian-backed President of the Chechen Republic, Akhmad Kadyrov, with a car bomb. In June Shamil Basaev led a raid against a Russian military garrison in Ingushetia. Russian units, frustrated by Chechen actions, continued to conduct punitive cleansing operations, known as *zachistki*, against villages in retribution for their soldiers killed in surrounding areas. *Zachistki* were the Russian tactic that was most feared and hated by the Chechens. Operations of this sort had been carried out since early in the first war and had become famous in the case of the Samashki massacre in April 1995.[7]

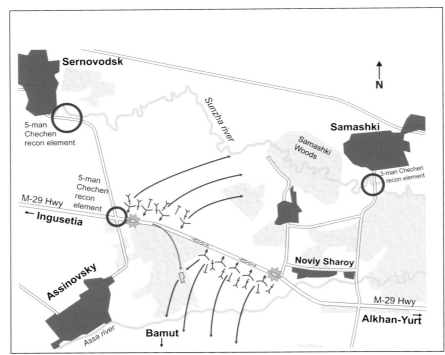

Ambush of Russian convoy on the M-29 Highway, August 2004.

Isa Manaev was still a commander with significant authority. After leaving Grozny he and his unit operated in southwest Chechnya. After conferring with deposed Chechen President Aslan Maskhadov regarding the Russian *zachistki* against the villages in his area, Isa went to work organizing a retaliation ambush. "This was truly revenge for the murder of our women and children, and for the suffering and humiliation of our people," Isa recalls. "The order was given not to take any prisoners."

According to Isa, the soldiers of the Russian column, whom the Chechens referred to as "death squads," were conducting *zachistki* in Alkhan-Kala, Zakan-Yurt, Samashki, and Sernovodsk and were heading back to their base near Grozny. It is not clear how the Chechens knew the Russian plan of action or that the Russians would take the M-29 back to their base, but Isa did know and prepared his ambush accordingly.

Isa tracked the Russian unit's zachistka but did not want to endanger the civilians from any of the villages. Rather than set up a communications link with the villagers, he placed small reconnaissance elements in multiple locations to keep him informed: near Sernovodsk; on the road junction from Sernovodsk and the M-29; and just south of Samashki.

Meanwhile, he moved his combatants into position along the M-29 between Assinovsky and Noviy Sharoy, using the apple orchards near the highway for concealment. In addition to the five-man reconnaissance element at the intersection, he ordered another 20 combatants operating in the woods around Samashki to move south and take positions north of the highway. He and his group of about 40 combatants from the mountains near Bamut moved north into positions south of the road, closer to the intersection of the road to Shamashki. All the ambush positions were staggered so they would not inflict friendly fire casualties in a crossfire.

Spread out in groups of twos and threes as the terrain dictated, the combatants readied their weapons and waited. Many were armed with RPGs and Mukhas, there were a few light machine guns [PKs], and the rest had automatic Kalashnikov assault rifles. The Chechens possessed no antitank mines. It was a formidable Chechen force for

any time of the war, and Isa was proud of being able to organize it this late in the second war. Still, it was perilous. There was constant traffic on the highway, including Russian military vehicles. Isa recalls lying in the same position for three days waiting for the column to return from its operations against the villages. "We ate dried meat and water, that's it." It was August. "At least it wasn't winter" Isa mused.

Midmorning on the third day the Russian unit moved out of its position in Sernovodsk. The column traveled south towards the M-29 Highway. Isa's reconnaissance team near Sernovodsk relayed the information to the team at the intersection, who soon saw the lead elements of the column. The Chechens north of the highway maintained their positions and let the column roll past them until the ambush was triggered. A kilometer to the east, Isa waited for the first vehicle to enter his own kill zone. As planned, Isa's group disabled the first vehicle in the column, a BTR, forcing the column to grind to a halt. More RPGs flew into the BTR. The group north of the road at the end of the column fired their own volley, striking a BMP at the end of the column. It was the signal for the rest of the Chechens to engage the middle of the column.

The Russian response was fierce and Chechen combatants were instantly killed and wounded. Amidst the chaos a Ural truck was hit, careened off the highway and drove through the Chechen position. A number of Chechens continued to fire at the truck. The driver was slumped over the steering wheel, dead. To the Chechens' surprise, the truck kept going. It was an odd sight to see it continue to roll into the orchard. The Chechens kept an eye on it. It continued moving aimlessly for a good part of the entire action before coming to a stop in the trees.

By now, the Chechens were running out of ammunition. Isa fired three bursts of tracer rounds from his machine gun to signal the retreat. As planned, the combatants at the north and rear of the column retreated northeasterly into the forest area around Samashki. Isa and the Chechens at the front of the column south of the highway retreated southward through open territory towards Bamut. They left, carrying their dead and wounded.

The retreating Chechens encircled the Ural that had strayed off the highway. Cautiously they approached. Six Russian soldiers were dead inside. The Chechens quickly pillaged the vehicle, taking hand grenades, four assault rifles, two Vintorez sniper rifles, and several thousand rounds of ammunition.[8] There was a brief discussion about confiscating the Ural truck itself, but since "we couldn't use it, we burned it and left," Isa recalls.

Having successfully retreated to the safety of the mountains around Bamut, Isa watched the Russians strafe and fire into the orchards adjacent to the highway for the next 24 hours. "They were shooting all over the place. I don't know what they were shooting at. They thought we might still be there I guess."

Commentary: Ambushes were still a vital part of the Chechen war effort. However, as the second war dragged on it became more difficult to mass numbers large enough to attack whole Russian columns like the Chechens did with greater success during the first war. Ambushes were still risky operations. Isa claims that the ambush claimed the lives of 40 to 50 Russian soldiers, which cannot be confirmed. Isa also claims only six Chechens were killed and eight wounded during the action.

The entire ambush lasted roughly 30 minutes and played out like other Chechen ambushes, driven by the need to attack and retreat quickly to avoid follow-on air strikes. By experience, Isa was acutely aware of when the window of opportunity would close and got his men out of the ambush site before Russian helicopters and tanks arrived on the scene to assist the convoy.

Isa emphasizes that they were also out of ammunition. "There was just no way to continue fighting even if we wanted to." There was some thought to running out onto the highway and stripping the disabled Russian vehicles of supplies, weapons and ammunition, but the lead BTR and BMP at the end of the column were burning

and Russian return fire from the middle of the column forced the Chechens to give up on that idea. Isa laments that his forces were not able to take more ammunition from the Russian column but was satisfied with sending a message regarding the Russian tactic of punitive cleansing actions against villages. According to Isa, President Maskhadov awarded him a pistol to commemorate the successful action.

Chapter Five Summary

When the terrain was constrictive, such as in a town or at a ridge or narrow road, the Chechens tried to take out one of the leading vehicles and the trail vehicle to bottle up the convoy. If the terrain did not favor this, they usually hit the middle of the convoy, where there were fewer armored vehicles. The Chechens constructed fighting positions wherever possible, since Russian return fire and artillery support could readily decimate an unsheltered position. Successful ambushes usually have a separate fire support group, a flank security group, an assault group and a spoils removal group. Most Chechen ambushes only had several assault groups under the nominal command of one of the group commanders. Some groups would use rehearsed exit routes, but often the ambush group would disperse into two-man groups and make their individual ways back to a link-up point.

When Chechens were ambushed, they relied on contact drills and the buddy system. Usually they would assault into the teeth of the ambush, relying on firepower, speed and daring-do to get them out of the kill zone. If this did not work they would then withdraw and disperse. In the second vignette, the Russian force was conducting aggressive patrolling when they happened upon the Chechens. They quickly assumed an ambush formation and effectively engaged the Chechens. Only the tree cover prevented a bigger Chechen loss from mortar fire.

6
DEFENSE OF LINES OF COMMUNICATIONS

The operational key terrain in Chechnya consists of the cities and major villages, the road and rail network, bridges over the major rivers, and oil fields and the oil pipeline transiting the country. None of these are in the mountains. The Russian-Chechen Wars started as maneuver combat before settling in on successive sieges of the cities and major villages. Preventing or delaying movement along the lines of communication (LOC) was a primary factor during these phases of the wars.

Chechnya is not Afghanistan and, although the Chechens successfully ambushed Russian supply columns, they were never able to block enemy LOCs for an extended period of time. The mountains are not in the right place for this to happen. Where the Chechens did manage to block the LOC for a period of time, they were aided by the deliberate, systematic advance of the Russian forces. The Russian Army was not about to hand any propaganda victories to the Chechens through precipitous action. For the Chechens, defense of LOCs was temporary – an attempt to buy time for another event to occur.

Russian combat columns advanced along roadways behind a lightly armored reconnaissance element. Reconnaissance was supposed to check out chokepoints, culverts, bridges and other

possible areas where Chechens might defend. They were also not supposed to delay the column unnecessarily. When possible, aerial reconnaissance also supported the advance. In those areas where the column was out of supporting artillery range, the Russian column brought its own artillery. Sappers and maintenance and evacuation vehicles were usually part of battalion-sized columns. After probing attacks, the Russian columns were careful to mass combat power before attacking well prepared Chechen defenses.

Vignette 16: Defending the Permykanie Junction on the road from Argun to Grozny, 15 October 1994

Sheikh M.

Background: By 1994 the Dudaev regime was opposed by various Chechen groups. Two major opposition groups, those of Beslan Gantemirov and Ruslan Labazanov, made several armed attempts to overthrow Dudayev and seize power during the summer and fall of 1994. Although the opposition failed to overthrow the regime, Dudayev was unable to eliminate the opposition. This was Chechen-on-Chechen violence, and religion and culture made it very difficult to simply wipe out or destroy another Chechen group. Many Chechens perceived Labazanov, a convicted murderer and escaped convict, as a modern day Robin Hood. They admired him for his crimes and for his resistance to the system. Labazanov openly established his headquarters in Argun, only 10 miles east of Grozny.

On 5 September 1994 Dudaev's forces attacked and drove Labazanov and his forces out of Argun. Labazanov and his followers relocated north in Tolstoy-Yurt. Ruslan Khasbulatov, another opposition leader and resident of Tolstoy-Yurt, extended sanctuary and assistance to him.[1] In order to limit Labazanov's influence and to counter an increasingly likely Russian invasion, the Argun proDudaev militia began fortifying positions and road blocks on the outskirts of the city. The intent was to block the Permykanie Junction to prevent an assault on Grozny along the Baku Highway. This junction sits on the primary road south from Petropalovsk and the M-29 Baku Highway, the primary east–west road in the region.

A native of Argun, Sheikh was one of the first volunteer members of the weeks-old Argun militia. "We formed the militia near the mosque. There was a large area there in the center of the city that everyone knew about." The order to block the Permykanie Junction came straight from Dudaev's headquarters and Sheikh was in charge of securing the objective. He requested support from an artillery unit from the nearby village of Shali, since his lightly armed combatants would be no match for enemy tanks. He placed the artillery commander in charge of the junction, and, with his guidance, he positioned some Argun militiamen and two mobile "mountain

guns," likely the M-99 76mm mountain gun or the Ch-26 57mm antitank gun,[2] forward at the bridge over the railroad.[3] It was nearly 1.5 kilometers due north of the junction, on the southwestern edge of Berkat-Yurt. The rest of his men, the command post, and one piece of heavier artillery were positioned in a ditch at the road junction. The south shoulder of the Baku Highway provided good cover.[4] In all, three guns and 20–30 militiamen covered the Petropalovsk Road from the bridge over the railroad to the Permykanie Junction.

On 15 October Gantemirov and Labazanov again attempted to overthrow the regime and seize President Dudaev's headquarters in Grozny. Gantemirov moved from the area southwest of Grozny while Labazanov's column moved south from Petropalovsk straight toward the Permykanie Junction.[5] Two UAZiks broke away from the column, and drove right past the bridge and straight to the Permykanie Junction, where they were stopped by Sheik's men.[6] Remarkably, Labazanov's wife and mother in law, ostensibly there as medical personnel, were in the first vehicle along with their driver. Sheikh recalls, "They were scared to death. The driver was shaking so bad [sic] he couldn't even talk. Apparently, they thought they had a clear path to Grozny." The other UAZik was full of Labazanov's men. They were killed by the militiamen at the junction.

The Argun militiamen deployed at the bridge were the first to spot the main element of Labazanov's armored column heading in their direction. They radioed back to the command post. Moments later they opened fire on the column at a distance of 200–300 meters from their position at the railroad overpass. The lead BTR was struck and careened to a halt, but the convoy continued forward. Facing tanks, the "mountain gunners" radioed back to the command

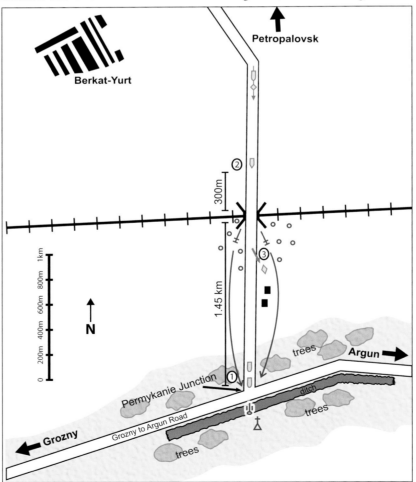

Defending the Permykanie Junction on the road from Argun to Grozny, 15 October 1994.

Labazanov pretended to be the right man for the job of overthrowing Dudaev but failed to do that. According to him, the Russians did not supply appropriate weapons, and the aging T-62 tanks and BTR-60s were outperformed by Chechen forces. This photograph shows a knocked-out T-62 from Labazanov's forces in Argun on 9 October 1994. The T-72 belonged to the Shali Tank Regiment of Chechen Republic. (Photo by TASS)

post that they had destroyed a BTR and were displacing south to the Baku Highway as planned. Sheikh ordered the militia accompanying the mountain guns to stay at the bridge, using their prepared positions and the trees and shrubs flanking the road for cover and concealment. The patrol watched as the first tank rumbled over the bridge past them, traversing its turret, searching for antitank positions on both sides of the road.

Two to three hundred meters south of the bridge, the heavier gun at the junction fired at the tank. The tank veered off the road, searching for cover among some trees and small buildings, but the fourth round found its target, destroying the tank.

Labazanov had lost one tank, one BTR and two UAZiks. His

A captured opposition T-62 tank pictured in Argun on 10 October 1994. According to both the Russian and Chechen versions, Labazanov's men simply abandoned their vehicles and ran without a fight. Who is wrong and who is right we will never know, but the fact is that the opposition attempt failed. (Efim Sandler collection)

column stopped and retreated northward looking for another way to Grozny. The Argun militia stripped the vehicles of weapons and ammunition. The medical prisoners, Labazanov's wife and mother in law, were taken back to the militia headquarters in Argun to be turned over to the DGB. They were detained for two hours, after which Sheikh was advised by an elder to release the prisoners into

his custody. This elder, whom Sheikh respected and considered a father figure, feared that the women would be raped and killed, should they be turned in to the DGB.[7] This decision caused Sheikh a lot of trouble with the DGB. "I won't hide it. They were going to take me to court over that." However, the morality of his decision won out and, in conjunction with the pending Russian invasion, the charge regarding his decision to release the prisoners was dropped. He kept the captured UAZik, full of medical supplies and weapons, for himself and the Argun militia.

Commentary: Much of the fighting among Chechen groups prior to the Russian assault has been overlooked, probably due to the miniscule scope of these inter-Chechen conflicts compared with Chechnya's war with Russia. However, as the multiple raids into Grozny by Gantemirov and Labazanov demonstrate, battles were taking place well in advance of actual contact with the Russian army. In many ways, these short skirmishes prepared Chechen combatants for war with Russia.

The defense of the junction by the Argun militia was largely possible thanks to artillery from Shali. Shali was home to an artillery and tank unit during the Soviet period. It was taken over by Chechen separatists when the Soviet Union collapsed. Although many Chechen combatants interviewed talk about the decrepit nature of the equipment at the Shali base, the defense of the Permykanie Junction proves that some pieces of field artillery were salvageable.

The Russian Army would later be criticized for being too road-bound, yet the Chechens suffered from this same tendency during this period. Further, Labazanov's reconnaissance element was too close to the main body and the first vehicle in line was a medical vehicle. The road junction was critical to his advance, yet he took no precautions to seize it early before the column arrived.

Many Chechens had served in the Soviet Army, but few of them were officers. They knew how to fire weapons but not how to coordinate movement and maneuver. These early skirmishes became on-the-job training for future commanders.

The destroyed BTR, tank, UAZik and combatants were important to the battle, but the captured UAZik, weapons and supplies were of more long-term importance. There was a chronic shortage of weapons, ammunition and vehicles. Seized enemy equipment from limited engagements like this one constantly supplemented Chechen logistics. This continued into the wars with the Russians.

Finally, although Sheikh's men were successful in defending the junction, this did not stop Labazanov's column from reaching Groxny. Rather, the column reversed course, eventually entering the capital through the Sunxa housing area in northeast Groxny. They linked up with Gantemirov's forces, but were again routed by President Dudaev's National Guard units protecting the headquarters. Dudaev's forces made a half-hearted attempt to destroy Labazanov's base in Tolstoy-Yurt two weeks later, on 27 October, but did not succeed and withdrew. Sheikh and the Argun militia continued to hold the Permykanie Junction.

Argun, seen in 2000. (Photo via Efim Sandler)

Vignette 17: Holding the Road to Shali (Part 1), late February–Early March 1995

Akhmed

Background: Many Chechens who defended and fought in Grozny against the Russian assault on the city were from the surrounding villages and towns south of the capital, Chechen-Aul, Belgatoi, Staryye Atagi and Novyye Atagi. Once the Chechens began to withdraw from the capital in early and late February many combatants returned to their home villages. Although the Chechen command had ordered all combatants to go into the mountains to regroup, many simply disregarded the order, went home and set up blocking positions and defensive positions at vital road junctions and bridges near their villages.

For the most part, these were disorganized forces. Aslan Maskhadov, Shamil Basaev, Ruslan (Khamzat) Galaev, and the other key military leaders of the Chechen resistance moved into the mountain bases and were executing plans based on what they considered the overall strategic need. In this sense, the Chechen combatants defending these villages south of Grozny were isolated. At the same time, however, the Chechen leadership recognized the need to slow down the Russian advance to give the larger Chechen resistance time to organize the defense of Argun and Shali and prepare the mountain base in Vedeno. There are indications that they were mildly supportive.

Akhmed was one of hundreds of Chechens who began digging a series of fortified trenches and positions centered on the junction of the P-305 road from Grozny and the road east to Shali. They set up a forward position facing an irrigation canal north of the road to Shali. They set up the command post and the main position south of the road and 300 meters east of a meat packing facility on the west

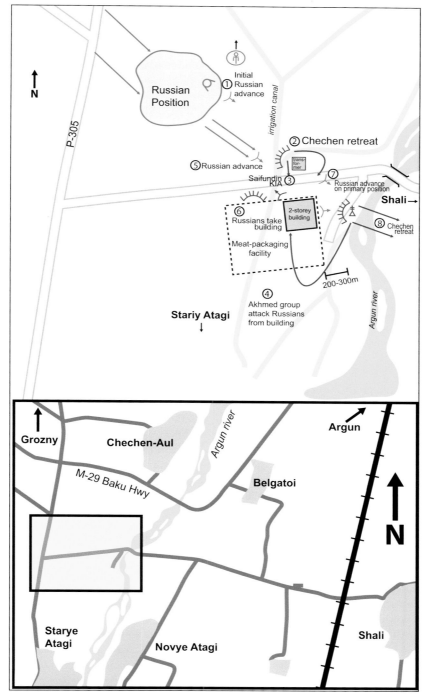

Holding the road to Shali (Part 1), late February/early March 1995

side of the Argun River. They dug additional trenches on the west side of the meat packing plant.

Akhmed estimates that there were 50–60 Chechen combatants milling about this block of defensive positions at any given time but "there was no one in charge, and when someone wanted to go home to eat or rest, they would just leave." The Chechens were also very lightly armed, considering that they were sure to face a Russian armored assault. "We had only two RPGs with only 20 rounds among all of us – that's it." The Chechens also had some light and medium machine guns. Most were armed with assault rifles, some fitted with an under-barrel grenade launcher.

Boredom and a feeling of helplessness convinced many Chechens to conduct attacks against the Russian positions being built south of Grozny. One night 15 combatants left this group of blocking positions. They were mainly from Chechen-Aul. They walked north

along the road, using a strip of woods as concealment as they snuck up on a Russian position at the intersection of the P-305 and the road to Chechen-Aul. They attacked using a couple of well placed RPG rounds and machine gun fire. There was a brief fight and then helicopters appeared and fired into the tree line. The Russian forward post retreated and so did the Chechens. "But nothing came of it. They [the Russians] returned a few days later."

Akhmed was in the forward trenches between the irrigation canal and a power transformer when the Russian armor began advancing down the P-305 towards his positions. Abruptly a portion of the Russian column swung off the road and into the fields in front of Akhmed (location 1 on map). The Chechens fired but, while the tank main guns could hit them, they were unable to engage the tanks effectively at that range. Within minutes they were forced to retreat. Akhmed jumped out of the trench and ran as fast as he

53

could towards the meat packing plant (location 2). Some of the Chechens ran around the power transformer using the structure for cover. A tank round exploded nearby just as they crossed the road. Debris covered Akhmed and the others. Akhmed's friend Saifudin dropped to the ground, killed by shrapnel (location 3). The rest of the defenders of the first trench line scrambled across the road and out of the line of fire.

There was a pause in the battle for a couple days as the Russians consolidated their position in the fields north of the meat packing plant. "They were only 600–800 meters away from us, but we could do nothing." Akhmed complained. The Chechens had previously decided to husband the two RPGs and remaining 20 rounds for a more opportune time. The Russian armor was in the middle of the field, just beyond effective RPG range, with excellent observation and fields of fire. Akhmed observed the Russians placing mines around their position. There was not much that the Chechens could do.

Over the next couple of days the Russians began shelling the Chechen positions. Akhmed hunkered down against the wall of one of the trenches they had dug. The Chechens were well dug in and suffered no casualties during the bombardments, but morale was eroding. For some, their frustration over their inability to strike effectively at the Russians, whom they could clearly see, was beginning to boil over.

During a lull in the shelling the Chechens decided to strike back. Some of the Chechens would go to the second floor of the meat packing plant and fire on the Russian position. They wanted to do something. Akhmed, with some 20 combatants, approached the building from the rear through a hole in the concrete fence that surrounded the facility (location 4). From the second floor, they could clearly see the Russian position spread out in the fields north of them. Elevating their weapon barrels to compensate for the distance, they fired a barrage of automatic and grenade fire. Observing through binoculars, Akhmed's buddy watched a Russian sentry scurry for cover. He also saw turrets rotate in their direction. "Get out now!" he yelled. Akhmed and the others ceased fire and scrambled down the stairs to the first floor.

The first tank round hit the second floor right above them. Plaster from the ceiling collapsed on top of Akhmed and a friend huddled next to him. Another round, and then another, hit the upstairs sending more debris down on them. The tank fire stopped five minutes later. Pulling himself out of the rubble, Akhmed helped a fellow combatant who was wounded by a piece of falling debris. They waited until the tank fire stopped before exiting the building.

Back at the primary trench position Akhmed and the others dusted themselves off. They were still excited and spoke quickly to each other, but as the adrenaline rush subsided Akhmed realized how tired he was. He had been in the trenches for some time now, and he was tired and dirty. He told the others that he was leaving, and then began walking home for a shower, clean clothes and hot food. He would return in a day or two. This was a typical routine by then for the Chechen combatants.

From his village Akhmed could hear the battle. The Russians were advancing on his group's position. He could see smoke and hear the chaos. Russian armor advanced south on the road and through the fields towards the meat packing plant (location 5). Artillery and tank fire pulverized the building, turning it into a heap of concrete (location 6). Chechen combatants were fighting from their trench positions 300 meters east but could not withstand the Russian attack. It was hard to determine what was going on but Akhmed could see a BTR burning between the meat packing plant and the trench position. It looked like the Chechens were fighting

from the primary trenches. Another Russian vehicle, a BTR, began to burn. There was nothing Akhmed could do but watch.

Commentary: The final Russian assault on these Chechen positions took two or three hours. Russian units seized the meat packing plant first and then the primary trench position. Although the Chechens did have some success, knocking out at least two Russian armored vehicles, they could not defend against the numerically superior Russian force. Many of the Chechen defenders did not escape, and for Akhmed the most painful part of the war was having to witness his friends and fellow village defenders killed on this day. "They were slaughtered like rabbits," recalls Akhmed.

The whole Chechen defensive plan amply illustrates a problem the Chechens repeatedly faced. In addition to the Chechen army, however loosely that is defined, there was an even more ad hoc military component buttressing the resistance. The village and friend-based units were not directly subservient to the military command and, although they were given orders, they often chose their own objectives, preferring time and time again to defend territory that, regardless of its military value, had direct personal value to them.

Akhmed's group was chronically under-armed and almost totally dependent on acquiring spoils of war. In this case the Chechens were not able to even bring their RPGs into the fight until the Russian advance was right on top of their position. There was simply no way to breach the Russian line to pillage equipment and supplies.

The battle also highlights another disconnect between these ordinary citizen combatants and the military forces of the Dudaev regime. Prior to the battle Shamil Basaev drove into the Chechen position and talked to the defenders. Akhmed claimed they begged him for weapons. Shamil said, "You'll get everything. I'll get you cannons, tanks, and everything… ." According to Akhmed, however, he did not do anything. Shamil likely had good intentions but simply could not give the Chechens defending that junction weapons that he did not have.

The Russians used their capture of the road junction up to the Argun River as the next staging area to attack south towards Staryye Atagi and east towards Shali. Still, their pace was slow and methodical, artillery and mortar followed by frontal armor attack. This continually gave the Chechens opportunity to displace further and further down the roads, giving up a little territory at a time and stalling the Russian advance on Shali, thus giving the Chechens time to get their men and materiel through Shali to the next significant line of defense – Serzhen-Yurt.

The Chechens defended with their backs to the river, and when the Russians advanced the Chechens were forced to retreat across a river under fire during daylight. This increased their casualties. The Russians were slow and methodical and so this Chechen defense held longer than it would if confronted with a determined advance. After the initial Russian defeat in Grozny, the Russian ground forces did not need any more bad publicity. They had superior strength and were content to push the Chechen resistance into the mountains and control the population centers, oil fields, pipelines, railroads and roads. This way they suffered no major defeats, but could publicly record victory after victory while privately working to fix the broken ground forces.

Vignette 18: Holding the road to Shali (Part 2), March 1995

Kair

Background: After the Chechens pulled out of Grozny, a substantial portion of them moved east to protect the city of Argun. Others moved south to establish blocking positions south of the M-29 or Baku Highway. Chechen units dug in north of Staryye Atagi and on the west banks of the Argun River. They dug additional positions on the road to Shali east of the Argun.

In addition to pushing their units east towards Argun in preparation to assault Chechnya's second largest city, the Russians also pushed units south from Grozny on the P-305 road, brushing aside a hastily-thrown-together Chechen position on the M-29 Highway intersection. Approaching the east–west road to Shali, the Russians split their force. Part of the force continued south towards Staryye Atagi, while part of the advance moved eastward, towards the west bank of the Argun River and a meat packaging facility.

When the Russians overran the Chechen positions near the meat packaging plant, surviving Chechens retreated and established secondary positions further east. One group of Chechen combatants positioned itself in a quarry north of the road to Shali on the east bank of the Argun River. Kair and his group of 12 combatants took up positions at the intersection near an insane asylum further east on the road to Shali.

Kair's mission was to block the road as long as possible and stall the movement of Russian forces towards Shali from the west. Having only 12 men and limited weaponry, he had no illusion of holding the road for long. Rather, he wanted only to slow down the Russian advance long enough to allow more Chechens to retreat from Grozny and Argun and go south through Shali and into the mountains further south. His small numbers were further limited by his modest arsenal. In addition to their personal assault rifles, his unit had one Fagot antitank missile, two RPGs, and a machine gun.

Kair's unit dug themselves in along the roadside in the fields adjacent to a tractor park to conceal their position and protect themselves from the Russian artillery bombardment that was sure to follow once the Russians began advancing eastward on the road. Russian artillery units were now established in the heights of Goyten-

Kyurt north of Belgatoi in support of Russian units advancing on Shali, Argun, Staryye Atagi and Novyye Atagi.

Kair and his men had been in their position for three days when the Russians consolidated their forces as well on the west bank of the Argun River and began to advance across the bridge. They did not move much farther east, however, and halted the column adjacent to the quarry where another Chechen unit was hiding. Observing the advancing column, Kair could not see any signs that the Chechens in the quarry were going to engage the Russian column. Rather, they seemed content to stay concealed and wait until the Russian column passed.

Surveying the road ahead and likely aware of various Chechen positions strung out ahead of them, the Russian column sent a tank forward to recon the road further at a spot on the road where an irrigation ditch ran perpendicular to the highway. The tank was now much closer to Kair's unit, maybe only 900 meters, "but still too far for a good shot." Kair also did not want to give up his dug-in position by using it to attack the tank – he would have to find a better position.

As Kair thought through the options, the tank lumbered forward and then stopped. For two or three minutes it sat there. No doubt a crewmember inside peered out at the horizon ahead of him using the vehicle periscope blocks or a Stickman Camera. The turret moved left to right scanning the horizon surrounding the roadway. The minutes passed and then the tank turned around and drove back to the column's holding position adjacent to the quarry.

Kair was not sure what the holdup was, but he thought the tank might come back again as armored reconnaissance before the main column began to move. There was a lot of discussion among his men. They all wanted to do something and attacking the tank seemed like a good idea if they could get within range and not risk exposing their position. Further, it was better to attack the lone tank before the column advanced rather than face the whole column. What good could his small number of combatants and their few weapons do against the larger Russian column? Kair's unit would be swept aside easily.

It was agreed. The Chechens would attack the tank the next day. Kair calculated that, although the Fagot's range was 800–900 meters, he would need to be much closer than that to be effective and justify the risk of initiating the attack. Getting within a few hundred meters

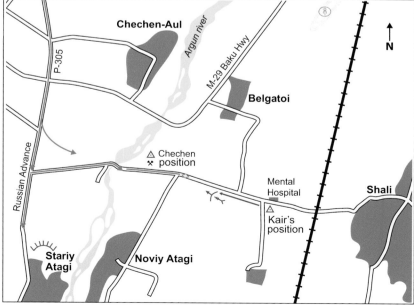

Holding the road to Shali (Part 2), March 1995.

would, however, put him in extreme danger from the tank's main gun and even its machine-gun. There was good concealment along the roadside and Kair moved west toward the intersection that night to get into position to strike the tank if it came out again tomorrow.

He and one other combatant crept out of their position under cover of darkness. Using the foliage beside the road as concealment, Kair and his assistant gunner inched their way westward. A few hundred meters away from the tank's previous position, the pair stopped and set up their gun. Kair lay in the brush next to his antitank weapon.[8] It was not as cold as it was a month ago, but the air was still brisk. Eventually he fell asleep.

The next day, as the Chechens had expected, the tank lumbered slowly up the road towards his position. As Kair had hoped, it stopped in roughly the same place as the day before and began scanning the horizon. Patiently Kair waited, but readied his gun. It looked as though the tank was looking right at him and the Fagot concealed in the brush. Kair held his breath. Attacking the tank head-on would be suicide. He needed to hit it when it was vulnerable to him, not the other way around. Eventually the tank began to turn around, preparing to head back to the column. This was the moment Kair was waiting for and as the tank spun around Kair pulled the trigger.

Kair struck the tank directly underneath the turret with a PTURS (antitank guided rocket round). It was a direct hit and the tank began to burn. The surviving tank crewmembers jumped out of the burning vehicle and ran back towards the protection of their column. This was not the first time Kair had attacked Russian tanks. He had fought them in the battles for Petropavlovsk in December and in Grozny in January. "This one was easy."

Kair had no intention of going after or trying to kill the retreating Russians and only gave them a cursory glance before retreating. He quickly folded up the Fagot and began to retreat back to the safety of his unit's dug-in position near the insane asylum.

"As I ran back the artillery started coming in all around the burning tank behind me." Kair thought of the Russian artillery positions in Goyten-Kyurt. The bombardment was not precise, but covered the region immediately surrounding the burning tank.

Kair and his assistant gunner were back in the relative safety of their positions when the artillery bombardment ceased and two helicopters arrived on the scene. They watched the gunships fly nose down back and forth past the tank, looking for targets. Kair felt his unit could have shot down the helicopters, but again he did not want to reveal his position, as it would surely bring another barrage of artillery down on them. His job was to observe and stall the Russian advance to Shali along this road. Taking out the helicopter would surely bring instant retribution from the Russians.

Commentary: Kair and his unit hunkered down in their position for the next two days as Russian artillery fired haphazardly up and down the road. At one point he noticed that the quarry was now being struck by Russian artillery. "They must have also attacked the Russian column," he thought. He did not know which Chechens were at the quarry, but it looked like they were being hit hard.

A close-up of an Mi-24 overflying positions of 245th Motor Rifle Regiment attacking towards Sernovodskoe in March 1996. Sernovodskoe was one of the lighter-held strongholds and was vacated by the Chechens after artillery and air strikes. The regiment then turned towards Goyskoe, which proved to be a hard nut to crack. (Efim Sandler collection)

The workhorse of Russian aviation in Chechnya – the Mi-8. (Photo via Efim Sandler)

"Perhaps they had attacked the column and had their own retreat planned." If not, "they were surely taking a beating" Kair mused.

At the end of the second day, during a lull in the artillery barrage along the road, a supply vehicle from Shali came to Kair's position. They were anxious for the resupply, including fresh food. The supply vehicle also brought a message to retreat back to Shali. There was nothing the small unit could do now to delay the Russians once they began a concentrated effort to move further east.

The Russians were well aware that the Chechens were going to hold them up wherever they could. Although the Chechens could not strike a heavy blow against the larger armored Russian column, they were able to destroy a vehicle here and there, inflicting a small, steady stream of casualties. This seemed to slow down the Russian advance along all the front, south towards Staryye Atagi, east toward Argun, and east toward Shali.

The Russian use of single tanks to scout ahead reflects the state of Russian infantry leadership early in the first war. There was no use of dismounted infantry patrols to protect the tank, check out the quarry and position their own ambushes in the vicinity where Kair set up his antitank ambush. Tanks have limited visibility and are vulnerable to infantry close attack. Russian infantry was clearly not up to the job at this point in the war.

Vignette 19: Fighting a delaying action while covering a withdrawal from Kurchaloy, late March–Early April 1995

Sheikh M.

Background: As the Russians captured the city of Argun on 22 March 1995, the defending Chechen force retreated south and east. Many smaller units, organized along family and village lines, retreated to the safety of their respective villages if these were still outside the Russian area of control. A large number of Chechen combatants, including hundreds of wounded, retreated to the regional hospital in Kurchaloy. The Chechens set up a headquarters in the hospital and began plans to move sufficiently recovered wounded to the safety of the mountains further south. The regional hospital in Kurchaloy was critical to the Chechen armed struggle following the fall of Argun, and it was necessary to block the Russian advance as long as possible to give the wounded a chance to be treated and recover before they were moved to the more austere mountain recovery areas. By late March the Russians had consolidated their gains in Argun and were advancing from the west, as well as from Gudermes in the north. The Chechen advantage was that the only way the Russian forces could get to the north to Kurchaloy was on a single road through Belorechie. The Chechens had to defend the road long enough to

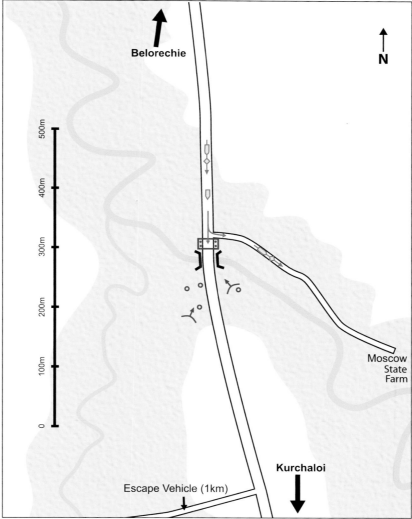

Fighting a delaying action while covering a withdrawal from Kurchaloy, late March–early April 1995.

evacuate the wounded from the regional hospital and thus preserve their force.

In preparation for the pending Russian assault, Sheikh and other commanders prepared defensive positions on the northern outskirts of Kurchaloy. The Chechens tried their best to mask their activity. They did not work openly during the daylight, but at night they walked from the city to these positions to build trenches and other fortifications for a positional battle that they hoped would not be necessary. The Chechen command knew that the Russians would still become aware of these positions, so the defenses were constructed far enough beyond the city limits to limit Russian artillery fire on the town and also on the hospital headquarters and wounded.

Sheikh also scouted the road north towards Belorechie, spending most of his time on a dirt road running parallel to the main artery but hidden by trees and brush. He was searching for a good place to slow down the inevitable Russian advance. Together with 18 combatants, Sheikh set up an ambush site at a small river crossing about four kilometers north of Kurchaloy. Tactically it was a great location, with ample coverage of the roadside. The road also narrowed at the bridge so that it was only wide enough for a single armored vehicle. If Sheikh could destroy a few armored vehicles at the bridge, it would force the Russian column to secure the area and then remove the destroyed vehicles before proceeding to Kurchaloy.

In a stroke of good luck, the position was next to a state farm [sovkhoz]. The caretaker brought them "meat, milk and sour cream" as they patiently waited for the Russians to advance. Another Chechen unit manned their previous positions outside of Kurchaloy.

Sheik did not have any heavy or medium weapons for his ambush. He had no RPGs, just assault rifles, some fitted with under-barrel grenade launchers.[9] He did have a few directional mines, and under cover of darkness his men mined both sides of the road north of the bridge, burying the mines and the wires in the gravel besides the asphalt.[10] Sheikh split his force and positioned them on both sides of the road in various concealed positions on the south side of the bridge. He also positioned a GAZ-66 truck about one kilometer down the road towards Kurchaloy.[11] It was parked under concealing foliage near a spring that he had spotted on the initial recon of the road. One of his men stayed with the truck.

Sheikh and his group were at the ambush site for about a week when they were awakened in the early morning by a Russian artillery barrage up and down the road to Kurchaloy. All they could do was hunker down in their trenches and wait it out. Eventually the artillery stopped firing and helicopter gunships began their aerial reconnaissance of the route. Sheik knew this was all in preparation for the ground assault on Kurchaloy and he prepared his men.

Sheikh could hear the Russian armor clanking its way down the road towards them, but the heavy vegetation that afforded such great concealment for his force also restricted his view of the road to only 30–40 meters beyond the location of the mines. This limited line of sight concerned the Russians as well. It sounded to him like the column was turning from the main to the left towards a state farm. "Perhaps the Russians were trying to encircle the village of Kurchaloy" Sheikh mused. Eventually he could see a string of vehicles moving away from his position on the far bank of the river, confirming his assessment.

However, the Russians had not sent the entire column towards the state farm. Rather, the column had broken in two. There was still a significant amount of armor heading in Sheikh's direction. The Russians first sent a lone BTR towards the bridge. Many of the Russian infantry were riding on top of the BTR so that they could see better and, in the event of encountering an antitank mine, might be thrown clear of the blast. Sheikh was frustrated. He had hoped to catch two or three armored vehicles in his hasty mine field.

As lightly armed as his unit was, he could not let the BTR cross the bridge and drive through their position. Sheikh's sapper detonated the mines, hitting the BTR squarely on the sides, and it came to an immediate stop. Russian soldiers spilled out from top hatches over the sides and onto the roadway. "I remember how the soldiers were sitting on the armor. When they were hit by the mines, they all began firing." The remaining column began to return fire, but "when they started, they fired everywhere. They didn't know where we were." The Chechens fired from their positions south of the bridge as well, but they also did not have a clear line of sight far beyond the disabled BTR.

"We fired for 30 to 40 minutes but we didn't have enough ammunition. No one was hurt on our side, Insha' Allah. I looked out beyond the bushes and down the road. I saw the Russian soldiers on the ground firing their weapons. No one was approaching. The [mine detonation] wire was valuable. I had to reel it in quickly and leave with it."

Sheikh radioed back to Kurchaloy that they were withdrawing from the position, but it was not a covered, deliberate withdrawal. He and his men were actually running beside the road through the foliage toward the waiting GAZ-66. This was the scariest part of the action. "We ran like hell. We probably had to run two kilometers." Fearing Russian helicopters, the truck full of combatants traveled parallel to the main road under cover of trees and bushes until it approached the outskirts of the town. Russian armor by this time had moved behind the disabled BTR to get a better line of sight and was firing down the length of the road.

Arriving in Kurchaloy, Sheik learned that all the wounded had been successfully evacuated from the regional hospital towards the mountains. Sheikh and his group drove south through Kurchaloy to catch up to the retreating force.

Commentary: The entire event lasted around five hours. None of Sheikh's force was killed or wounded in the delaying action, and it is unclear how many Russian soldiers were killed and wounded. "We blew it up and began firing. How many died and what else happened, we don't know." The engagement was a tactical success. The delaying action stalled the Russian advance long enough to move the headquarters and evacuate the last of their wounded from the regional hospital and redeploy into the mountains. "We counted on destroying the first armored vehicle and the rest wouldn't be able to get through. And that is how it happened for us." Selecting the ambush site at the bridge crossing gave Sheikh a tactical advantage, since the road narrowed and a single armored vehicle could block the roadway, as the destroyed BTR proved. However, the site selection was not lost on the Russians and they minimized their losses by not committing the whole column, but rather only a single BTR. Delaying actions were a staple of Chechen tactics as the much larger and better armed Russian force carried the day in nearly every engagement. "Getting away" rather than destroying the enemy was victory enough. Finally, Sheikh remained very fearful of the helicopter threat and countered this using concealment when constructing the defensive positions north of Kurchaloy, choosing the ambush site and parking the GAZ-66 getaway truck.

Although the Russians bombarded and then overflew the route of advance prior to sending the column, they did not follow up with additional artillery once the column had been ambushed. The area around the bridge site would make an ideal target box and should have been plotted before the column set out, but it appears that the Russian force preferred to use the bridge rather than destroy it with their artillery. The river was not wide and Sheikh believes the Russians probably should have skipped the bridge and forded the river elsewhere. The Russian command may have felt that, having scouted the route, the column would be more than capable of clearing the action of any small unit that might not have been destroyed or detected prior to the column's advance. For whatever reason, the bridge site, while scouted by the lone BTR, was not targeted in advance or once contact occurred.

Chapter Six Summary

A combatant's best friend is frequently his shovel. Tales of daring-do and valor focus on the moment of impact, the minute that the weapons begin firing. Success in defensive combat, however, depends on time and the shovel. A good commander is able to read the terrain, understand the enemy and understand the strengths and weaknesses of his own men. The digging should start only after evaluating the terrain and determining where the enemy will come from, what he will do and how he will deploy. Properly sited and

camouflaged positions give the defender significant advantages over the attacker and can put steel in the backbone of tired or novice combatants. Too much digging produces exhausted combatants.

Rehearsed, marked routes of escape and on-hand transport are also a good idea. In the first vignette, artillery was positioned in direct-lay at the forward defensive positions. As the wars progressed, artillery was too valuable and cumbersome to be risked at forward positions. Mines were available in the first and fourth vignettes, but otherwise were not always on hand. Mines are also difficult to recover when a position is being overrun.

Commanders in the defense have to deal with boredom, fear of the unknown and exaggeration of the enemy's capabilities and strength. There is a tendency to keep the men digging so that they will be too tired to entertain these thoughts. Strong defenses are great, but afterwards rehearsals, training, aggressive patrolling and forward ambushes can do much to offset "bunker mentality" while improving the defense. Rotation of units, when possible, can also pay dividends.

7
DEFENSE OF A RIVER LINE

Defending a river line is a complex problem. The best place to cross a river is at a bend in the river that turns away from the attacker and surrounds the defender on three sides. This puts the high bank and the deep channel of the river against the attacker's shore, where he can more easily deal with the attacker and can then anchor the far end of his bridge in the shallower water with a more-gradual approach in slower current. These bend areas often open onto flatland, which further complicates the defender's efforts. Use of sand bars in the river also helps an attacker anchor a bridging effort, as long as the current is driving the bridging away from the sandbars.

The first step in defending a river line is determining where the enemy is most likely to cross. The defender's next dilemma is whether to defend forward along the river line or picket it and build the main defenses further back where he can better engage the enemy. The temptation is always to hug the river bank, since it is an obvious obstacle. However, the obstacle quality of a river varies from river to river, as well as with the season of the year and the weather. In summer, raging mountain-fed rivers can dry up and prove no obstacle at all.

Defending a river line requires many people, much equipment and an overarching command. The Chechens fielded excellent platoon-sized bands of combatants, but tying the entire effort together in a workable plan was often difficult. Audacity is one thing, effective war fighting at brigade and higher level is another.

Vignette 20: The Failed Defense of Argun 21–22, March 1995

Sheikh M.

Background: After their organized withdrawal from Grozny the Chechen forces deployed to surrounding towns and villages, taking control of remaining vital transportation links not under Russian control. A significant number of Chechens redeployed into the city

of Argun, some 10 miles east of the capital, and along the critical east–west M-29 Baku Highway. The Russians had attempted to take Argun on the way to Grozny in late December 1994, but then bypassed the city due to significant Chechen resistance.[1] Now, with Grozny under their control, Argun became the next major Russian objective. Argun is on the east bank of the Argun River, affording the Chechens a natural defensive barrier against Russian forces coming from the west. The Russians had cleared the way to the western bank of the river, consolidating their positions at Berkat-Yurt and Komsomolskoye to the north and south of the Baku Highway. The Russians had learned valuable lessons in the fight for Grozny, specifically not to send in troops without significant preparation. Russian artillery, as well as Grad and Uragan rockets, pounded Chechnya's second largest city for weeks, so much so that a common joke amongst the Chechen defenders was, "the weather here in Argun is good, either rain or Grad!"[2]

Shamil Basaev was in overall command of the defense of Argun, but, as was customary for the Chechens, the city was defended by multiple units that, while pursuing the greater defense of the city, fought independently, with varying degrees of coordination with adjacent units. Some units were assigned sectors to defend, but how they prepared, defended and fought in those sectors was left to them. While Sheikh and the Argun militia maintained their headquarters in the police building on Lenin Street across from School Number 1, Shamil never established a permanent headquarters, rather remaining mobile, moving unit to unit to issue commands.

Having intimate knowledge of the city, Sheikh and the Argun battalion were central to the defense planning. The Argun militia only numbered around 100 combatants, but other units flooded into the city. The Naursky Battalion had only 50 to 70 combatants, while units from Mesker-Yurt, Tsatsan Yurt and Shali arrived with roughly 20 members each. Sheikh estimates that the Chechens had 200–300 combatants committed to defending the city. However, the number of Chechen combatants was fluid, as they were constantly

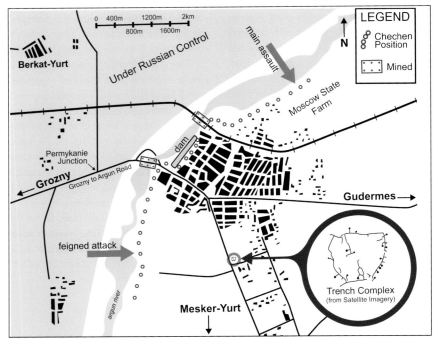

The failed defense of Argun, 21–22 March 1995.

coming and going. It is likely that the numbers actually swelled once the Russian assault began, as Chechen volunteers poured into the defenses as they had in Grozny once the battle was joined.

In preparation for the expected Russian assault, the Chechens blew up one of the two Baku Highway bridges over the Argun River and mined the other bridge, as well as the only railroad bridge over the river north of the highway bridges. The Chechens expected the Russian main assault to occur from the dairy farm southwest of the city and north of Komsomolskoye. They put considerable effort into preparations to defend the southwestern portion of the ring around the city. They established defensive positions, primarily trenchworks, on the river's edge in an arc around the south, west and north of the river, paying particular attention to the levee, and adjacent to a dairy farm southwest of the city. They also deployed mobile patrols with fixed fighting positions along another dairy farm northeast of the city, where their numbers were few. They dug trenches where possible, but Chechen fighters were few and strung out to about 10 men every 50 meters, so the position lacked density.

On 21 March 1995, in a last-ditch effort for a peaceful resolution the Russians raised a white flag over their positions and met the Chechens on the surviving bridge over the Argun River. They attempted to persuade the Chechen combatants to surrender the city and the road between Grozny and Argun, a vital line of communication. The Chechens, in turn, demanded that the Russians surrender their weapons and promised safe passage back to Russian territory. The Russians fumed and both sides returned without an agreement. Russian shelling was more intense following the failed surrender negotiations.

The same evening Russian units started moving into assault positions. While the Chechens could hear movement across the river up and down the front, they were unable to assess the situation and determine where the Russians were massing their forces and where they would attempt to breach their defenses. Russian artillery and multiple rocket launcher (MRLS) units had been shelling the city for weeks, forcing the Chechens to keep their heads down and effectively denying the Chechens the ability to observe much of the Russian activity on the other side of the river. What little intelligence

the Chechens were getting suggested that the Russians would attack from the southwest.

As the Chechens expected, the Russian bombardment on the southwestern approach to the city was heavy and the men hunkered down while the outgunned Chechen artillery answered the Russians. Sheikh's brother, deployed on the northeast approach to the city, was leading a mobile patrol that first detected the initial assault. It was 0500 and, to their surprise, the Russians had already nearly completed putting a pontoon bridge across the river. It was a complete intelligence failure for the Chechens. The Russian assault was not on the southern approaches, but rather clear around on the northeast side of the city, toward the other dairy farm. It was the weakest part of the Chechen perimeter, with few fixed positions and few mobile patrols.

Hearing his brother's unit on the radio, Sheikh set out immediately with a reserve of 24 combatants to help defend the northeast corridor against the river crossing. By the time he arrived, Russian troops had already crossed the river and were engaging his brother's unit. The fight for the dairy farm was fierce and lasted all day. "During this battle, this farm, the dairy farm, changed owners three or four times. It was in their possession, then we took it back and fought them off." They fought building to building, walking over Russian dead as they advanced. They carried off their own dead and wounded as they retreated.

At the end of the day, Russian firepower and ability to mass forces proved too much for the limited Chechen defense at the dairy farm. Sheikh lost his brother during this battle. "The first to die in the battle were from that patrol. My brother and four people from the Naursky Battalion died in that trench."

While the fighting was heaviest to the northeast, the Russians probed other points along the perimeter. Early in the evening the order went out by radio to withdraw from the city. The Chechens gave up their defensive positions on the bridge and to the south and west of the city, leaving Argun open to the Russian advance.

Commentary: The battle for Argun lasted all day before the Chechens withdrew their forces. As in previous battles, most of the Chechen volunteers went home, including the smaller units from the surrounding villages like Mesker-Yurt. Sheikh puts Chechen losses at roughly 100 killed and many more wounded, but the fluid nature of the Chechen volunteer ranks prevents accurate assessment of casualties. Sheikh's brother and four additional men from his patrol were among the first killed during the battle for Argun as they tried to prevent the Russian advance across the pontoon bridge. Sheikh was not able to retrieve his brother's body.

Russian artillery preparation in advance of the assault was significant, but the Chechens learned how to dig and prepare their fortifications to withstand the bombardment and save lives. It wasn't until the actual assault that the Chechens were forced to give up ground once again. At times Chechen intelligence was good and helped the Chechens score tactical victories, but, as in the case of Grozny, defending a city against the full brunt of Russian military might, an estimated 50,000 soldiers at the time, was too much for the Chechen defensive positions to bear. The Russians also did a very good job of pinning down the Chechens with constant bombardment in the weeks previous to the assault on the city, not allowing them to observe the Russian preparations on the other side of the Argun River.

The only chance that the Chechens had to punish the Russians was to conduct an urban fight within Argun, yet the Chechens put all of their efforts into building a long, under-strength perimeter along the river banks and mostly outside of the city. Perhaps the relatively small size of Argun convinced the Chechen leadership that block-by-block urban fighting would not be as effective as it was initially in Grozny. Or the costs associated with holding Grozny may have convinced the Chechen leadership that they could not afford the high attrition rates that would be inevitable in another urban fight.

The lessons of the Chechen initial success at Grozny were apparently lost on Shamil Basaev, and, consequently, the Russians were able to conduct a battle of maneuver on relatively open ground. This was the Russians' strong suit. The Chechen plan was to hold the river line, but they had developed no alternate plans and positions for a Grozny-like urban fight, where they could negate Russian mass and technology.

Vignette 21: Defending Against a River Crossing, September 1999

Sheikh M.

Background: By September 1999 Russian forces had moved their armored columns into the Cherlyonovsk area for a pending assault into Chechen territory across the Terek River to seize the city of Tolstoy-Yurt. Chechen sappers responded by destroying a section of the bridge over the Terek on the road linking Cherlyonovsk to Tolstoy-Yurt. With the bridge not passable, Sheikh and his twenty-odd fighters, part of roughly 100 Chechen fighters from four or five different units deployed between the road to Tolstoy-Yurt and Cherlyonovsk. They were ordered to hold a section of the south bank of the Terek River.[3] Surveying the location between the disabled bridge to the west, and the village of Vinogradnoe to the right,

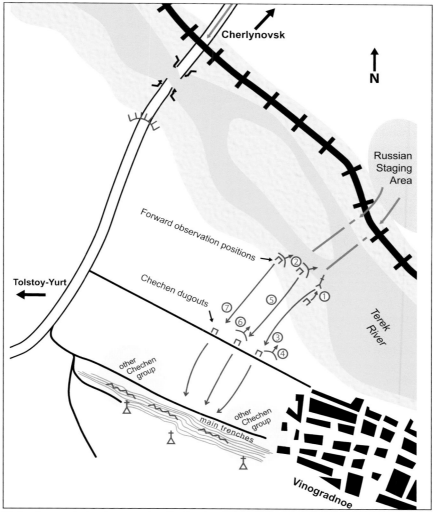

Defending against a river crossing, September 1999.

Sheikh recalls, "We were ordered to defend against any attempt by the Russians to cross the river in this area. We knew they would try to cross here because the river west of the bridge was too fast and deep." Ichkerian intelligence believed that the Russians would attempt a forced river-crossing across the Terek River by pontoon bridge, as they had done to start the first war in 1994. There was a large sandbar in the river, which would provide anchorage and allow the Russians to push a pontoon bridge across the river quickly. The Terek is an easterly flowing river, so Sheikh decided to defend against a crossing at the eastern end of the sandbar. This was the logical site, since the Russians could readily float their pontoons into position by launching them to the west. The crossing site would allow the Russians to avoid getting tangled in the village of Vinogradnoe, yet still have access to the local road network.

Working with his subordinate commanders, all of whom were veterans of the first war, Sheikh laid out a network of observation positions (OPs) and trenches. The forward positions were nothing more than firing pits for two men, dug into the brush and reeds roughly 30 meters from the southern bank of the Terek. They were not more than 100 meters apart and close enough to be able to signal each other by sight if necessary. Sheikh's men dug these positions in one night in response to the Russian build-up across the river. Two Chechens occupied each position, one armed with an RPG, the other with a standard assault rifle. They stockpiled many RPG rounds in these positions. The teams stayed hidden during the day to conceal their positions, and had orders that under no circumstances were they to fire from their position and give away their location until the Russians actually began to cross the Terek River. "These six men were supposed to harass the Russians. Harass them and then leave, so that the return fire would be directed at their positions." The Chechens in the first positions did not need or seek orders to probe the enemy, and often one man or two-man teams snuck out of their positions under cover of darkness, crossing the shallow river to raid and gain intelligence about the Russian positions across the river.

Sheikh's men clandestinely dug another set of positions another hundred or so meters further south, in the fields of the Moscow State Farm. This set of positions was not occupied, but instead was referred to as the "second line" or "retreat positions." These second positions were constructed to save the lives of the fighters retreating across open territory towards the primary Chechen fortifications further south. "The tactics of the first war taught us that if the guys in the OPs begin to shoot, they'll attract fire to themselves. When one of the OPs comes under fire, the other OPs will open fire, shifting the Russian fire onto themselves while the first OP retreats to the second line of defense. When those guys reach the second line they start firing on the Russian positions, and when the Russian fire shifts to them the guys in the other OPs can now retreat to the second line of defense. In this way all the guys in the forward OPs can cover each other."

Finally, they built a third and final line of defense. This was the main base for Sheikh's fighters guarding this stretch of the Terek River frontier. It was a set of trenches and bunkers dug into a hillside on the only commanding elevation over the Moscow State Farm and the Terek River.[4] The Chechens had learned the hard way during the first war that, while bigger trenches were more comfortable, they were not safe. These fortifications were small, with dugouts cut into the side of the main trench line in which one or two men could shelter from artillery and air strikes. They constructed three larger subterranean bunkers at the end of the trench line to use as a tactical operations center, field kitchen and medical facility. The total distance to the Terek River from the hillside base was less than two kilometers.

The situation during the first week and a half was static while Sheikh's unit maintained its positions. Periodically Chechen teams crossed the river at night to gather intelligence and raid, if possible, while Russian artillery and Grad multiple rocket launcher batteries would fire on anything that moved on the roads.[5] The Chechens operating in the OPs had radios, but were under strict orders not to turn them on and contact headquarters until the Russian pontoons were halfway across the river. It was 0500 when one of the OPs turned on its radio and sent the message that they all knew was inevitable: "The pontoon bridge is halfway across the water."

Signing off, the two-man team crept out of its OP and towards the river's edge. Hiding in the reeds, up to their waists in the chilly autumn water, they waited for the bridge-laying operation to get within effective RPG range. It was conventional wisdom among the Chechen fighters that, although an RPG had a maximum range of over 500 meters, anything over 300 meters was a gamble and not an efficient use of precious ammunition. "We had to wait, to be patient. The rounds were like gold to us." The gunner waited until enough pontoons were laid to bring the bridging unit within effective range. A first RPG round hit the pontoons but did nothing to stop the Russian engineers from continuing to construct the bridge. The assistant gunner quickly loaded another round. The second hit the vehicle laying the pontoons; it caught fire and rolled on its side.[6]

Return Russian fire was immediate, and the RPG team used the cover of the reeds and bushes to make its way south towards its OP. The OP nearest the team in retreat opened fire to draw Russian fire, and, the OPs evacuated their positions near the river, giving each other covering fire during the withdrawal. The Russian artillery barrage was heavy and Sheikh and his men had no choice but to hunker down in the relative safety of their field fortifications. They continued to take a beating from Russian artillery, Grad rockets, and helicopter fire for another week and a half before they were withdrawn from the line, replaced by another Chechen unit. Sheikh himself was instructed to return to Argun, and again, as in 1995, he was ordered to prepare for the defense of the city.

The Russians did not try again to launch a pontoon river crossing in that location. The pontoons that had been laid before the RPG strike remained in the water until well after Sheikh and his group left the area, albeit they were now stretched a little to the right as the current swept them away. Rather, the Russians redirected their efforts, fighting another Chechen unit for control of the disabled bridge on the main road to Tolstoy-Yurt. Eventually they gained control of the bridge, repaired it, and drove their armor across the Terek River, entering Chechen territory, on their way to Tolstoy-Yurt.

Commentary: Although the Chechen positions and fortifications were well devised, constructed on knowledge gained during the first war, Chechen tactical objectives remained limited and betrayed inherent weaknesses in the overall Chechen military capability. Although weapons were laid up before the war started, there was an acute shortage of ammunition and the realization that attacks had to be limited. Slowing down the Russian advance was the objective, not stopping it. In this case, however, the Russians gave up on the pontoon river crossing, opting to take and repair the bridge further east. Further, overwhelming numerical advantage belonged to the Russians. Sheikh and his 20 men, nor the combined Chechen force of 100, would ever be a match for the thousands of Russian troops, armor and artillery Russia would eventually throw at the Chechen positions. Finally, while the Chechen small units were effective at striking Russian positions, the overall strategy was one of retreat rather than advance. "We knew we wouldn't be able to stand our ground against the tanks, but we could, nonetheless, not allow them to cross into Ichkerian territory unhindered."

The Russian force, on the other hand, was very timid or unconcerned. There is no indication of probing Russian patrols across the Terek. After selecting a river crossing site, the commander needs to move reconnaissance across the river and follow this with an assault force to seize and expand a bridgehead before the bridging is attempted. Even if the commander expects an unopposed crossing, he should position forces on the opposite shore as or before he starts bridging. The Russians needed to control the adjacent village before they crossed, since it could have been a danger to their flank. The Russian commander was fairly passive and, once he met resistance, did not push across, but chose to rely on long-term artillery fire, which had little effect on the dug-in positions. The Russians were held in place by a Chechen force of roughly 100 men holding the terrain between the road and the village, specifically Sheikh's group of 20 at the point of contact, something that patrolling and reconnaissance should have disclosed. Despite all the time available since the first war, the Russian tactical intelligence effort was lagging.

The Chechens could have done more. Incorporating the village into the defense would have complicated a determined river crossing, but, in deference to the villagers, the Chechen units stayed out of the village. The demolition of the highway bridge evidently did not include the footings, since the Russians were able to put it back into service fairly quickly.

Chapter Seven Summary

The Chechen defense of a river line was usually conducted forward along the immediate water's edge, with fallback positions prepared to the rear. Sometimes consideration for the safety and property of the civilian population prevented the Chechens from conducting an effective defense once the Russians had crossed the river. Regardless, once the Russians crossed the river at one point, the entire river defense was most often abandoned.

Multiple river crossings are an effective tactic, but require a lot of resources and additional security on the part of the attacker. Usually the Russian forces were content with a single crossing site, since the Chechens lacked the ability to mass against an established bridgehead. Since the Chechens were content to hold defensive positions, the Russians were content to pound them for weeks to soften them up before conducting a river crossing.

These river crossings were not the vital crossing battles of the Great Patriotic War (World War II). There were seldom serious consequences for delaying crossings until conditions were more favorable. Russian forces waiting to cross kept Chechen forces pinned down and unavailable for other tasks while air attacks and artillery fire attempted to reduce the size and effectiveness of these forces. A successful defense of a river line relies on a strong mobile reserve. The Chechens lacked the equipment and manpower to constitute such a force.

8
MINING AND ANTITANK

Land mines and improvised explosive devises (IEDs) were a favored weapon of the Chechens and produced many Russian casualties once the Chechens switched to guerrilla war. Initially, most IEDs were made from 152mm artillery rounds or 82mm mortar rounds. Later, as the supply of these rounds dwindled, the IED makers switched to dud bombs and rounds, as well as industrial explosives.

There is some evidence of later cross-pollination between the IED bombers in Iraq and Chechnya, with much of the information originating in Chechnya and then surfacing in the Middle East and other regions via video compact disks during the first war and more recently the Internet. There has been much reporting of Chechen bomb-makers working in Iraq and Afghanistan, but there is little, if any, evidence to support those claims. Chechen bomb-makers, like the vast majority of Chechen combatants, were solely focused on the war with Russia. Incidentally, a small number of foreign combatants arrived in Chechnya in the spring of 1995, most notably the Arab al Khattab, fresh off Jihad in Tajikistan. It was he who was said to have offered training to the Chechens on combat tactics, including mining operations, not the other way around.

The primary targets for Chechen miners and IED makers were Russians and documentation was considered critical. One Chechen IED team leader who operated during the second war only described his unit as a five-combatant force. However, the only responsibility of one of these five was to make sure he had the camera, tape and batteries capable of documenting the mining incident. These strikes against Russian armor would then be disseminated abroad.

The primary focus for Russian miners was protecting Russian outposts and checkpoints with antipersonnel mines. Occasionally they targeted dismounted Chechen units that habitually used certain trails.

Defeating Russian armor was a major challenge to the Chechens. They mainly used RPGs and IEDs for this. However, IEDs are not too mobile and the maximum effective range of the RPG is limited. The Chechens created a cottage industry manufacturing primitive but effective antitank weapons.

Vignette 22: Mine Warfare near Chiri-Yurt, Summer 2000

Vakha

Background: The Russian Army had focused and improved by spring 2000, and had inflicted two devastating defeats on the Chechens (the withdrawal from Grozny and the decimation of Ruslan Galaev's force in Komsomolskoye). In early summer 2000 the Chechen high command gave the order to abandon all fixed positions and conduct guerrilla warfare against the Russians much like they had done in the summer of 1995 following the loss of Vendo. Although they had now lost or given up the major hilltops, the Chechens continued to establish multiple lookout positions in the mountains to monitor the Russians operating on the valley floor. One such lookout was positioned in the hills near a clay pit east of

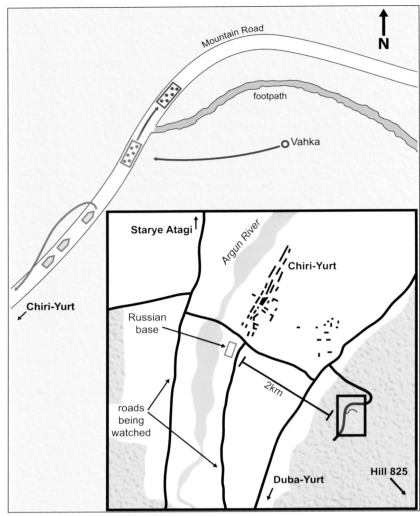

Mine warfare near Chiri-Yurt, summer 2000.

the main roadway between Chiri-Yurt and Duba-Yurt. From this position the Chechens could monitor Russian columns moving up and down the main road in and out of the Argun Gorge, while also keeping an eye on the Russian base established on the flat land just south of Chiri-Yurt.

Observing the Russian positions during the afternoon was particularly dangerous for the Chechens east of the Russian position south of Chiri-Yurt, because periodically the Russians would see the reflection of the binoculars that the Chechens used to survey the area. Binoculars, the sheen of a gun barrel, an ammunition belt slung over the shoulder – all of these items could produce a reflection alerting the Russians below. The Russians were well aware that the Chechens were watching them from the heights, and small units from both sides fought many skirmishes as each side moved in and out of the mountains searching each other out.

The Russians shelled the area east of Chiri-Yurt often, trying to disrupt Chechen observation. Finally, they sent a detachment from their base to mine the dirt road near a footpath. The Russians were sure that the Chechens were using the path and road to move through the area.

Vakha, who had fought in many battles during both wars, including operations in Grozny and most recently the fighting for Hill 825, now acted more or less alone. He had proven himself a valuable scout and spent many days and weeks on his own tracking Russian units in the mountains. "I carried two weapons [a machine gun and a sniper rifle], because you would always have to take out the radio operator before a battle. Or if you stumble upon a recon group you need the machine gun. Of course it's important to take out the radio operators. As soon as I see the antenna, I take him out. Their communications are very important, so they try not to let anyone get to him. When they don't have communications, they have no way to call for help, especially if it is a scout platoon."

From a position of safety Vakha watched as the small Russian convoy slowly drove up the road towards his position. It was about two kilometers as the crow flies from the base to his position, but easily double that taking the roads. As the Russians ground to a stop a short distance below him, Vakha made his way towards their location to get a closer look. Climbing down from his position, he began walking in the direction of the road. He knew these hills well. He could hear the Russian soldiers talking as he got closer. He thought to himself, "We would never make that much noise. How stupid are those guys?" As he got closer he could hear the sound of shovels. They were digging something.

Vakha crept closer and hid in the thick brush and scrub pine while waiting for the Russians to leave. Eventually the soldiers got back into their BTRs and headed back down the mountain road. He walked out to the spot where the Russians were working and surveyed the ground. They had "placed the mines right there so that we would run into them as we left the road [going] in this direction, toward the forest."

It was obvious where the mines were. The overturned ground was still dark, not having had time to dry out and blend in with the sunbaked dirt of the road. Vakha got on his hands and knees and carefully unearthed one of the mines. His first thought was to defuse it and the others and then put them in his rucksack so that he could use them elsewhere. However, upon examination, he realized that he could not disarm this particular mine. "It was impossible to defuse the mines. They were antipersonnel mines that can only be armed once."

Unable to diffuse and take the mines away, Vakha began digging them up one by one. Surveying the road he picked a likely spot. "I just took the mines and placed them about 10 or so meters to the rear. I buried them just like they did. They thought they were right here, but I moved them." Finished, Vakha melted back into the concealment of the thickly forested hills.

A couple days later Vakha came back to the location. The dirt now looked all the same. Standing by the location of the previous Russian mine field, he took a hand grenade off his vest and pulled the pin. He tossed the grenade towards the location of one of the mines that the Russians had laid out. He hoped to lure the Russians back to the minefield. "I am sure they heard it and said, 'Someone stepped on a mine. Maybe we can catch one of their wounded.'"

The Russians did respond, sending four or five vehicles quickly to the location, thinking that they were going to capture a wounded Chechen combatant. When they arrived and did not find anything but the scarred road where the grenade had detonated, they spread out and began walking further up the road. They knew where they had placed the mines and walked with confidence on the road beyond where the footpath broke off. As Vakha had hoped, they walked right into the new minefield he had planted. The third or fourth soldier stepped on the first mine, which blew off the lower part of his leg. The Russian soldiers were in a panic. Another soldier stepped on a mine, disabling him.

There was immediate chaos. Soldiers fired their weapons into the surrounding forest. When there was no return fire, the soldiers picked their way out of the minefield, loaded their wounded onto the BTRs and rushed them back to base. Vakha continued to observe the Russians from a safe distance. Predictably, as the vehicle cleared the area, Russian artillery rained down on the road where first the Russians and then Vakha has placed the mines.

Commentary: Mine operations were an important force multiplier for both the Russians and the Chechens. The high casualties that the Chechens suffered leaving Groxny in January 2000 resulted when the Chechens had to move through a minefield to escape the city. It was during the withdrawal that Shamil Basaev, perhaps the most notable Chechen field commander, lost his leg below the knee to an antipersonnel mine.

Like other weapons, the Chechen mines were constantly in short supply. Moving them like Vakha did was frequently considered necessary, although incredibly dangerous. Not all sappers fared as well as he did, and on occasion were blown up trying to do precisely the same thing.[1]

Vakha considered his little ruse a success not because of the two injured Russians, but because he denied the Russians the territory. "From that time forward, they never did come back to this location. They just fired on it using their artillery. Their soldiers won't come here anymore on foot as long as there are mines here."

Emir Khattab briefing his men on operations. Khattab, who had already fought Soviet forces in Afghanistan, was an advocate of partisan warfare. He believed there was no sense in attempting to go head-to-head with Russian firepower as happened in Grozny, but instead recommended focusing on the rear and supply lines. (Efim Sandler collection)

Vignette 23: Shaitan (Devil) Rocket Launcher

Multiple Interviewees

Since they were short on weapons and ammunition, the Chechen insurgency had numerous, decentralized, ad hoc weapons-production programs. The Krasnyy Molot (Red Hammer) Factory in Grozny already manufactured the 9mm Borz sub-machine gun, as a Chechen Republic of Ichkeria-sponsored state-run small arms industry, but the weapon's quality was poor and its production ceased once the war reached Grozny in January 1995. The Chechens produced other types of weapons from necessity as the war progressed. The Shaitan was one such weapon. Desperate for antitank weapons, the Chechens fashioned many makeshift antitank launchers, using the Russian S-5 and S-8 air-to-ground rockets and the fixed- and rotary-wing aircraft launch tubes from which the Russians typically fired them.

The Chechens shot down at least two dozen Mi-24 helicopters during the wars, and in many cases the Chechens were able to retrieve the UB-32 launch pods. They would then strip the undamaged tubes (up to 32) from each pod. This may have provided a few hundred tubes, but there were not enough and Chechens looked for alternatives. Many makeshift launchers were fashioned from the drive shaft covers of vehicles. The Soviet-era MAZ truck driveshaft cover fit the 57mm S-5 rocket well, while the Ural truck drive shaft cover was fitted to launch the 80mm S-8 rocket. Chechen combatants estimate that there may have been a Shaitan launcher tube in each unit. According to Kair and others, "there wasn't one launcher tube, there were many. One person made one, others saw it and then they made their own. It was widespread among our units, but to count all of them is difficult. They could have been in every group. If not one, then two. This wasn't unusual. It was a normal weapon that we Chechens had. We didn't have anything else. That's why we had to find our way out of this situation. We had to invent weapons as we went along."

It is difficult to determine if one system was used more than the other, but more combatants talk about the S-5, while fewer mention the S-8 (this could be a random result of those interviewed and have no actual bearing on how many of each rocket size were used). The S-5 rocket (first designated the ARS-57) was developed by the Soviet

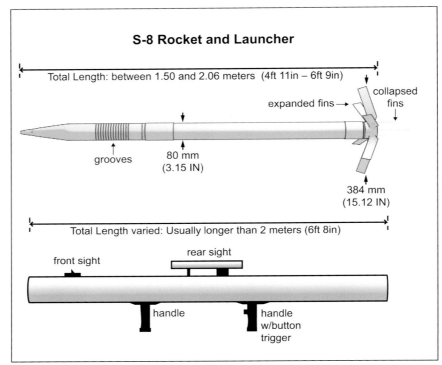

S-8 Rocket and Launcher

Total Length: between 1.50 and 2.06 meters (4ft 11in – 6ft 9in)

expanded fins →

collapsed fins

grooves

80 mm
(3.15 IN)

384 mm
(15.12 IN)

Total Length varied: Usually longer than 2 meters (6ft 8in)

front sight

rear sight

handle

handle
w/button
trigger

Shaitan (Devil) rocket launcher.

Air Force and used by military aircraft against ground area targets. It is in service with the Russian Air Force and various foreign services. It is produced in a variety of models with different warheads, including HEAT antiarmor (S-5K), high-explosive fragmentation (S-5M/MO), smoke, and w/button incendiary. Each rocket is about 1.4 meters (4 foot 6 inches) long and weighs about five kilograms (11 pounds), depending on the warhead and fuze. The range is three to four kilometers (1.9 to 2.6 miles), depending on the model.

The tube for the S-5 is approximately 58 millimeters in diameter, just the right size for S-5 rockets. Kair recalls that the men in his group who made these Shaitan launchers cleaned out the inside of the tube, and lubricated it. "It was a tight fit. The rounds would barely fit, but if it was loose in the tube, then the round would chatter up against the sides before leaving the barrel and be less accurate. The tube itself was usually up to two meters long. You don't need it to be any longer because the round itself, the helicopter round, doesn't exceed two meters. If you put the round in the tube it's enough for the tube to cover the round. It's a close fit. If the tube is any bigger in diameter, the round is going to fly out, no problem. But the accuracy will be bad. It might strike the wrong target. Secondly, when the rocket flies out of the tube, it could injure the shooter. When it's fired, it produces a recoil and creates a pocket of air which can injure a person. The tube was produced so that this doesn't happen and in order that the round securely exits."

Everything on the launcher is homemade. In most cases the trigger mechanism was simply a button attached to a handle with wires leading to the rear of the tube. The wires are connected to a battery that sends the signal down the wire. "The operator presses the button and the battery that's attached to this stand starts to work, the electricity goes to the rear of the rocket and the phosphorous automatically ignites. And then the rocket flies out of the tube." Many operators came up with their own ways to fire the rocket, but, according to users, they all incorporated "two wires attached to the end of the tube to ignite the phosphorous at the rear of the rocket, which starts the rocket engine of the round."

There were a variety of sights that were attached to the tube, but they all basically copied the RPG sight. "Let's say a person is standing up. He puts the tube on his shoulder, and they then attach the sight where it suits the gunner. Half of a binocular, a night vision scope, or something else is attached as the rear sight. The shooter acquires the target, aims, and can adjust for farther distances through the rear sight, like on an RPG. If he determines that the distance is one kilometer, he automatically raises the point of impact in the sight and determines 'Aha, it's possible.' This sighting method worked very well."

A forward handle was attached to the barrel for additional control and steadiness while aiming the weapon. Recalling the battles early in the first war, Kair felt that the Shaitan launcher gave the Russians pause when the Chechens first used it. "The Russians didn't understand what had hit them. They didn't know what kind of weapon it was."

Makeshift weapons and inexperienced gunners are a risky combination, and many gunners were wounded by the Shaitan launcher. Backblast was a serious issue and Shaitan gunners were seriously burned and wounded firing the weapon. "When the round flies out of the tube, it produces a lot of fire. The flame shoots out from the rocket engine. And when it ignites, it immediately produces flame. If a person is standing behind it, he can get burned. And when the round flies out of the tube, this flame can burn the gunner. To prevent burns, the gunner usually wore a fire-resistant camouflaged coat. He added a hat to this, preferably a hat with earflaps, and goggles or glasses to protect his eyes. Gloves were worn to prevent burning your hands." While Shaitan gunners did what they could to reduce injury, the benefit was considered far greater than the risks. "When the rocket leaves the tube, it only lasts a second and then it's gone."

Despite the challenges and potential of serious injury, the Shaitan was used in hundreds of battles and skirmishes. There were also some humorous moments. Aslanbek recalls shooting down a helicopter and retrieving the pod full of S-5 launch tubes and rockets. "We took the pod. From the pod, we took out a launch tube, put it on our

A BMP-2 of 84th Separate Reconnaissance Battalion from 3rd Motor Rifle Division, captured during the ambush in Duba-Yurt on 31 December 1999. (Efim Sandler collection)

BMP-2 of 84th Separate Reconnaissance Battalion from 3rd Motor Rifle Division, destroyed during the ambush in Duba-Yurt on 31 December 1999. During the fight, 84th Battalion lost 10 killed, 41 wounded, three BMPs and a BRM. The trapped battalion was relieved by the tanks of the 160th Regiment. (Efim Sandler collection)

Abu al-Walid, a Saudi militant who was one of Emir Khattab's deputies and took part in the Duba-Yurt ambush. Al-Walid took over the command of Khattab's units after his death and was in turn killed by Russian forces in 2004. Abu al-Walid was the most famous Saudi participant of Chechen resistance. (Photo via Efim Sandler)

shoulder and fired rockets from it. Once there was a BMP driving along and one of our guys wanted to hit it with his Shaitan from over here. But this weapon, the Shaitan, is unpredictable, they aren't guided missiles. He fired the rocket. The recoil threw him backward and the rocket didn't fly straight. It started to do all sorts of zigzags. Either it was damaged or I don't know. It flew past the Chechen positions several times, there and back. There was a Russian command vehicle directing the battle from the rear. Finally, the rocket landed directly on this BMP. The Shaitan gunner had been shooting at someone else altogether. The rocket started swerving and finally hit one of theirs. I am not lying!"

Vakha, a combatant in Khamzat Galaev's group, recalled there were a few of the larger S-8 rockets and Shaitan launchers in his unit. Like other units, they struggled with not only injury from the backblast, but also transportability. They came up with an ingenious way to break down, pack, and transport the tube. "The tube is a little over two meters long. We cut it into three pieces and used a sleeve and bolts to fasten the sections together when we wanted to use it. Or you can fold it up when you need to break it down and travel. You can put it in your backpack. When you need it again, you assemble the three sections and the launcher tube is then more than two meters long. Then you put the S-8 ammunition in the tube and use an ordinary battery to fire it with a button switch."

Vakha's unit also made an effort to minimize facial injury from the rocket flame, fashioning a protective shield out of plastic or out of glass. "That's it. You put it on your shoulder and from 2.5 kilometers I can fire a rocket from my homemade shoulder-fired launcher and hit Russian armor." It was an evolving process of trial and error, but the shield seemed to do the trick of protecting the gunner's face from the blast.

It is hard to determine how many Shaitans were in action, and how many rockets were available. In addition to the rockets retrieved from downed helicopters and even the occasional Su-25, the Chechens relied on the Russians themselves to keep supplied with rockets. Chechen combatants talk about buying hundreds of S-5 and S-8 rockets from Russian soldiers, especially during the first war. In many cases, the rockets and other weapons were bought through third parties, mostly local children. Chechen combatants claim that soldiers at checkpoints and garrisons around populated areas would tell the kids that they had weapons and ammunition to sell or trade, often for vodka. The children would then go to the combatants and the combatants would confirm the arrangements (where to leave the rockets and goods being traded) through the children.

While this seems incredible, most Chechen combatants have at least one story about swapping goods for weapons with the Russians – again, especially during the first war.

By all accounts, the Shaitan launcher proved a valuable weapon system. Combatants claim that, in addition to destroying tanks and armored personnel carriers, they also shot down helicopters with the weapon. At the very least this makeshift weapon helped keep the Chechens on the battlefield. According to Kair, "We did everything we could, we thought up everything. Weapons are one of the Chechens' hobbies. It's been that way since the beginning of time and will always be."

Chapter Eight Summary

Mines are a favorite weapon of the guerrilla. It is a relatively inexpensive way to attack vehicles and personnel. Mines and IEDs were valuable, so they were seldom emplaced and left unattended. The Chechens normally combined offensive or defensive actions

An action shot of a Su-25 attack on Chechen positions in 2003. (Efim Sandler collection)

9
ATTACK

Frequently it is difficult to distinguish between a Chechen attack and a raid. Both are designed to gain a position, but the attack normally plans on holding that position for a period of time afterwards. Chechen attacks were normally conducted by platoon-sized groups with a common affiliation-village, school, family, clan, neighborhood or religious fervor. The group leader was part of that group and commanded by personal influence, reputation and demonstrated performance.

Fire and maneuver and assault by bounds were evident among the more-seasoned groups, but a normal attack consisted of 15–50 combatants moving in the same direction, firing as they went. Fire discipline and fire effectiveness was a problem among the less-seasoned groups as combatants tended to fire full-automatic and then stop and change magazines at the same time. Primary weapons during the attack were the Kalashnikov assault rifles and RPG-7 grenade launchers. In this chapter's vignettes, the attackers hold the objective for varying amounts of time. Due to the limited time at the objective, the night attack might also be characterized as a night raid.

Regardless, Chechen attacks might or might not be preceded by mortar or RPG-7 fire and might or might not be covered by supporting machine gun fire. Chechen attacks usually involved several small groups acting in a somewhat coordinated manner. The attackers relied on the impact of suppressive small arms fire on the enemy as they advanced. Sometimes they swept past the objective and then fell back and consolidated on the objective after Russian artillery had finished firing on their former positions. Sometimes they just halted on the objective and sought shelter before the artillery fell. After occupying the objective, the first order of business was to treat or evacuate the wounded and resupply ammunition from the enemy stocks. Attacks were a high-risk option to the Chechens, since an attacker often suffers more casualties than a defender. As the wars continued, the supply of willing, healthy Chechen manpower dwindled and the attack option looked less and less appealing.

with their mines and IEDS and tried to move them at the end of the action if they were not detonated. Once the mines and IEDs were in place, the Chechens covered them with direct fire. Naturally, to the resource-poor Chechens, Russian defensive minefields were a tempting source of resupply. The Russians put in anti-lift devices or used mines that could not be defused to combat Chechen forays into their minefields.

As a general statement, Chechens like weapons and Chechens like to tinker. Mines and IEDs were all "product-improved" by tinkering, and many Chechen males are missing appendages from such attempts. The Chechens also liked inventing antitank devices – not a project for the faint of heart and unimaginative. The Shaitan is a prime example of tinkering that can go wrong, yet the final product is serviceable, even if not up to the loosest safety standards.

Vignette 24: Pinning down Russian control point during the Battle for Grozny, 6–10 March 1996

Elimpash

Background: Nearly eight months had passed since the truce following Shamil Basaev's attack on Budennovsk. Although there were periodic breaks in the ceasefire, a status quo developed on the battlefield with both sides holding the positions they gained during the first six months of fighting. The Chechens utilized the time to recuperate and rebuild their forces. They also began planning an operation designed to demonstrate their ability to continue the fight. The plan called for a three-day operation to enter Grozny, bloody the Russians, broadcast their tactical victory from the capital, and retreat back to the relative safety of their mountain bases. The Chechens were to enter the city from three directions and put all Russian positions in the city under fire. Shamil Basaev had operational control of the entire operation. Ruslan (Khamzat) Galaev commanded the Chechen combatants entering the capital from the west from Chernorechie.

Like many Chechen combatants, Elimpash had returned to his home after the June 1995 truce. He was periodically asked to participate in actions but had decided against all of them until he learned of the March operation against the capital. Other men from his area were preparing to depart to the staging area in Alkhan-Yurt and he joined them. From Alkhan-Yurt Elimpash's group approached Grozny through the back roads in the Chernorechie Forest. Dozens and dozens of Chechen groups were entering the city from all directions, each targeting their designated Russian positions.

According to plan, Elimpash's unit reached its staging point at the western bus station south of the Sunzha River round 0500. The Chechen offensive against the Russians would begin at 0600, but already Elimpash could hear intermittent fire echoing across the city. Other Chechen groups set about fortifying the bus station,

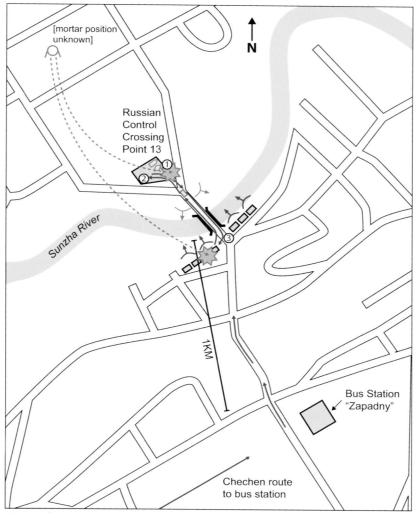

Pinning down Russian control point during the Battle for Grozny, 6–10 March 1996.

while Elimpash and his group of 25–30 fighters left the bus station for their designated position on the south bank of the Sunzha River. The position was more than one kilometer north of the bus station and they were careful not to fall into any Russian traps en route. The Chechens had been gathering intelligence for months and there were not supposed to be any Russian units between the bus station and the objective. A Russian patrol of three BTRs drove by the bus station almost immediately after they had all arrived. "What if they had noticed us?" Elimpash thought as they moved north toward the Sunzha. They advanced briskly but warily toward their objective.

Nearing the Sunzha, Elimpash could see the Russian position. There was a pillbox directly across the bridge, in the middle of the road. It was made of concrete slabs and blocks and equipped with firing slits. Beyond the pillbox was a former garage. The entire complex was now a fortified Russian control-crossing point equipped with machine guns. Intelligence reports indicated that there was one BTR and one tank inside the control point. Elimpash's group split into two. Elimpash and 12 combatants occupied a house on the west side of the road leading to the bridge, while the other half of the group occupied a house on the east side of the road. Elimpash peered out the window toward the Russian position. The pillbox in the middle of the road was probably 100 meters away. The main Russian position was another 100–200 meters beyond that. From his vantage point, it looked to be very well fortified. The Chechens did not waste any time. By now the entire city was under attack. They began firing to let the Russians know that they were there and

that the Russians would not be able to advance south across the bridge. That was Elimpash's objective to prevent the Russians from advancing south across the Sunzha.

The control point and Chechen position exchanged fire intermittently during the first day. Elimpash was relieved that no Russian reinforcements arrived to help the control point. "Thankfully, the other Chechen units must also be doing their job," he thought.

The Chechens continued to fire on the Russian position on the second day, but suddenly "large caliber mortars began to fall all around our position. The house next to ours was hit and exploded in a ball of flames. We went down into the basement for cover." He was thankful that the building he was in had a cellar. Sitting there in the dark basement, he thought that there must have been an open gas line in the house that went up in flames. As the shelling quieted down, Elimpash and the others in the basement went upstairs to re-engage the Russian position. At that moment, the Russian position took a direct mortar hit on the roof. It landed on what he believed was the Russian command post at the corner of the position, "Ah, someone is directing this mortar fire," Elimpash thought. Everyone cheered, and the Chechens resumed their fire, heartened by the mortar strike (location 1 on map).

The Chechens continued to observe the Russian position that night, but there was no visible movement. Everyone took turns sleeping. The next morning, the Chechens again observed no activity coming from the Russian position. They probed the position with fire but there was still no sign of life. It was decided that half of the group would cross the bridge and assault the position. Elimpash and the other half covered their movement and were ready to engage the Russians. The Chechens set out across the bridge. Nearing the pillbox, they broke into a run, firing at the pillbox as they ran by. There was no return fire. Cautiously a Chechen peered through the firing slit. The pillbox was abandoned.

They continued on to the control point. Approaching gingerly at first, they reached it without incident. The Russians had likely abandoned the position after the mortar strike the day before. Elimpash and the other half of the group now crossed the bridge and joined the others scavenging through the Russian position for equipment and supplies (location 2). They found a Fagot antitank weapon with two rounds and a box of grenades and ammunition. There was nothing more to do but return to their positions and wait for the order to withdraw from the city. They also wanted to keep the river between them and a Russian counterattack to retake the control point (location 3).

Commentary: The order came to evacuate the city late that night. Elimpash and the rest of the unit packed their equipment, including their trophies, and made their way back to the bus station just after midnight. Linking up with other Chechen units still holding the bus station, they abandoned that position too, retreating in a southwesterly direction, back through the Chernorechie Forest to Alkhan-Yurt. Dozens of other Chechen units around the city were also retreating. Elimpash returned to his home the next day.

Russian accounts of the March 1996 attack claim that at least three of their control points on the Sunzha were destroyed or had to be abandoned during the Chechen offensive. Control point 13 was one of them. Elimpash is not sure why the Russians abandoned their position, since the whole city was under attack. "There was nowhere for this unit to go. The war was being fought all over the city." He thinks that after the mortar strike the Russians felt that they had been targeted and would be under continual fire, and that is why they left. The Russians appear to have been in a hurry to leave. They did not mine or booby-trap their position as they exited, and even left a weapon and some grenades and ammunition.[1]

The March 1996 raid on Grozny was a tactical and emotional victory for the Chechens. They were able to meet all their objectives and in many cases exceeded them. In addition to acquiring much-needed supplies, the Chechens gathered valuable intelligence all over the city. Interestingly, Chechen accounts of the August 1996 attack on Groxny, which ended the first war in Chechnya's favor, imply that the Russians did not change much, if anything, in their defense of the capital from the March 1996 attack. This was a huge advantage for the Chechens, as they simply reattacked the same Russian positions that they had attacked months before.

Elimpash's account confirms the impression that the Russian forces "went to ground" during the Chechen raid and did little to patrol and regain control of the city. Instead, the Russians relied on artillery fire and airstrikes to retain some degree of control outside their individual strong points in the city. An intact bridge across the river was clearly valuable, but the Russian control post was abandoned with no apparent ability to reoccupy it or to control the area from another location.

Vignette 25: First Battle for Hill 825, Fall 1999

Vakha

Background: When the second war began in Chechnya in 1999, Chechen units controlled the crowning heights dominating the narrow passage leading into the Argun Gorge. Known as the Wolf's Gate, the passage was important because it offered a direct route to the Chechen-controlled southern area, including Shatoi, and was a back-door route to Vedeno and other Chechen strong points. During the first war (1994–1996) the Chechen leadership was caught by surprise when the Russians used the banks of the Vashtar River between Hills 825 and 776 to move men and armor into their rear areas to disrupt their supply lines and safe havens.

Referred to by their elevation in meters on the map sheet, Hills 825, 835, 950, and 776[2] would become crucial battlegrounds during the first months of the Second Chechen War. Realizing that they could not withstand Russian air strikes, the Chechens maintained lightly manned lookouts on all these elevations, keeping most of their force nearby in numerous small mountain bases near these vital hilltops. In most cases, the Chechens were only a few hundred meters from the heights, close enough to defend the positions from any Russian assault when required.

By late fall, the Russians controlled all the plains area below these crucial hilltops, including the town of Duba-Yurt at the mouth of the Wolf's Gate, where they established a key checkpoint [blockpost in Russian] with a direct line of sight to Hill 825. The hill could be reached using a dirt road that snaked half way up the mountain. The road gave way to a footpath that continued the rest of the way to the hilltop.

One night, in late fall, sometime before the first snow, Russian forces attacked Hill 825. There were only four Chechen combatants on the hilltop at the time, which was standard practice. They were forced to withdraw under fire from a Russian BMP-1. It had driven as far as it could up the mountain road to a position from which it was able to pound the hilltop with direct fire from its 73mm smoothbore "Borz" cannon. Meanwhile, Russian infantry ascended the hilltop using night vision goggles and seized the hill. Since the four Chechens had withdrawn, the Russians took Hill 825 without a casualty.

The Chechen garrison near Hill 825 was located in positions only hundreds of meters from the hill. They were stunned by the Russian success and were determined to take back the hilltop the next day before the Russians had a chance to further consolidate their position. Vakha estimates that an entire company of soldiers was settling in, frantically digging in and fortifying their positions preparing for a Chechen counterattack.[3]

The hilltop ridge itself was 30–50 meters wide. The Russians fortified their position with two lines or echelons of defense with their southern flank protected by the steep face of the ridge. The first Russian line was roughly 30 meters below the second defensive position, located on the ridge's high ground. Both defensive positions were laid out in an irregular semicircle, using the steep cliffs on the southern side as a natural defensive barrier and focusing all their defensive efforts to the north and to the western gently sloping left flank.

The Chechens were well trained and experienced in combining numerous smaller groups into a coherent force when necessary. The Chechens massed about 100 combatants for the attack to retake Hill 825. They planned to attack along both the eastern and western slopes, flanking and hitting the Russian first defensive line. "We

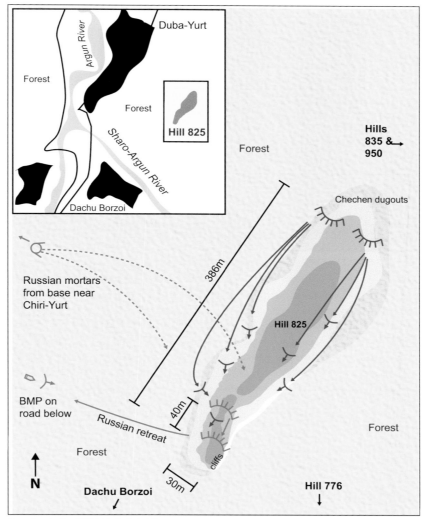

First Battle for Hill 825, Fall 1999.

Duba-Yurt, also called the 'Wolf's Gate'. (Photo by Boris Tsekhanovich)

A member of a Ministry of the Interior sapper team with his dog, 1999–2000. (Photo via Efim Sandler)

One of the IEDs found on a Chechen route. (Photo via Efim Sandler)

were determined to take back the hill and we threw our full force at it!" recalls Vakha. The multiple Chechen groups were combined and then divided into two parts. One group would converge on the Russians from the right and the other from the left. Each attacking force, comprised of small units, would move forward, providing mutually supporting fires as they bounded towards the Russian lines. "You shoot and when you need to reload someone covers you. Then the rear moves forward."

The Chechen advance was steady and determined. "In close quarters combat, you continue to strike your opponent hard and don't let him raise his head, which brings you success. You still have to fire rounds intelligently so that he doesn't have a chance to raise his head. The goal is to not allow him to shoot at you accurately. To fire and to fire accurately are two different things."

Chechen casualties began to mount, despite laying down continual fire on the Russian first and second defensive lines. Eventually the Russian first defensive line broke and the Chechens were able to overrun and occupy the trenches. Vakha knew that they could not sit in the first trench for long – they had to keep moving. The Russians targeted their positions in case they were overrun. As soon as the Russians in the second line of defense radioed for support, mortars would be raining down on the first defensive line in seconds. They had to get to the second and final Russian position.

But Vakha had other concerns. Many of the Chechen combatants were new to combat and their inexperience was apparent. "In the middle of a battle, this guy close to me yelled 'throw me a magazine.' I threw him one, and then he yelled 'throw me another.' I threw him one more. He looked at me, and I threw him another one – a third magazine! I yelled, 'what are you doing – littering?!' It is poor practice to fire automatically. I always said 'fire one shot at a time.' You can still fire single shots in quick succession." These were lessons the new recruits would have to learn.

Pinned down in the first trench line, with a steady stream of fire coming from the second Russian line, the situation looked bleak. Then the mortars started falling and a BMP on the road below with direct line of sight started pounding their position with its 73mm gun.

Vakha looked around. He had been wounded and a few of the men in his group were dead, lying on the ridge line behind him. It had been a fierce assault so far and it was not getting any easier. At that moment, a young Chechen combatant sprung up, "I don't know, something must've triggered him, he threw his rifle down, threw everything down, and took out his ancestral dagger. He

was literally 30, 40 meters away from the Russian second line of defense. He jumped out of the trench and ran toward the Russians." Other Chechens rushed from the trench after him. "I looked up and remember seeing the fear on the Russians' faces. The Russian soldiers just broke and ran. You could say this guy, without a single shot, armed only with this dagger, took the peak."

The Chechens had secured the hilltop once again, but at a steep price. Twenty-seven Chechens were killed during the assault, two fell to their deaths off the sheer face as they advanced from below, south of the ridge. The knife-wielding Chechen was the first to reach the final Russian position. "This guy sprang into an uphill fighting position. There was a mine in the fighting position. The Russians knew that sooner or later they would give up this position and they mined the whole area. That was their tactic. He was blown up by the mine in the Russian entrenchment."

Commentary: The victory was short lived. The BMP-1 on the road below continued to fire onto Hill 825. The Chechens tried to attack the BMP, but it was well protected by mines to the left and right of the road, while the road itself was protected by the BMPs main gun. The Chechens simply could not get close enough. It was too far away for their RPGs to be effective. Russian aircraft also began to pummel the ridge, forcing the Chechens to abandon the hilltop. The Chechens withdrew back to their small bases near the hilltop, preferring to put only a couple of combatants on the position at any one time to observe the Russians on the plains below.

Some weeks later, sometime after the snow started falling, Russian infantry attacked the hill again. Incidentally, there were only three Chechens manning the hilltop at the time. "About 400 meters away there were some foxholes that were warm. These three were freezing, so they said, "Let's run over there and eat, and then we'll come back." All three of them left, and at that exact moment the Russians reached the ridge. Both times the Russians took the hilltop without firing a single shot. Our soldiers just left their post."

The Chechen attackers suffered 27 dead and two missing who had fallen or been shot and fallen off the steep slopes near the top of the hilltop. This was a significant loss to a fighting force that could not afford to take 20–30% casualties every operation. Vakha's small unit itself had suffered five dead. Respecting the dead, Vakha and the others in his unit carried the bodies down the mountain to the village of Ulus-Kert, where they buried their dead in the village cemetery.

The Chechens did not establish a support-by-fire position along the top of the ridge, where machine guns could have provided continual suppressive fire in addition to the interrupted suppressive fire from the bounding teams. This was probably due to the ad hoc nature of the Chechen force, as well as the uneven level of training in the Chechen force. Lifting and shifting supporting fire requires good communications, extensive practice and experienced machine gunners who can engage the enemy without endangering their own force.

Vignette 26: Night attack on a temporarily-positioned Russian tank and Ural trucks, January 2000

Vakha T.

Background: By January 2000, Russian forces controlled large sections of Grozny, but there were still significant numbers of Chechen combatants operating in the capital. These individual pockets of Chechens were often too small to conduct attacks against Russian targets without combining with other groups. Vakha was a member of Isa Manaev's group, located in the Zavodskoy Rayon in Grozny. One day in January another Chechen commander entered Manaev's bunker to solicit his support for an attack on a Russian T-90 main battle tank near the village of Alkhan-Yurt, southwest of Grozny.

After concluding it was a good idea, Manaev called out the names of 13 individuals from his bunker. Manaev recalls, "Each was selected based on individual skill and what the mission required."

Vakha watched anxiously, hoping he would be selected for the mission but he was not. His friend Timor was. Vakha asked Manaev for a moment and pleaded with him to be part of the operation because, "Timor and I, we've always fought together and I do not want to be separated now." Manaev consented but there was still one problem. Vakha had no weapon or field gear. He had lent them to another Chechen, who had been killed in combat a couple days ago. He was unable to recover his weapon. To Vakha's surprise, Manaev gave him his own assault rifle and pack.

It is unclear how the group got from their bunker in Zavodskoy to the area between the Chernorechie Intersection and Alkhan-Yurt, but the long winter nights afforded ample time to travel under cover of darkness. Eventually they reached the location. Two scouts broke from the unit to assess the Russian position and confirm the target. It was just as the Chechen commander had indicated: a T-90 main battle tank and two Ural trucks, one hitched to a mobile field kitchen. The vehicles were parked near the rise of a foothill and positioned with the two trucks in front of the tank, as if to hide the tank. The scouts reported seeing only two sentries guarding the vehicles.

The group split up and moved out to their positions according to the plan they devised back in Manaev's bunker. The 13–16 men split up into four loose groupings.[4] From left to right, the first group consisted of three men armed with an RPG, a Mukha, and an assault rifle. Islam, part of a second team of three, was 70–80 meters to the right, armed with another RPG. The second man carried a shortened special assault rifle with a silencer.[5] His job was to creep up and take out one of the sentries. The third man operated a PK light

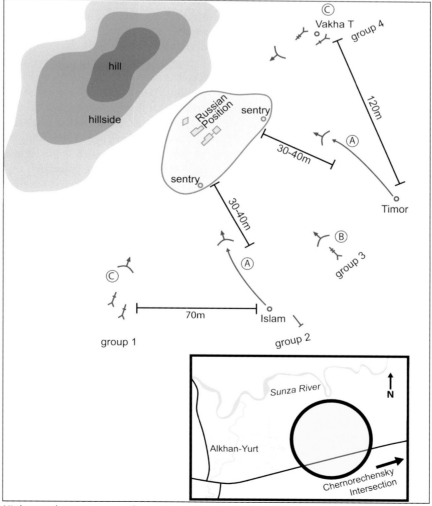

Night attack on a temporarily-positioned Russian tank and Ural trucks, January 2000.

machine gun, or Krasavchik, as the Chechens referred to the weapon.[6] The Krasavchik would not see any action if the operation went well, but if turned bad, the machine gun would lay down covering fire while the rest of the group withdrew.

Dead center, looking straight on at the Russian vehicles was the Chechen commander who had alerted Manaev's unit to the target. His team was armed with not only RPGs but also the "Vampire" RPG-29, which fired a heavy tandem round designed to penetrate the reactive armor of a tank.

A little further to the right

A BMP-2 of the 693rd Motor Rifle Regiment destroyed by an IED near the village of Borze, Shatoi District, on 29 July 1996. The blast killed four of the crewmembers. (Photo via Efim Sandler)

was Vakha's friend Timor, also armed with a silenced assault rifle. He would take out the second sentry when the time came. Finally, Vakha was in the group to the far right. He was armed with the assault rifle Manaev had given him. Another man had a couple of Mukhas. The third man was armed with an RPG. They also had a fourth man armed with an SVD sniper rifle.[7]

Once the teams were all in place, Timor and the other Chechen with the silenced weapon crawled forward to within 30–40 meters of the sentries. They took them both out with single shots. They were careful to maintain silence, having also tied the orange tourniquet band from the standard Russian medical field kit to the bolt to prevent it from noisily retracting.[8]

Once the sentries were eliminated the Chechen commander in the center position fired the first RPG, followed by a single volley of RPG-7 and RPG-29 shots from the various positions. Vakha claims that "only four or five shots were fired," two or three RPG-7 rounds for the trucks and two RPG-29 rounds to finish off the tank.

The Chechens withdrew as fast as they had mobilized at the point of attack. "The whole operation took less [than] four minutes. No more," claimed Vakha. As hoped, the Krasavchik was never needed. The Chechens retreated as quickly as they had arrived. They were afraid, with good reason, that the Russians may have sighted and laid weapons on the location in the event that it was attacked. Others in the group were worried about Russian artillery fire, possibly out of Khan Kala.

Commentary: The whole raid took less than five minutes and resulted in at least two Russian KIA (the sentries), and one T-90 tank and two Ural trucks (one with field kitchen) destroyed. There were no Chechen losses. The Chechens felt that the Russian position was temporary and a target of opportunity that would have to be acted upon immediately or they would miss their chance. Recon scouts went forward first and surveyed the situation and placement of the Russian vehicles. The 13–16-man force then moved up the middle and the left and right flanks, closer to the Russian position. It is not clear what kind of concealment the Chechens were able to use. The area in question is a patchwork of fields and wooded area with relatively little changes in elevation. The position of the Russian vehicles against the hillside must have been a good choice by the Russians, since the Chechens also did not attempt to attack from the direction of the hill. Vakha recalls that, "it was too difficult to attack

from that direction." However, the Russians did not appear to have prepared forward defenses against a possible attack.

The Chechens were also never clear on where the rest of the soldiers might have been. They assumed that they were in the vehicles. There was also some talk that there might have been sentries on the other side of the Russian position, on the hill, but the Chechens could not locate any other sentries prior to the attack and did not stay to find out after the attack. Thinking about the event, Vakha suggested, "we all want to live. If there were other Russian sentries at the position, they probably hid themselves until it was over and we were gone."

The attack seems to have been motivated as much by the specific target as a desire to strike Russian forces. The Chechens were aware that the T-90 tank was the newest tank in the inventory, there were very few of them and they represented a substantial financial cost to the Russians. It would be a psychological victory. The Chechens also appear to have been husbanding their stockpile of the RPG-29 warheads for attacks such as this. It is unclear where they acquired the RPG-29 warheads or launcher.

Finally, both Isa and Vakha were cognizant of Russian artillery capability and the mission was designed for the Chechens to conduct it quickly and then retreat to the safety of their bunker in the Zavodskoy Rayon in Grozny. "It was our way, attack, retreat, attack, retreat. Get out of there. That's it." Isa recalled.

Vignette 27: Second Battle for Hill 825, January 2000

Vakha

Background: The battles for the key hilltops surrounding the Wolf's Gate grew more intense in early 2000. The Chechens determined that they needed to retake Hill 825 for the second time. They made preparations for an assault. However, the memory of the first assault to recapture the hill was on everyone's mind. They had taken far too many losses in the first attack. The Chechens were sure that the Russians were prepared to defend against another attack similar to the first one.

There were multiple groups in the mountains around Hill 825, including Vakha's group of 15 combatants. This time Vakha was elected to lead the entire assault. "I was in charge the second time.

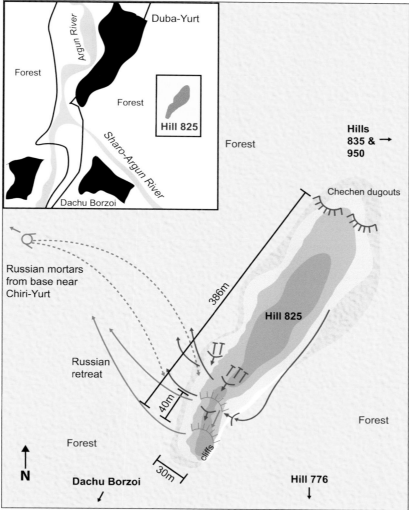

Second Battle for Hill 825, January 2000.

There were two or three groups involved, but I took command because I understood the situation better because of my experience." Still the preparation was pretty relaxed, "how should I put this? As we were planning, we just said 'you do this and you do that,' and then we went about our business."

The losses of the last assault on the hill weighed heavily on Vakha and he was concerned about throwing all the men at his disposal into a frontal attack uphill against the Russian positions. Thinking it over, he devised a new plan. "The first thing I did was deploy 19 fighters with machine guns across the width of the ridgeline facing the Russian first line of defense. They engaged the Russians in the first line of defense."

The close proximity was not unusual, and both the Russians and Chechens could often hear each other even though they could not always get a clear line of sight due to the terrain features. On many occasions the Chechens and the Russians had taunted each other from nearby positions. For their own safety, the Russians rarely ventured forward of their defensive position. Instead of mining the ground in front of them, the Russians relied on their ability to call in mortar and artillery fire from the plains below. The Russians still had a BMP positioned below on the road to Hill 825 with direct line of sight on the second Russian defensive position at the top of the hill, but it could not help them much in front of the first defensive position.

Vakha placed a second group of Chechens a bit further back and to the right of the first group. Their mission was to lay down

suppressive fire on the second Russian defensive line on the hilltop. "There were very rocky places right here, and the second group fought with these Russians in the second line of defense. The distance to this group was about 80–100 meters." About 400 meters down the ridge there were an additional 40 Chechen combatants in dugouts. "I did not activate them because it was close combat, and the more people that were in the battle, the more casualties we would have sustained." Still, they were there if needed and this reassured Vakha.

Finally, Vakha and three other Chechens would traverse and then climb the steep cliff face to the southeast of the forward line of Russian positions on the ridge in an attempt to flank them from the unexpected side while the first and second Chechen positions kept the Russian defensive lines occupied with suppressive fire. If Vakha was successful and outflanked the first line, his attack on the Russian right side would be the signal for the Chechens in group one to join the assault on the first trench line.

Everyone checked his gear and ran to his position. Vakha and his small team began the treacherous climb along the south face. At H-hour the machine-gunners began firing up at the Russian defensive lines. In response, "drunken conscripts yelled down to us, 'Let's go, you bearded goats!' Some of the young men with me yelled back 'Ivan, change your diapers, we're coming!'"

The second group of Chechen shooters began firing at the second defensive position on the hilltop. The Russians fired back and called in mortar and artillery on the Chechen positions only 30 to 60 meters from their first defensive line. Vakha and his fellow combatants could hear the battle raging above them. As they continued along the steep rocky ledge, two of Vakha's group (friends of his) stopped to pray. Glancing back at them, Vakha had an overwhelming sense of foreboding. "When I looked at them, I immediately understood that these guys would soon leave this world." He looked back up the hill. They had to continue their ascent.

Eventually they reached a position adjacent to the Russian first line. Scaling the few meters to the top, Vakha and his small group appeared on the first defensive line's flank, just as they had planned. "I saw the Russians who were yelling at us earlier. One soldier, as soon as he saw us, jumped out of his position, and we shot him. Another soldier saw me when I appeared from behind the cliff face and our eyes met (we were about 10 meters apart). He looked at me and was so scared that he pulled the trigger of his rifle and shot three of his own fellows in a row."

The Russian first line was in jeopardy and began to collapse. "The Russians didn't understand what was happening – they now had no first line of defense." Soldiers ran from the position down the hillside to their north, while others ran towards the second and final defensive line. "The first line retreated and communicated to the others that the 'Chechens have occupied our positions.'" Russian mortar teams then began to fire right on the Russian lines. "We hadn't yet taken the second defensive line, but the Russians themselves helped us. The second defensive line was higher up, and the confused Russians fired mortars at their own positions. All we had to do was climb up, and the rest of the Russians in the second defensive line retreated."

The experienced Chechens had learned early in the first war to stay close to the Russians, although they sometimes could not convince the younger, more-inexperienced Chechens of the necessity until they experienced it themselves in combat. "If you are winning in a close combat situation, the Russians will retreat and call in the coordinates of your location. At that point, you need to either withdraw or, even better, move toward the Russians because they will give the coordinates of your location to their artillery. So the closer you are to them, the less chance you have of being hit by artillery or aircraft fire. The closer you are to the Russians, the better chance you have of surviving. If you panic and retreat or stay in the same location, you will be buried by large-caliber rounds. The best thing to do is move in the direction of the enemy."

The Chechens did not stay to occupy the hilltop, however, because mortar fire and fire from the BMP-1 on the road continued to hit the hilltop now that the last surviving Russians had retreated. Instead, Vakha followed the retreating Russians. "I climbed down a little following the same path of the retreating Russians and observed the BMP on the road below through my binoculars. I wanted to get to the BMP, but Russian snipers began firing at me. Snipers also began targeting the positions on top of Hill 825."

As the sun disappeared below the mountains to the west, the mortars stopped. The Chechens foraged through the Russian position. There were many dead soldiers.[9] There were also some luxuries, including thermoses of boiling water. "Can you imagine? When we drank our little bags of tea, it was wonderful. I remember that the moon was out. It was a very light night."

Commentary: The retaking of Hill 825 had taken two hours.[10] Vakha was adamant that it had to be secured before dark and it was. His men did not have the advantage of night vision technology and

The common reality of the war in Chechnya was that there was either an IED planted during the night, or an occasional RPG fired from the roof. The problem for the Russians was that their forces' activities were limited by political agreements of so-called 'clean' villages. If a village was marked as 'clean' or 'under agreement' no force could be used inside. (Photo via Efim Sandler)

A convoy of Russian forces. The first three BTRs belong to troops from the Ministry of the Interior, the T-72B tank belongs to a motor rifle unit of the Russian Army. (Photo via Efim Sandler)

he knew that the longer the Russians stayed on the hill the more risky it was to his operation. Chechen losses were remarkably low, only two or three according to Vakha. Vakha's two friends, who had stopped to pray as they climbed towards the Russian positions, were dead, just as Vakha's premonition had indicated.

The next day Vakha and a few others set out on the path down the slope towards the plains below in the same direction as the Russian retreat off the hilltop the day before. He found three dead Russian soldiers from the previous day's battle. He was still looking for a way to strike the BMP that was causing them so much trouble, but could not reach it due to the minefields the Russians had placed on both sides of the road leading to it. There was little he could do but continue to observe it through his binoculars. Before heading back up the hill the Chechens collected all the dead Russian soldiers' ammo and equipment.

Rather than assault the position again, Russian fixed- and rotary-winged aircraft pummeled Hill 825 steadily for weeks afterwards. The Chechens never relinquished Hill 825 again until the Chechen command ordered its forces to abandon all fixed positions and begin guerrilla warfare. Then Vakha and his men moved off the elevation, and by summer of 2000 the Russians once again established themselves on Hill 825.

Looking back on the operation, Vakha recalls multiple factors led to their success. "We kind of tricked them. We went up the steep cliff. The Russians at the top thought that we had already overrun the first line of defense. If we had taken more combatants with us, more would have died, you know? But to win the hilltop while losing three people . . . even our senior commanders were amazed that we took the hilltop and lost only three people. It was our military abilities and luck. Luck played a big role. It worked out for us."

This time the Chechens established two support-by-fire positions to engage the two Russian defensive lines simultaneously. There is no indication how the fires were controlled. The commander was not able to do so directly, since he was leading the assault with a small group in advance of the main attack force. Vakha probably communicated with a Motorola hand-held radio or similar short-range communications device.

Vignette 28: Chechens attack ring of villages along mountain frontier, 16 August 2002

Isa
(with supporting material from Russian statements and press accounts)

Background: By late summer 2002 Chechen forces operating in the mountains found it nearly impossible to reach out across the plains and attack the Russians. Further, they were now faced with pro-Russian Chechen forces who were loyal to Moscow and Putin-appointed acting Head of the Administration Akhmad Kadyrov.[11] Kadyrov's Chechens fought alongside the Russians and secured the plains. Instead of fighting them, the Chechen combatants, under the command of the interwar Chechen-elected President Aslan Maskhadov, fought Russian forces in or near the mountains, which have always been safe havens for guerrillas, lawbreakers and rebels. Chechen small-unit attacks diminished and were gradually replaced by mine warfare. The IED was, according to many Chechen combatants, their only effective weapon and tactic. Many combatants found it distasteful but nonetheless necessary. Periodic strikes against the new regime in Grozny were occasionally conducted, but the decreasing number of these attacks, plus their limited success

and combat power, caused the Russians to declare publicly that the Chechen insurgency was incapable and a spent force.

Until summer 2002 Isa was commander of the Southwestern Front. However, sometime during the summer Doku Umarov was named commander of the Southwestern Front. Still, Isa's units remained active in the area.[12] In 2002 Isa was summoned to the Vedeno area for a meeting with President Maskhadov and the other commanders. "I traveled through the mountains to this meeting, where we finalized a plan to seize several villages, including some in the Southwestern Front. Maskhadov assigned me to seize the villages of Shalazhi, Gekhi-Chu and Roshni-Chu. Other commanders were going to seize other villages in their sectors. We were ordered to hold the villages for 24 hours."

Geographically, the southern edges of the villages were nearest to the mountains. Shalazhi was almost nestled into the hills, giving the Chechens an initial advantage, since they were able to use the forested heights for concealment and cover. Isa combined many small groups as he organized his men into a force of 300 to 400 combatants. "In order to capture three villages and hold them, that size of a force is needed. For larger operations, we quickly combine smaller groups." He then split the large force into three independent commands and prepared them for a coordinated attack on all three villages. Isa established his own command post at a position from which he could look down on the villages. "We assigned a group to the Roshni-Chu area, one to Shalazhi, and a third group to Gekhi-Chu. I was in the center in order to control everything. I wanted to see and control all of the troops."

Isa positioned snipers on the heights near all three villages to target the Russian and pro-Russian Chechen personnel in the villages. Isa claims there were Russian garrisons in all three of the villages on his target list, but other sources indicate that the villages were garrisoned by Chechen special police (OMON), other pro-Kadyrov Chechen forces and a very limited amount of Russian federal forces. However, Russian forces in Shalazhi included a detachment of the Omsk OMON located at a checkpoint set up at the juice bottling plant within the town.

Isa's forces were aware of his internal and external "enemies" in the villages below. "We do not need to conduct reconnaissance in our own territory. Our reconnaissance force consists of the patriots who are always watching the situation and any movement, every minute, every second. In these mountain villages we didn't need it, because we have several dozen people in each village." As for Roshni-Chu, Isa was even more confident, "we had many soldiers that were from Roshni-Chu."

The infiltration and attack began in the evening of 16 August. In Shalazhi the 100 Chechen combatants broke into three main groups. The first group took the prominent heights to direct sniper and mortar fire onto the Russian positions in the village. A second group moved in to attack targets within the village, including the houses of pro-Kadyrov Chechen police and officials. A third group moved north past the village to block off the road and prevent Russian reinforcements from entering the village.

Russian response was immediate but restrained. There were no artillery strikes on the Chechen positions. Instead, Spetsnaz and MVD [Ministry of Internal Affairs] forces rushed to reinforce their compatriots in Shalazhi and cut off Chechen escape routes into the mountains. In the early morning, nine volunteers from the Vologodsky OMON and three BTRs from the 47th MVD Regiment rushed towards besieged Shalazhi from the regional MVD headquarters. The small column was minutes from the village

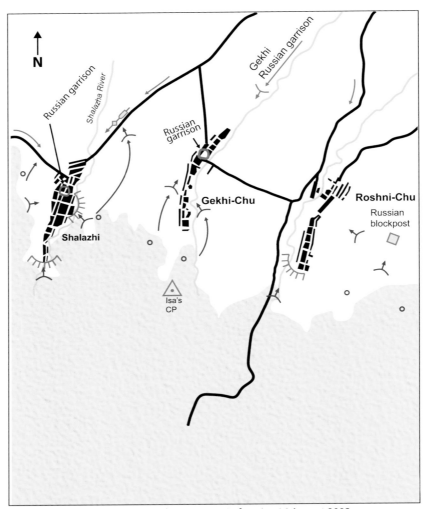

Chechens attack ring of villages along mountain frontier, 16 August 2002.

outskirts when they saw Chechen combatants moving into position to attack them and stop them from reaching the village.

The column slammed to a halt and began to engage the Chechens on their flank. The lead BTR immediately became separated from the others. The Chechens could not overrun the column, but the Russians could not advance past the Chechen positions. The battle wore on for a couple hours and both sides took casualties. The Russian commander ran out to drag a wounded man out of the line of fire. After tucking him away safely, the commander returned to the fight. He was hit by a sniper's bullet and died on the spot. Shortly afterwards a second convoy of reinforcements arrived, forcing the Chechens to retreat.

Meanwhile another battle in the heart of Shalazhi raged near the Russian garrison at the juice bottling plant. The Chechens had been able to use the houses and their knowledge of the village to get within 30 meters of the Russian post. They did this by flanking the Russians through a nearby lumber yard. Desperate, the Russian OMON commander went on the offensive. From the ground he directed his BTR to crash through the gates of the lumber yard. He then led a 12-man maneuver group through the gate and into the lumber yard. It appeared the Chechens were breaking contact as the OMON forces pressed the advantage. A moment later, the OMON forces stepped into heavy machine-gun crossfire. The soldiers were forced to retreat and the OMON commander was killed moments later.[13]

In nearby Gekhi-Chu, the Chechens initially had a somewhat easier time. There were federal forces around the village, but, according to Isa, "there was no Russian garrison in Gekhi-Chu."

In either case the Chechens seemed to take the village easily, digging in to withstand an inevitable Russian counterattack. As in Shalazhi, local Chechens working for the Kadyrov government were being drawn into the fight while federal forces moved to block the Chechens dug-in around the village perimeter.

Little is known about the battle for Roshni-Chu, but, according to multiple reports and statements in the Russian media, the Chechen forces under Isa's command completely destroyed a Russian checkpoint on the eastern side of the village and were able to hold at least part of the village for the 24-hour period that Maskhadov's order specified.

Commentary: Tactical detail on the action is lacking. While Isa is able to provide operational background and a large-scale picture of the fighting, many additional sources are thankfully available to provide some additional detail regarding the situation in Shalazhi. There is even less information on the situation in Gekhi-Chu, and very little information on the battle for Roshni-Chu, although various sources confirm that there were battles in all three villages. "We held the villages for 24 hours, and left in the evening on the second day. We left with only one wounded and sufficient ammunition and weapons. We then went back into the mountains. You could say that getting back into the mountains was also a successful operation."

The reported numbers of Chechen combatants, numbers of Russians and pro-Russians garrisoned in the villages, and the number of dead on both sides fluctuate wildly. Statements by pro-Kadyrov Chechens claim that 32 Chechen insurgents were killed carrying out the action. Local statements made after the fact honor eight pro-Kadyrov policemen who died, while other reports detail the death of the Russian OMON officers. There is no mention of casualties associated with the reported destruction of the Russian checkpoint east of Roshni-Chu.

The impact of the action is also hard to measure. Though the Chechens did not appear to suffer significant losses, it is unclear how it helped their war effort. Losses on both sides appear to have been minimal. Rather, the entire operation was meant to be psychological or demonstrative in nature. Insurgencies are nasty. Targeting pro-Kadyrov Chechens meant that Chechens were killing Chechens. Isa makes a point of saying that he gave explicit orders not to attack pro-Kadyrov Chechens while in the villages. However, additional sources claim they were attacked. It could be a question of perspective. In most of the additional accounts it is clear that the pro-Kadyrov forces in the villages responded to the insurgent attacks, and that would have put them in the battle at that point. However, other accounts state that the Chechen combatants actively sought out and targeted village administrators and policemen in their homes.

This action stands out in comparison to other Chechen actions against Russian forces that occurred during the wars as a result of circumstance or opportunity. In this case the operation was planned and was carried out across a broad front. The Chechen commanders met in council to plan out the attacks. Even the information arm of the Chechen resistance was involved. From the initial moments of the battle the Chechen website, Kavkazcenter.net, under the direction of Movladi Udugov, pushed out its own version of events to counter Russian or Kadyrov statements.

Incidentally, Kadyrov got it right. He claimed the coordinated attacks were not carried out to seize and hold the villages for any length of time. Rather, he called the whole exercise a stunt to demonstrate the insurgency's ability to conduct military operations.

According to Isa, the attacks were carried out because the Russians had been saying that the Chechen insurgency "was combat incapable." The operation was designed to refute that appraisal.

Tactically, the fighting demonstrated that each town was a separate fight and the insurgents were only able to support the fight in their sector. Isa apparently did not have a reserve or supporting firepower, so his role was reduced to communications, supply and an attempt to coordinate the actions of three separate commands. The Russians showed restraint in the use of airpower and artillery, since many of the Chechens in these towns did not support the insurgent cause. After a brief occupation, the Chechens withdrew in good order and the war moved back to the mountains.

Chapter Nine Summary
The Chechens seldom rehearsed their attacks before they conducted them. Consequently, coordination among units and with fire support often developed avoidable glitches. Successful attacks required logistics support if the Chechens were going to hold onto their gains. The Chechen logistics system was village-based and not always up to the challenge of maintaining a force following a successful attack. This was particularly true if the attacking force was not from the area. Often, the combatants arrived on the objective with little food, water or ammunition, and these were slow in arriving. If the attacking unit intended to stay for any period of time, they needed shovels, sandbags, firewood, bedding and other basics – again depending on a stressed logistics system.

Large-scale Chechen attacks, such as the attack on Grozny, required much planning and were high-risk options, since they exposed so much of the Chechen combat power to destruction. Their purpose was primarily political. By the time that the Chechens moved into guerrilla warfare, their ability to conduct significant attacks had diminished considerably.

10
SHELLING AND SNIPING ATTACKS

Early in the war, the Chechens conducted shelling attacks with artillery, mortars and rockets, but as the war continued, Chechen ammunition supplies dwindled. Initially, Chechen attacks were against Russian compounds, outposts and checkpoints, but the targets became more selective as the Chechens husbanded their ammunition for high-value targets. The Russians were quite effective in finding and destroying Chechen artillery and rocket launchers, so the later Chechen shelling attacks were mostly with mortars. In a pinch, the Chechens also used the ubiquitous RPG-7 antitank grenade launcher. Depending on the type round, it will self-destruct 900–1,000 meters from launch. The Chechens would "stand-off" this distance from the Russians and fire elevated rounds so that the rounds would explode in air bursts over the heads of the Russians.

There is more to conducting a shelling attack than setting up a mortar and lobbing rounds at the enemy. Entry into the firing position needs to be surreptitious. Enough ammunition needs to be carried to the firing position, but no more than necessary, since the crew does not carry ammunition when fleeing the area. The crew needs to register the weapon on target before they fire it for effect. This gives the enemy ample warning unless the firing sites have been

surveyed and used before. After the rounds have been fired, the crew has to leave rapidly, with the weapon. Since mortar barrels get very hot during firing, this can be an adventure in itself.

Sniper actions are also tricky. Snipers need to operate covertly and need a spotter and security. Weapons with telescopic sights are great, except that slight bumps will destroy sight alignment. Most manuals recommend that, after transporting a weapon with a telescopic sight over rough terrain, the firer confirm that the sight picture is still accurate by firing several rounds to confirm the "battlefield zero." Snipers do not have that luxury. Naturally, snipers prefer to engage high-value targets after all the work they do getting into position and then waiting. Radio operators, crew-served weapons gunners and officers were the prime targets, but after a long period of time any Russian soldier would do.

The vignettes that follow are from the second war and show the selective nature of Chechen targeting.

Vignette 29: Mortar attack on Russian armor position, sometime between December 1999 and Mid-January 2000

Vakha

Background: The Russian Army had established an extensive operating base on an elevated plain west of the Kirova housing area. The position offered commanding views of Kirova, Aldi, Chernorechie and other suburbs of western Grozny. The terrain was barren, offering no concealment and affording the Russians extensive fields of fire. The location was also impervious to frontal assault from the wooded area and tree-lined streets of Kirova, as potential attackers would have to scale the height in plain sight to get to the Russian positions above. It was a near-perfect location for a division or brigade headquarters, although the position was vulnerable to sniping and indirect fire.

Isa Manaev's group, operating in the Aldi, Kirova, Chernorechie areas, often broke up into smaller detachments to carry out specific missions, including mortar attacks. One of Manaev's soldiers, Ruslan, was an excellent mortar man. It is unclear where Ruslan gained his expertise – he may have had previous mortar experience in the Soviet Army. He operated a homemade light mortar that he had fashioned himself from an existing mortar tube with rusting supports and missing base plate. He used two pieces of rebar to construct a makeshift bi-pod and welded on an additional piece of metal that served as the base plate. In Ruslan's hands, it was a reliable system and he became very proficient with the weapon. It is unclear what size rounds he was using, but Vakha recalls that they were hard to come by. Ruslan was always in search of more ammunition.

Manaev's men knew the Kirova housing community well and used this knowledge to position spotters in the houses and factory buildings in the area. From his position on the fourth or fifth floor of an industrial building Musa monitored the Russian positions 300–400 meters away. He regularly noticed soldiers digging trenches and fueling stoves with wood. On this particular day he noticed a BTR and Ural truck parked near the ridgeline in plain sight and within

Ruslan's mortar range. Musa radioed headquarters and Ruslan and a mortar detachment were called into action. Musa continued to monitor the Russian position while waiting for the team to get in place. Saydan, a fresh recruit, would man the Krasavchik to draw fire away from Musa, should the Russians identify the mortar position. It was Saydan's first time in battle. Finally, Vakha. would support and cover Saydan with his 5.45mm-caliber assault rifle if necessary.

It did not take long to get ready. Musa positioned his mortar to the right of Ruslan, perhaps a bit closer than 300 meters to the Russian position. Saydan was roughly halfway between Musa and Ruslan with the Krasavchik to provide covering fire for Ruslan to retreat if necessary. Finally, Vakha. was close to Saydan and the machine gun. "My job was to cover the Krasavchik if necessary. All team members took advantage of the terrain, foliage and buildings to find appropriate concealment."

Ruslan dropped the first round into the tube. He had only 13 rounds and he wanted each one to count. Musa called it in, "8 meters to the right!" Ruslan adjusted and put another round in the tube – it was a dud. Quickly he put another round in the tube. Off it went and Musa again corrected his fire. The rounds were "right on target," radioed Musa. Ruslan fired all 13 rounds but four were duds, so only nine were effective. Musa continued to watch the target area as the team began to displace. The Russian position was a flurry of action. Both the BTR and the Ural were burning. Musa observed many dead and wounded.

The whole action took only a few minutes and the group prepared to displace from their individual positions. Ruslan had packed up the mortar and began to retreat when he was surprised by PK fire coming from Saydan's location. Vakha was startled as well and turned in time to see Saydan running toward the hillside firing up at the Russian position yelling, "let's storm them." This was not in the plan and, desperate to get his attention, Vakha picked up a rock and threw it at Saydan yelling, "what are you, crazy, abnormal?" Saydan continued to run up the hill until he emptied his ammo can. Realizing his vulnerability, he quickly reversed course, running back down the hill to the safety of the wooded area and the Kirova housing settlement. Remarkably, Saydan and the others were not hit by Russian fire, but they were forced to take extra precautions

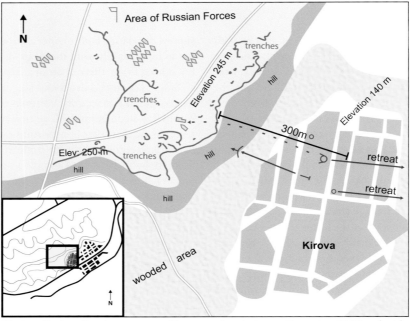

Mortar attack on Russian armor position sometime between December 1999 and mid-January 2000.

retreating from their positions. After a hasty retreat, Vakha did not know whether to laugh or curse, "the intent was to not give away our position – and then Saydan starts running up the hill firing and yelling at the Russians!"

Commentary: The mortar attack ended well for the Chechens despite Saydan's breaking ranks to attack the Russians on his own. Saydan had only recently joined the insurgency after the Russians killed his wife and children, and he lost himself temporarily in his zeal to strike back at the Russians. These types of events happened often among the Chechen combatants, many joining the fight after a traumatizing event like the death of a family member. This occurrence is significant because the Russians claimed during the first war that the Chechens were a better-trained force. This may have been true for a small but significant cadre of soldiers and militia, including Shamil Basaev and Ruslan Galaev and the soldiers under them who had fought in Abkhazia prior to the war with Russia. However, Saydan personifies the other half of the Chechen resistance, those who join the war effort because they have lost everything. They are poorly trained, if at all, and have emotional issues that can destabilize an operation. Vakha notes that Saydan was very old to be fighting with them, 44 years old.

The mortar itself is a mystery. Some Chechens claimed they manufactured homemade mortars and rocket launchers from various materials, including the drive shaft casing from KAMAZ trucks.[1] Others claim to have done the same with the drive shaft covers from ZIL trucks. Mortars and other weapons were also said to have been made during the interwar years, 1996–1999, in the half-destroyed Krasnyi Molot and Elektropribor factories and in the Pischemash factory in Argun.[2]

Vakha's account does not put much emphasis on Russian return fire. The fact that all four members of the mortar detachment were able to successfully retreat might suggest the Russians were unprepared to respond or simply did not have any way to locate the mortar position. Russian counterbattery radar was not utilized, but with these systems it is always a question of the unit being turned on, calibrated and pointed in the proper direction. If Ruslan's mortar was smaller than an 82-mm mortar, counter-mortar radar would have difficulty acquiring the shot and trajectory. The Soviets used a 50-mm mortar during World War II. Vakha remembers the raid lasting 10 to 12 minutes. Saydan's run towards the base of the hill firing would surely give the Russians a chance to fire on him effectively. Still, he was able to retreat under fire and get away with the rest of the detachment.

Vignette 30: Sniping attack on a Russian senior officer, sometime between December 1999 and January 2000

Vakha

Background: The high plateau west of Kirova was the perfect staging point for the Russian forces advancing into Grozny from the west. At 250 meters above sea level, it sat nearly 100 meters above the Kirova housing settlement below. Beyond the Kirova settlement lay the vast belt of industrial factories. More than a kilometer away the Chechens positioned themselves on the higher floors of these buildings to observe the Russian positions and snipe at them when feasible. Russian tanks positioned on the plateau fired on the Chechen positions when they could find them.

Zhelen lay in the ruins of the attic in a cottage that had taken a tank round some time earlier. He peered through his binoculars. He counted 120 pieces of Russian armor in various positions. It seemed the whole Russian Army lay before him. Although he had never set foot on the Russian position, he knew it well, as he'd had "eyes on" the target for weeks. In the next building on the third floor lay Musa, a sniper. Musa peered through the scope of his SVD sniper rifle through the branches of a tree growing up past the window. The men in the unit teased him about his rifle because he treated it like a baby. He would not let anyone touch it and he was constantly caring for it. Some time ago it had fallen out of his hand during a narrow escape and was banged up. Vakha and the others were impressed with Musa's effort to fix it.

Vakha and his friend Timor were also in the building, on the same floor with Musa. Their job was to cover the corners. They also peered out towards the Russian position, but it was 1,100 meters away. Between them and the plateau lay Kirova and then a strip of woods. To the rear of the building were three exterior stairwells. They planned on exiting the building down these stairwells and out through another partially destroyed building directly behind them.

Vakha is not sure who noticed it first, but Zhelen and Musa were talking to each other over the radio and seemed to be excited. The

Shamil Basaev (left) and Aslan Maskhadov (right) during the Second Chechen War, sometime before January 2000 when Basaev lost a foot during the failed withdrawal from Grozny. (Photo via Efim Sandler)

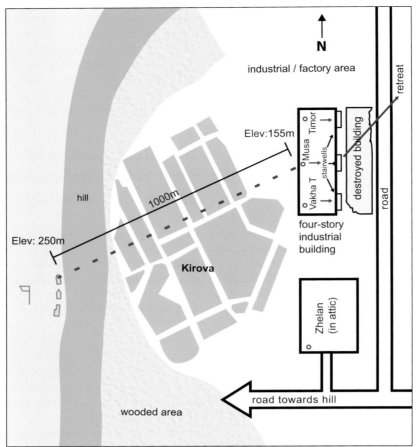

Sniping attack on a Russian senior officer, sometime between December 1999 and January 2000.

Russian camp had just come alive with the arrival of a UAZ, a BTR, and a Ural truck. Soldiers stumbled out of their tents and dugouts, some were still putting their boots on. Others were tucking in their shirts and buttoning jackets. "This guy has to be important" Zhelen thought. The figure stepped out of his vehicle and both Zhelen and Musa recognized the wide red stripes of a general officer down the sides of his pants. Apparently he had come to present something to someone, but had put himself in plain sight of Musa and his beloved SVD sniper rifle.

Musa compensated for the distance, 15, 20 centimeters. He fired a single shot and the officer slumped down. Vakha recalls, "he crashed like a spineless animal, like a snake or an invertebrate." Musa fired a second round at the general's body slumped on the ground. There was no lingering to celebrate the kill. Musa jumped back from his position and raced to the back of the building. He met Vakha and Timor on the second floor as they made their way to the back of the floor and down the stairwell. They felt the building take the impact of a tank round. Pieces of concrete and brick showered down over them. They continued to run down the stairwells as another tank round hit the building. In a moment they were off the stairwell, running across the broken heap that was once the building behind them.

Commentary: All four of the Chechen combatants involved in the sniping incident were able to withdraw successfully from their positions. This was a particularly successful operation not only because they were able to kill a Russian general, but also because they had only been in their position for two hours. Sometimes they would stay in their positions for days waiting for a target to materialize. "Usually you have to wait for an opportunity like that,

sometimes for days, and still nothing happens." recalls Vakha. Musa often spent weeks looking for noteworthy targets without ever firing a shot.

The Russians were able to pinpoint Musa's location quickly, likely on the second shot. Vakha thinks it could not have been more than 20 seconds before incoming fire destroyed the third floor. Vakha went back to the location the next day to survey the building. The holes in the wall were over two meters in diameter. There was concrete rubble strewn about.

Chapter Ten Summary

Logistics was a major problem for the Chechens during both wars. Although there was some outside financial support from fundamentalist Islamic groups in the Middle East, there was no external logistics support organization across the border providing ammunition, medical care, maintenance support and the like. At the start of the first war the Chechens were fairly well supplied with heavy weapons, small arms, vehicles and ammunition, but they had no surviving organization providing replacements for destroyed, captured and broken weapons and equipment and certainly no ammunition-manufacturing facilities or external supplies of ammunition. Over time the Chechens became a less robust force with far-fewer heavy weapons and combatants. Shelling and sniping attacks were one way of striking back at the enemy and contesting turf, but the Chechens lacked the ability to follow this up with a concerted effort. The conversion from a conventional force backed

by local militias to a guerrilla force is difficult, and the Chechen resistance clearly had problems. Shifting to guerrilla warfare is a confession of weakness, and, as the enemy keeps the pressure on, the guerrilla force has difficulty improving and growing.

11
CONCLUSIONS

The first post-Soviet Russian-Chechen War pitted a larger, poorly-supported, poorly-trained modern mechanized force against a smaller and motivated force backed by village and neighborhood militias (primarily light infantry). The Chechens defended Grozny, concentrating on mobile strong points covering the central Presidential Palace. After the Russians pushed them out of Grozny they then took the fight to various urban centers. The Chechens started the conflict with a good supply of modern weapons and ammunition, but, as the conflict continued, the major weapons systems and vehicles broke down or were captured or destroyed. Ammunition stores dwindled and the Chechen National Guard (regular army) and militias began to blend into a generic light infantry, backed by local food, medical and repair facilities. Chechen "battalions" were often platoon-sized. Still, following a successful March 1996 reconnaissance by force into Grozny, the Chechens withdrew and then again infiltrated into Grozny, surrounded the Russian garrisons and began a campaign of multiple sieges within the capital city in August 1996. The Russians were not in mutually supporting positions. Moscow finally negotiated for withdrawal and granted Chechnya its independence.

Thus, the first post-Soviet Russian-Chechen War ended with a Russian withdrawal and a putative Chechen victory. However, the ability to win the peace and govern themselves eluded the Chechens. There was no plan to run the government and society when the shooting stopped. Massive unemployment and lawlessness defined the young men's roles and kidnapping for ransom became an accepted activity among many of the former combatants. The divisions in Chechen society, which had been papered over by the presence of the Russian occupiers, were now all too visible. During the first war, the President's command over the National Guard was tenuous at best. The various National Guard commanders retained a great deal of autonomy. They had united out of necessity, but historically the Chechens seldom unite unless they are fighting a war. *Adat* kept Chechen society together, but years of war eroded this societal infrastructure.[1]

The Russians were much better prepared for the second post-Soviet Russian-Chechen War. They had added a supporting rail line in neighboring Dagestan, their supply and maintenance posture was greatly improved and the troops were better trained and equipped. They brought overwhelming firepower and forces. The Chechens, on the other hand, were left with their weapons from the previous war and little ammunition. Maskhadov's government had enough other problems without reconstituting the police and armed forces, which had not previously been responsive to government demands.

The Chechens intended to fight the Russians in the same manner as during the first war – first a defensive battle of attrition in Grozny, then a shift to fight further defensive battles in the other urban centers. This fit their light infantry force. The Russians intended to let the Chechens fight this very war – concentrating their forces into urban kill zones where massive, prolonged aviation and artillery strikes would annihilate the Chechen forces from a distance before they systematically reduced the urban areas. The Chechen forces were decimated during the retreat from Grozny and further reduced in the ensuing smaller urban fights. As Vedeno, the Wolf's Gate, and other strategic positions fell, the Chechens reverted to local guerrilla

warfare and terrorist attacks into Russia. The Russians pursued the Chechens into the mountains and, in 2009, proclaimed that the counterinsurgency campaign was over. The war was not over – it was just much lower key and had spread across the region into Dagestan and Ingushetia.

Technology
The Russians mostly used tried and true technology. Their aviation and artillery strikes were delivered by cold war systems except for some large-caliber mortars which they introduced. Europe experienced its largest and longest artillery barrages since World War II. Artillery-delivered fuel-air explosives were used for the first time in combat on European soil. Tanks and infantry fighting vehicles were legacy systems, but effective. During the Second Russian-Chechen War, the Russians introduced new small arms for the close urban fight – replacing the supersonic, light-weight 5.45mm bullets with 7.62mm rounds that would penetrate load-bearing walls and not ricochet around the room. Combat shotguns, urban sniper rifles, flame projectors, modern breaching rounds and other modern tools were issued to the infantry soldiers.

The Chechens had no reliable source of new armaments or ammunition. They used what they could capture, manufacture or purchase from corrupt Russian servicemen. They built antitank launchers, land mines and blast mines (improvised explosive devices or IEDs, in the current parlance). Internationalist money was important, but without a friendly border over which weapons and ammunition could enter, Chechen technology was limited – and became more so as the wars progressed and supplies and materials diminished.

Role of Military Professionals
The Russian Army was considerably hampered by the lack of a professional NCO corps. The fight was carried on the backs of teenaged conscripts and slightly older lieutenants. The Russian Army had not adopted their hard-won lessons learned fighting an insurgency in the mountains of Afghanistan. The Russian Army leadership used a conventional war approach, even when the Chechens reverted to guerrilla war.[2] Only in the second war, as the Russian Army got better, did they use rigorous small-unit patrolling by airborne, air assault, and Spetsnaz forces to push into the mountains and contest and interdict the insurgent lines of communication, supply and retreat. The failures of the first war brought a willingness to rebuild and retrain the bankrupt post-Cold War army and adapt to the lessons of the first war.

There were few military professionals in the Chechen ranks. Most of these were former Soviet military or National Guard commanders. Still, most Chechen males had served conscript service with the Soviet Army and were familiar with weapons and rudimentary tactics. Many had even served on the Soviet side of the Soviet-Afghan War and proudly showed their medals and decorations to anyone who would show interest. Others had gained combat experience in Abkhazia in 1992–1993. Chechen units were most effective at the platoon-size level (30 to 40 men), where the personality of the commander drove the unit. It was not an army of rules, regulations or tables of organization and equipment. The few real military professionals rose to prominence, primarily in major staff positions. This fact hampered the Chechen war effort repeatedly.

Tactics

The Russians preferred to dominate the plains with their mechanized forces and engage the enemy with artillery and aviation. The RPG-7 was an effective antitank weapon and the Russians used preparatory fires to destroy or disrupt these gunners before they moved within close combat range. Once the war entered the mountain guerrilla phase the Russians engaged heavily in winter campaigning. The forests of Chechnya are largely deciduous and guerrillas could be detected and tracked when the ground was bare or snow-covered.

All warfare, guerrilla or conventional, is about controlling one's own lines of communication, supply, advance and retreat while threatening those of the enemy. On the plains, roads and urban areas, the Russians established control using fortified permanent and mobile control points (*blokpost*) and raids. The Russians became adept at identifying key mountain terrain (roads, passes, water-crossing points and high ground controlling these). They would seize and garrison these with elite forces and then dispatch patrols to interdict guerrilla lines and ambush guerrilla groups. Mountain guerrilla warfare is dependent on fixed bases. When the Russians identified guerrilla mountain bases, they used airstrikes, artillery and raids to deal with these priority objectives.

During the first war, the Russians preferred contiguous lines and predictable, methodological advances. This led to a series of bloody frontal attacks against defending forces in urban terrain. In the second war, the Russians began holding the defending Chechen force in place with a limited attack while bypassing this defense to capture an objective beyond the Chechen defense. This would unhinge the Chechen defense and provide an opportunity for Russian aviation and artillery to punish the bypassed, retreating Chechens. The Russians continued this leapfrogging until they had small garrisons holding key terrain along the southern mountain border with Georgia.

The site of an ambush of the 451st Motor Rifle Regiment on 26 April 2000. This was one of a myriad of such ambushes that haunted Russian forces well into the 2000s. The hit-and-run tactics in woods and mountains worked well, though they never stopped Russian forces. (Efim Sandler collection)

A BMP-2 of ODON (Separate Operational Division, also known as 1st Division of Dzherzhinsky), destroyed by an IED on 18 March 2001. (Photo via Efim Sandler)

The main Chechen tactics were the defense, raid, and ambush. The Chechens rapidly learned the value of prepared defenses, covered zigzag trenches, obstacles, railroad embankments, river lines and a predictable enemy. Except for the spectacular raids described in the history chapter, Chechen raids were usually semi-rehearsed small-unit actions within a few kilometers of the starting point. The ambush became the mainstay of Chechen tactics. It was used to slow Russian advances, inflict damage and supply the Chechen force. Still, the Chechen ambushes never developed the organization and effectiveness of the Mujahideen ambushes that the Soviets experienced in Afghanistan. The Chechens were never lacking in courage or audacity. They all wanted to be in the assault group, never the support group or covering force. They often lacked the patience, discipline and cohesion necessary for effective ambushes. There were notable exceptions, including al Khattab's ambush and destruction of an entire Russian armored battalion in spring 1995 and Musa's ambush on the road to Vedeno as described in chapter four.

As a rule, in the usual tactical fight (company, platoon and below) the Chechen combatants were older and more experienced than their Russian opponents. Many were veterans of the Soviet Army, some of Afghanistan, and some of the fighting in Abkhazia. The maturity of the Chechen force was often a deciding factor when two equally-matched forces met. The Russians preferred to keep the Chechens at least 300 meters away (out of the range of the AK-47 and the RPG-7 against a moving target). The Chechens, however, tried to "hug" the Russian forces whenever possible so that they could use their RPGs while avoiding Russian artillery and aviation supporting fire.

Logistics

Tactics determines battles while logistics determines campaigns. The Russian logistics structure for the first post-Soviet Russian-Chechen War was inadequate, especially for the initial urban slugfest in Grozny. The Russians had their logistics in order for the second war and even added an additional rail line from Kizliyar to Karlan Yurt in Dagestan. This line paid dividends in support capacity during the second war. The Russian side had what they needed when they needed it and guerrilla ambushes never seriously slowed the logistics delivery.

The Chechen logistics system was based on the local village or region, which supplied food, medical support, lodging and some maintenance. The Chechens started the first war with an impressive collection of tanks, artillery, personnel carriers, mortars and logistics stockpiles that the departing federal forces had left behind. These were expended during the first four months of fighting. The Chechens had no way to replace weapons or expended ammunition. Limited "garage-manufactured" weapon production helped, but the Chechens fought most of the wars with inadequate stocks of ammunition and working weapons. International aid, mostly in the form of Salafi money, was important, but there was no access to an outside source of ammunition and weapons. Some venal Russian soldiers sold ammunition, weapons, fuel and medicine to the Chechens (usually through a child intermediary), but this was never enough to sustain the Chechen effort beyond one or two tactical engagements. Any Chechen hope of support from the West died after the Beslan hostage-taking raid.

Guerrillas cannot live off of the land – and do anything else. Survival is a full-time job. Guerrillas can live off of the local population, but the Russians became better at buying up surplus crops at premium prices in critical areas and otherwise denying the guerrilla access to the locals. Russia's move to install a former insurgent, Kadyrov, to rule Chechnya pitted Chechen against Chechen, severely undermining the population's support of the insurgency. Further, locals can provide food and shelter, but they cannot provide mortar ammunition. In the final equation, guerrilla logistics often ended up as a family matter, and Chechnya was full of Tolstoy's "unhappy families."[3]

BIBLIOGRAPHY

Akhmadov, Ilyas and Miriam Lanskoy, *The Chechen Struggle: Independence Won and Lost* (New York: St. Martins's Press, 2010)

Babchenko, Arkady, *One Solders War* (London: Portobello Books, 2007)

Baiev, Khassan, Ruth Daniloff, and Nicholas Daniloff, *The Oath: A Surgeon Under Fire* (New York: Walker Publishing, 2003)

Bodansky, Yoseff, *Chechen Jihad, Al Qaeda's Training Ground and the Next Wave of Terror* (New York: HarperCollins Publishers, 2007)

Dudayev, Umalt, "Chechnya's Homemade Weapons Fuel War: Rebels are using improvised and home-made weapons to continue their guerrilla war," *CRS* Issue 227, Institute of War and Peace Reporting, 21 February 2005.

Efimov, M. et al., *Chechenskaya voyna: Rabota nad oshibkami* [The Chechen War: Working on the Mistakes] (Moscow: EKSMO, 2009)

Gall, Carlotta and Thomas de Waal, *Chechen Calamity in the Caucasus* (London: Macmillan Publishers, 1998)

Hughes, James, *Chechnya: From Nationalism to Jihad* (Philadelphia: University of Pennsylvania Press, 2007)

Isby, David C., *Weapons and Tactics of the Soviet Army* (London: Jane's Publishing, 1981)

Knezys, Stasys and Romanas Sedlickas, *The War in Chechnya* (College Station, Texas: Texas A&M University, 1999)

Kulikov, General Anatoly Sergeevich. Appendix B, "The First Battle of Grozny." Russian Ministry of Internal Affairs briefing in Olga Oliker's *Russia's Chechen Wars 1994–2000: Lessons from Urban Combat* (Rand, 2001)

Lieven, Anatol, *Chechnya, Tombstone of Russian Power* (New Haven, Conn.: Yale University Press, 1999)

Murphy, Paul, *The Wolves of Islam, Russia and the Faces of Chechen Terrorism* (Dulles, Virginia: Potomac Books, 2004)

Nivat, Anne, *Chienne de Guerre: A Woman Reporter Behind the Lines of the War in Chechnya* (New York: Public Affairs Books, 2001)

Schaefer, Robert W., *The Insurgency in Chechnya and the North Caucasus From Gazavat to Jihad* (Santa Barbara, California: Preager, 2011)

Seierstad, Asne, *The Angel of Grozny, Orphans of a Forgotten War* (Oslo: J.W. Cappelens Forlag, 2007)

Smith, Sebastian, *Allah's Mountains: The Battle for Chechnya* (London: I.B. Tauris, 2001)

Documentary Films

Chechnya: Separatism or Jihad?. Dir. Dodge Billingsley. Combat Films and Research for The David M. Kennedy Center at Brigham Young University, 2004.

Immortal Fortress: Inside Chechnya's Warrior Culture. Dir. Dodge Billingsley. Combat Films and Research, 1999.

NOTES

Preface

1   See Lester W. Grau, *The Bear Went over the Mountain: Soviet Combat Tactics in Afghanistan*, Washington: National Defense University Press, 1994; Ali Ahmad Jalali and Grau, *The Other Side of the Mountain: Mujahideen Tactics in the Soviet-Afghan War*, Quantico, Virginia: US Marine Corps Studies and Analysis Division, 1996; and *The Soviet-Afghan War: How a Superpower Fought and Lost*, written by the Russian General Staff with translation and commentary by Grau and Michael Gress, Lawrence: University Press of Kansas, 2001.

Chapter 1

1   Russia officially announced an end to counterterrorist operations in Chechnya on 16 April 2009. However, this admission by the Russian leadership has not stopped the conflict between pro-Moscow Chechen forces under the command of Chechen President Ramzan Kadyrov and insurgent combatants under the command of Doku Umarov.

2   The Khasavyurt Agreement was first signed on 30 August 1996 by Alexander Lebed and Aslan Maskhadov in Khasavyurt Dagestan. A final version of the accord was signed by Boris Yeltsin and Aslan Maskhadov on 12 May 1997 in Moscow.

3   Interestingly, our interpreter, who remained in Chechnya after I left in late December 1997, was kidnapped by Chechens with whom we stayed. He was held in a pit for months, given very little to eat and was beaten and traumatized repeatedly. There was one other person being held with him, an Ossetian, the brother of a well-off Ossetian businessman. On one occasion, the kidnappers cut off the Ossetian's ear and sent it to his brother in Vladikavkaz, seeking a ransom. The wealthy Ossetian appealed to Maskhadov and then Basaev for help securing his brother. Basaev eventually tipped off and his men surrounded the kidnappers' house. After the threat of a gun battle the victims, including our interpreter, were pulled from the cellar. Basaev wasn't even aware that our interpreter was being held and thought that he had just left Chechnya shortly after our departure.

4   I was on the Terek River on that day and could hear the battle, but had no idea what was going on. Shortly after the attack started, we heard Russian helicopters nearby. Eventually, some of the combatants retreated right past us, over a partially destroyed pipeline crossing the river. They told us to leave the area immediately as Russian forces were in pursuit. They expected that the Russian helicopters would fire on anybody in the line of retreat.

5   There was also a set of apartment bombings in Russia that occurred in September 1999. Some analysts and commentators on the war see the hand of Russia's Federal Security Service (FSB) in the bombings, others believe the bombings are the work of al Khattab, and still others see the attacks as distinctly Chechen. Looking at the various sources ascribed to all the conspiracy theories surrounding the bombings, it is evident that each source's theory is a reflection of its long standing position on the Russian-Chechen Wars and, therefore, the individual theories on the bombings must be seen in that context.

6   To ascribe Basaev's notions of a united Caucasus to Islam is tricky. He was known to believe in a trans-Caucasus political entity of some sort as early as 1992. He took his followers to fight in the war in Abkhazia in 1992–1993 and was a supporter of the Confederation of Mountain Peoples of the Caucasus—another organization operating at the time with vague notions of a united Caucasus.

7   Author's conversation with Basaev at his Grozny residence in December 1997.

Chapter 2

1   A rayon is an area or region, a second level subdivision, found in all former Soviet republics and states, including Russia proper.

2   For an inside glimpse of the location of the Chechen command during this part of the war see Ilyas Akhmadov and Miriam Lanskoy, *The Chechen Struggle: Independence Won and Lost* (New York: St. Martins's Press, 2010), p.32.

3   Phone interview with Ilyas Akhmadov, 4 April 2011. Ilyas was well positioned to comment on the battles of the Vedeno front, as he was part of Maskhadov's command at the time.

4   It is unclear exactly where Hill 541.6 is located, but it is likely to the east of Serzhen-Yurt. Seizing it did not provide the Russians easy access to the town, since its western edge is a sheer drop-off, nor did it provide good positions for fire support.

5   Mohmad is the way Chechens traditionally transliterate Mohammad into English.

6   Kair, like many of his contemporaries, cannot recall with accuracy the exact dates of particular events. However, there are numerous Russian and press accounts that corroborate the Russian advance being on 17 May. This timeline also fits with other Chechen accounts.

7   See special vignette in chapter 7 regarding the Shaitan.

8   There is some confusion as to when and where Tutashkh's unit was overrun. Some accounts recall that they were encircled while at their second position near the Zhelimkhan monument the next week in the second Russian push for Serzhen-Yurt (see "Second Phase of the Battle for Serzhen-Yurt").

9   See Knezys, Stasys, and Romanas Sedlickas, *The War in Chechnya*, (College Station, Texas: Texas A&M University, 1999), pp.153–154.

10   The Shmel [Bumblebee] is the RPO rocket-propelled flame projector that can fire a flame canister accurately out to 600 meters. It has a flame, thermobaric, and smoke round.

11   Follow-on phone and skype interviews with Ilyas. Ilyas was well positioned to comment on the battles for Serzhen-Yurt, as he was part of Maskhadov's command in Vedeno at the time.

12   See "Ambush of Russian Column Between Benoi and Vedeno."

13   On 14 June Shamil Basaev led a group of Chechen combatants on a mission into Russia. Posing as a Russian convoy carrying "Cargo 200" (Russian dead) from the war in Chechnya, the convoy was stopped in the Russian town of Budennovsk. There was a shoot-out with Russian police and the Chechens took refuge in the city hospital, taking more than 1,000 hostages. A five day siege resulted. Eventually, after numerous attempts to dislodge the Chechens failed, the Russians agreed to a cease fire in Chechnya and the safe return of Basaev's group to Chechnya. Many Chechens claimed that this event saved the war effort, as it allowed the Chechens to rebuild their strength during the ensuing cease fire, before retaking Grozny for good in August 1996.

14   This date is questionable. Although the combatant in question was quite active during this time, it is possible that his account is a retelling of the battles for Bamut in 1996. There were both significant battles for the village in both 1995 and 1996.

15   I traveled to Bamut after the first war and could not find a single undamaged building or house in the village. Most of the structures had only one or two walls remaining. Russian tanks littered the single road running through the center of the village. Turrets, with their reactive armor still intact, littered the roadside, lying dozens of meters from the hulls of the tanks that lost them. Of all the locations I visited in Chechnya after the first war, only the Grozny city center around the Presidential Palace sustained more damage.

16   There is some discussion of what effective range is for the RPG. All Chechens interviewed considered maximum effective range roughly 500 meters, while other sources consider 300 meters maximum effective range.

17   As with the preceding "Defending Bamut" vignette, it is possible that this is an account of Musa's unit during the battles for Bamut in 1996.

18   The "Mukha" [Fly] is the RPG-18, a short-range, single-shot, disposable light antitank weapon similar to the US M72 LAW (Light Antitank Weapon).

19   First name unknown.

20   Multiple other Chechen sources put the total number of Chechen combatants in the village at around 350 personnel.

21   In addition to Hasmohmad's account, which is more focused on his particular sector, a handful of the Chechen combatants interviewed took part in the battle for Goyskoe, including Isa Manaev. Other former combatants interviewed that were not at the battle but were part of General Maskadov's command staff and were aware of the details include Ilyas Akhmadov and Khuseyn Iskhanov. Additional details are also available at adamalla.com.

22   Khuseyn Iskhanov was a member of General Maskhadov's command staff and, as such, was put in charge of coordinating the two different

Chechen fronts. He made numerous trips across Chechnya in 1996, relaying messages to and from Dudaev, who had command of the western half of the republic, and Maskahdov, who had command of the eastern half. Khuseyn was captured just weeks after the battle of Goyskoe and sent to Moscow. He was released more than a month later as part of a prisoner exchange.

23 This may be the account that spawned the urban legend (possibly true) and led so many in Chechnya to claim that Russian aviation often fired on their own infantry to prod them to battle. Every Chechen to whom I have spoken while in Chechnya and since then claims to know this to be a fact. A full accounting from the Russian side is necessary to validate these claims. Or could the helicopter attacks on Russian armor have been a case of friendly fire? As farfetched as it may sound, there is precedent found in the US invasion of Iraq in March 2003. Advancing to the Line of Departure, or the Iraqi border, Alpha Co tanks attached to 3/7 Marines were struck and disabled by Hellfire missiles fired from Marine Corps Cobra attack helicopters. This occurred while still in Kuwait, before the tanks even reached the Iraqi border.

24 Another reason Chechens put forward for the three-day pause is that, in defiance of orders, the regimental commander of the 324th Motorized Rifle Regiment refused to lead his men to storm the village and was replaced. This has not been verified from Russian sources.

25 The commanders of the three groups forced to retreat were Dikaev, Hamid, and Magamadov.

26 Russian order of battle is not fully accounted for and nor are their total losses. Chechen sources and claims based on testimonies of captured Russian soldiers, estimate two entire motorized companies destroyed by the end of operations on 4 April.

Chapter 3

1 GAI (*Gosydarstvennaya Avtomobil'naya Inspekhtsiya*) is the State motor-vehicle inspectorate, which had permanent police traffic control sites located at key intersections inside and outside of cities.

2 Khassan Baiev, Ruth Daniloff, and Nicholas Daniloff, *The Oath: A Surgeon Under Fire* (New York: Walker Publishing), p.293.

3 There are many accounts of the bloody withdrawal from Grozny. Many of them are at odds with each other regarding various parts of the story, including the route chosen and whether or not there was a prior deal with the Russians in which the Chechens were misled or double-crossed. However, no Chechen combatant I have met who participated in the withdrawal believes that any communication or deal had been arranged with the Russians. For a good account of the aftermath in the city of Alkhan-Yurt see *The Oath* by Khassan Baiev, and *Chienne de Guerre* by Anne Nivat.

4 Isa is referring to the *Tambovskaya Otdelnaya Brigada Spetsialnogo Naznacheniya* [Tambov Separate Special Designation Brigade], the legendary 16th Spetznaz Brigade formed on January 1st, 1963.

Chapter 4

1 This Russian unit is likely part of the 129th Motorized Rifle Regiment (1,619 men, 40 tanks, 6 BMPs, 70 BTRs, 11 BRDMs, 15 mortars). It was part of the group "Vostok" [East].

2 The AKS is a folding stock version of the AK-74. The AKS was originally issued to airborne forces and vehicle crews, since the folding stock shortened its length by 10 inches until it was ready to be used.

3 Novyy Tsentoroy [New Tsentoroy] is a relatively new development and does not show up on many Chechen maps. It was built to provide housing to victims of an earthquake that occurred in Chechnya in the mid 1980s. Since there is already a village of Tsentoroy, the settlement was named Novyy [New] Tsentoroy.

4 The *Grad* [Hail] is the BM-21 Multiple Launcher System that fires 40 122mm rockets before it requires reloading. It is an effective area-fire weapon. The Chechens often referred to the 122mm round as the Grad.

5 Musa cannot recall when the event occurred, but press reports put the Russian tanks on the square and the Chechen command still in the Presidential Palace on 10 January. Chechen General Maskhadov gave the order to evacuate the Palace on 18 January, and the last fighters exited the building during the early morning hours on 19 January.

6 The PK machine gun can be fitted with ammo belts of 100, 200, or 250 rounds. Elimpash said his had a rectangle box that had either 90 or 110 rounds. He said he didn't take much ammo with him. There are different PK models, the PKM (Modernized Kalashnikov Machine Gun) and PKT (Tank Kalashnikov Machine Gun) use the

aforementioned ammo boxes. Elimpash states that his machine gun wasn't heavy; only seven kilograms – which, incidentally, is about how much the PKM weighs (7.5 kilograms without ammo. The PKT weighs 10.5 kilograms). It appears that Elimpash carried a PKM.

7 The artillery piece in question is likely the D-30 122mm. Pre-war analysis concludes the Chechens under Dudaev were in control of some 80 D-30s previously taken/bought/acquired from existing Russian/Soviet bases in Chechen territory.

8 Usually Russian tank crews kept one man in the vehicle in defensive positions unless they were on full alert. A Russian tank is not roomy nor comfortable and the crew rested in shifts outside the tank.

Chapter 5

1 Ilyas Akhmadov, in his book *The Chechen Struggle: Independence Won and Lost*, recalls this feature of the Chechen resistance vividly, describing units that would leave their assigned positions just because they thought they could get into more action against Russian forces elsewhere or because they were bored. This fact was also highlighted in additional interviews I conducted with former Chechen combatants who chose to defend Staryye and Novyye Atagi against President Dudaev and General Maskhadov's orders to give up the plains and retreat to the defensive safety of the mountains following the Chechen withdrawal from Grozny.

2 Normally the scouts would have traveled a kilometer or so ahead of the main column. Musa makes no mention of being in position and waiting for the scout vehicle to pass. Rather he talks as though he was concerned that he would run into scouts even days before the main column traveled the road. He might have been referring to reconnaissance elements rather than scouts. In any case, he seemed perplexed, but happy, that he never saw the scouts on the day of the ambush or before.

3 The AK-47 and AKM Kalashnikov fire the 7.62mm round. The AK-74 fires the 5.45mm round.

4 The GP-25 40mm grenade has a maximum range of 400 meters.

5 Seventy-seven pounds.

6 Isa recalls the exact date to be August 27, 2004. However, this may not be accurate as his memory of dates is not good. Other actions he was involved in are verifiable via additional sources, including Russian, but in almost every case he is off by a year or two.

7 "It is reported that a massacre of over 100 people, mainly civilians, occurred between 7 and 8 April 1995 in the village of Samashki, in the west of Chechnya. According to the accounts of 128 eye-witnesses, Federal soldiers deliberately and arbitrarily attacked civilians and civilian dwellings in Samashki by shooting residents and burning houses with flame-throwers. The majority of the witnesses reported that many OMON troops (Chechen government special police] were drunk or under the influence of drugs. They wantonly opened fire or threw grenades into basements where residents, mostly women, elderly persons and children, had been hiding." (Bold face type in original.) Commission on Human Rights, Fifty-second session, *The situation of human rights in the Republic of Chechnya of the Russian Federation: Report of the Secretary-General*, 26 March 1996, paragraphs 58 and 59.

8 The VSS Vintorez is a special operations weapon with an integral silencer. It fires the 9x39 subsonic cartridge with a 16 gram bullet to maximum effective range of 400 meters. It is designed for urban and forest stealth actions and was very popular with Spetsnaz and OMON forces.

Chapter 6

1 Khasbulatov and Labazanov formed an alliance earlier the same year when Khasbulatov felt he needed a local armed force.

2 Sheikh is not an artilleryman and cannot recall what these actual guns were; rather he knew it only as a "mountain gun." The M-99 is a likely candidate, as it was assigned to the Soviet units stationed in the Caucasus and abandoned during their withdrawal. However, Sheikh may also have been describing the Ch-26 57mm antitank gun that was also widely available.

3 Sheikh does not recall the name of the artillery commander, but confirms that he was killed at a later battle during the first war.

4 Sheikh is again unsure what type of gun it was. He did state that a ten-man crew manned the gun and that it was capable of traversing two or three meters in either direction left to right. It was most likely a D-30 122mm howitzer. Russian commanders have estimated that the Chechens were in control of up to 80 of these systems, left behind in

Chechnya after the collapse of the Soviet Union. See *Russia's Chechen Wars 1994–2000: Lessons from Urban Combat*, Appendix B, "The First Battle of Grozny," General Anatoly Sergeevich Kulikov, Russian Ministry of Internal Affairs, Rand, p.39.

5   Ruslan Labazanov reportedly had 300–400 combatants with him. He claimed up to 600 followers at one point.

6   The UAZ-469 is a rugged 4X4 "Jeep" that the Ural Automobile Factory produced for military and civilian use. It is affectionately known as the UAZik.

7   The DGB was the Department of State Security of the Republic of Ichkeria, roughly equivalent to the KGB. It was Dudayev's secret police.

8   Normally a Fagot antitank team would consist of three personnel, primarily to help carry the rounds. However in many cases the Chechens operated these weapons with one or two men depending on location, the need to displace, and number of warheads required. Kair can't recall exactly but thought that he only had two Fagot rounds with him on the day of the attack.

9   The "Podstvolnik" is similar to the 40mm GP-25 and GP-30, which are designed to attach to the Kalashnikov assault rifle. The sights for the GP-25 are on the left side and the GP-30 on the right side. The GP-25 is designed for direct and indirect fire (out to 400 meters) while the GP-30 has only a direct-fire capability. The Podstvolnik is a rifled, single shot, front-loading caseless 40mm grenade projector which arms at 40 meters and is accurate out to 150 meters and has a lethal bursting radius of five meters.

10   Either the MON-50 or the MON-100 antipersonnel mines. The MON-50 is very similar to the US Claymore mine, while the MON-100 is a larger version. Neither is effective against armored vehicles.

11   The GAZ-66 is a rugged, light-utility two-ton, 4X4 truck produced by the Gorky Automobile Plant.

Chapter 7

1   Vitali Noskov, *"Sneg na brone," Chechenskaya voyna: Boevye operatsii* ["Snow on the Armor," The Chechen War: Combat Operations], (Moscow: Yauza, 1999), pp.230–235.

2   Grad means hailstorm. It is also the nickname of the BM-21 122mm multiple rocket launcher. Its 80-round launcher is mounted on a URAL-375 or other 6X6 truck and is a deadly area-fire weapon out to 20 kilometers. Uragan [Hurricane] is the BM-27 220mm multiple rocket launcher. Its 16-round launcher is mounted on a 8X8 ZIL-121 truck and fires out to 40 kilometers.

3   Sheikh was serving in the MVD (Ministry of Internal Affairs — National Police) of the Government of Ichkeria at this time and took his orders from Aidamir Abulayev, head of the MVD.

4   Approximate location of main trench complex 43°28'15.16" N 45°50'04.36" E.

5   MRLS (multiple rocket launcher system) is a generic term covering a family of rocket artillery that is fired from a ground launcher or a launcher mounted on a truck bed or ship deck. It is a direct descendant of the Soviet Katyusha [Little Kate] rockets of World War II. The MRLS is used to hit a large area with concentrated high-explosive fire or to lay instant smoke screens. The two systems used in Chechnya were the BM-21 Grad [Hailstorm] and the BM-27 Uragan [Hurricane]. The BM-21 has 40 launch rails that can direct 122mm rockets to a distance of 20 kilometers. The rockets can be fired individually or the entire 40 rounds can be launched in 20 seconds. It has been in production since 1963. The BM-27 has 16 launch rails that can direct 240mm rockets to a distance of 35 kilometers. These rockets can also be fired individually or the entire 16 rounds can also be fired in 20 seconds. There are many models of rockets for each system, but the smallest high-explosive warhead for the BM-21 weighs 18.4 kilograms, while the smallest high-explosive round for the BM-27 weighs 90 kilograms. These systems can create havoc on a defending force that is not dug in.

6   The pontoon system the Russians deployed was likely the PMP (pontonno-mostovoy park), or pontoon bridge set, the standard Soviet-era tactical bridge. The basic pontoon link system consists of four hinged accordion-folded pontoon sections, which automatically unfold when they hit the water. Crews then have to join the sections together. In Soviet times a division usually had half a PMP set with 16 river and two shore links and six boats — enough to construct 118 meters of a 60-ton bridge, 22 meters of a 20-ton bridge, or two 170-ton, three 110-ton, four 80-ton, or six 60-ton rafts. Full crew strength for assembly is traditionally 70 80 personnel. (see David Isby, *Weapons and Tactics of the Soviet Army* (London: Jane's, 1981), p.343.

Chapter 8

1   In 1997 in Vedeno I met a Chechen sapper who during the first war had lost both hands trying to defuse and move an antipersonnel mine laid by Russian forces. His face was also disfigured and he was completely blind in one eye and partially blind in the other. The burden that this permanently disabled veteran put on his family and community is significant. Multiply him by tens and hundreds and one can see that the burden of taking care of wounded combatants and civilians in Chechnya has had an impact far beyond the actual number of disabled.

Chapter 9

1   There are a variety of Russian sources confirming Chechen actions against the various Russian control-crossing points. Elimpash's description of events seem to correspond to these accounts of the fight for Russian Control-Crossing Point 13. According to Boris Karpov in the online journal VV: Kavkazskiy Krest – 2. "Blokpost-13 Vyzyvaet 'Storm,'" the 13th Block Post (called "Storm") was described as "the least fortunate" of the block posts. The author goes on to say that it was ill-suited for prolonged fighting. The concrete slabs only gave an "appearance of reliability," but it would only take a few hand grenades to destroy it. At this post were a good number of OMON officers (Special Police). On 6 March reports show that there was a concentration of Chechen fighters in the industrial area, which was "literally across the street" from the Russian unit (the block post). The Chechens did not attack it head-on, rather they attempted to starve the Russians out. While the 18th and 19th block posts were able to call in accurate artillery strikes because their zones had specific coordinates, the 13th did not, despite its being on an important road. The artillery men used a ruler on a map to determine where to fire and basically had to call fire upon their own men. It was a risky move, and the shells landed very close to the Russian position at the 13th block post. As a result, the report says, the Chechens were beaten back. By the morning of 7 March the 13th Block Post was almost entirely destroyed, but the Russians were still alive. They evacuated in a damaged BMP that could drive but not shoot. The report says the Chechens didn't even notice them leave due to how quick and unexpected the maneuver was. They drove to the Komendatura, and upon arriving realized that five of their men were missing.

2   The Chechens wiped out the entire 6th Company, 104th Parachute Regiment of the 76th Airborne Division on Hill 776 in February 2000.

3   There are multiple conflicting sources regarding the battles for these hills. In many cases there seems to be confusion as to which details belong to the battle for which hill, or which battle the details belonged to, since there were multiple battles for a single hill that occurred during the first months of the second war.

4   The number of Chechens that took part in the operation is unclear. Vakha T. firmly remembers 13 being called out by Manaev. He also recalls that the Chechen commander came with two of his own. That would bring the total Chechen force to 16 combatants.

5   Probably the A-91 compact assault rifle with sniper scope and silencer.

6   Krasavchik literally means "pretty boy," the term most Chechen combatants used for the PK light machine gun. The Chechens also used the term to refer to the NSV Utios 12.7mm heavy machine gun. But in this case, it is probably the lighter and more mobile PK light machine gun that was used in the operation.

7   SVD or Snayperskaya Vintovka Dragunova, a 7.62mm Dragunov Sniper Rifle.

8   There would still be noise, but the difference would be that of a round fired from a single-action rifle versus a semiautomatic rifle. A silencer would further deaden the noise.

9   It isn't clear how many Russian soldiers were killed in this operation, or even what unit they were in. According to gorod.dp.ua. Thread entitled "Ochen interesnyy vzglyad na sudbu 6 roty VDV." http://forum.gorod.dp.ua/showthread.php?t=138550&page=1, "The Russians were able to capture hills 835 and 950 without losses, but lost a whole company of untrained new recruits trying to capture 825. By the middle of winter 2000, the Russians hadn't quite taken hill 825, and 950 was lost." Another Russian source states, "Big loss of Russian troops on Hill 825. . . . Inglorious failed attack for 825, laid down a whole company." There is some confusion as to which Russian company this is.

10   This fact is also corroborated by Ratiborov, Konstantin. "Budanov v Tyurme i na Voine". No. 15(332). April 11, 2000. http://www.zavtra.

ru/cgi/veil/data/zavtra/00/332/32.html. "Hill 825 was captured by the Chechens after a two-hour battle." The same source puts the date of the attack as 15 January 2000. Vakha only remembers it being during Ramadan, which took place 9 December 1999 to 8 January 2000, so there is some discrepancy as to when the action occurred.

11 Kadyrov had been appointed acting head of administration in July 2000, and was later elected Chechen President on 5 October 2003. He was killed in a bomb attack by Chechen separatists on 9 May 2004.

12 It is not known whether or not Isa took orders from Doku Umarov after the command change, or if Isa's clout permitted him to be an equal for all intents and purposes. In any case, the credit for these battles for Shalazhi, Gekhi-Chu and Roshni-Chu goes to Umarov. In many sources, the battles for these towns are mentioned in conjunction with the battle for Martan-Chu. As Isa states that he only had command for Shalazhi, Gekhi-Chu and Roshni-Chu, it is possible that Umarov had command of the battle for Martan-Chu, in addition to other locations.

13 Multiple Russian sources state that two officers from the Omsk OMON were killed fighting the Chechens during the battle: Lieutenant Colonel Igor Suyarov, the detachment commander, as noted above,

and Lieutenant Nikolai Fomin. For example, see http://www.ortrk. ru/?story id=A565.

Chapter 10

1 Umalt Dudayev, "Chechnya's Homemade Weapons Fuel War: Rebels are using improvised and home-made weapons to continue their guerrilla war," CRS Issue 227, Institute of War and Peace Reporting, 21 February 2005.

2 Email correspondence with Umar, 10 December 2010.

Chapter 11

1 *Adat* means "custom" or "common law." It compliments Sharia law and sets rules for the daily life of clans and families. It is moral norms and traditions that form a code of conduct.

2 Or, having lost at least two companies air-dropped into the mountains during the first war, Russian tactics were an indication of the level they were capable of fighting at with the army that they had at the time.

3 "Happy families are all alike; every unhappy family is unhappy in its own way." This is the opening sentence of Leo Tolstoy's 1878 book, *Anna Karenina*.

ABOUT THE AUTHOR

Dodge Billingsley, is the Director of Combat Films and Research, a fellow at the David M. Kennedy Center for International Studies at Brigham Young University, and a senior faculty member at the Naval Post Graduate School's Center for Civil Military Relations.

A long time observer of many conflicts, Mr Billingsley has spent considerable time in the Caucasus where he first became familiar with Chechen insurgent/separatist forces during Georgia's war with Abkhaz separatists 1992–1993. He has produced two documentary films based on his experiences with Chechen combatants and recently conducted a number of interviews of former Chechen combatants for his current work, *Fangs of the Lone Wolf: Chechen Tactics in the Russian-Chechen Wars 1994–2009*.

Mr Billingsley has also spent extensive time in both Afghanistan and Iraq. He was present at the Qala I Jangi Fortress uprising in November 2001 and won both the prestigious Rory Peck and Royal Television Society awards for Best Feature for his footage in the film House of War. Months later he landed with US troops in the Shah i Kot Valley in eastern Afghanistan for Operation Anaconda. His film *Shah I Khot: Valley Redoubt*, which accompanies *Operation Anaconda: America's First Conventional Battle in Afghanistan*, co-authored by Mr Billingsley and Mr Les Grau, is a result of his coverage of that operation.

In 2003 he embedded with 3/7 Marines for the invasion of Iraq and his subsequent film *Virgin Soldiers* was again nominated for the Rory Peck Best Feature category. He embedded with 3-2 Stryker Brigade in Mosul in 2004 for the BBC and in December 2011 he accompanied 46 Infantry for the closure of Al Asad Air Base and the final withdrawal of US forces from Al Anbar Province, western Iraq.

His most recent film (2013), *Unfortunate Brothers: Korea's Reunification Dilemma*, examines the prospects of Korean reunification through the testimony of experts and the experience of a North Korean defector living in Seoul.

Mr Billingsley lectures extensively to both academic institution and military installations and is a long time contributor to *Jane's Intelligence Review*. He has a BA in History from Columbia University and a MA in War Studies King's College, London.